SEXUAL CULTURES IN EUROPE
National histories

MANCHESTER
UNIVERSITY PRESS

SEXUAL CULTURES IN EUROPE

National histories

edited by
Franz X. Eder, Lesley A. Hall & Gert Hekma

Manchester University Press

Manchester & New York

distributed exclusively in the USA by St. Martin's Press

Copyright © Manchester University Press 1999

While copyright in the volume as a whole is vested in Manchester University Press, copyright in individual chapters belongs to their respective authors, and no chapter may be reproduced wholly or in part without the express permission in writing of both author and publisher

Published by Manchester University Press
Oxford Road, Manchester M13 9NR, UK
and Room 400, 175 Fifth Avenue, New York, NY 10010, USA
http://www.man.ac.uk/mup

Distributed exclusively in the USA by
St. Martin's Press, Inc., 175 Fifth Avenue, New York,
NY 10010, USA

Distributed exclusively in Canada by
UBC Press, University of British Columbia, 6344 Memorial Road,
Vancouver, BC, Canada V6T 1Z2

British Library Cataloguing-in-Publication Data
A catalogue record for this book is available from the British Library

Library of Congress Cataloging-in-Publication Data applied for

ISBN 0 7190 5313 7 *hardback*
0 7190 5314 5 *paperback*

First published 1999

05 04 03 02 01 00 99   10 9 8 7 6 5 4 3 2 1

Typeset in Monotype Bell
by Koinonia, Manchester
Printed in Great Britain
by Bell & Bain Ltd, Glasgow

Contents

CONTENTS

Contributors

Efigenio Amezúa is the Director of the Instituto de Sexología, Madrid, an archive resource and research centre on contemporary sexuality, which also provides postgraduate courses on sexology. He has published a number of monographs on sexuality in the *Revista de Sexología*.

Richard Cleminson is a lecturer in Spanish Studies at the University of Bradford, UK. He has published on eugenics and on homosexuality in contemporary Spain with particular reference to the anarchist movement. He has compiled an anthology of 1920s/1930s anarchist articles on homosexuality published as *Anarquismo y homosexualidad* (Huerga y Fierro, 1995).

Ralf Dose MA (b. 1950) is co-founder of the Magnus Hirschfeld Society and its secretary since 1983. He is editor of *Mitteilungen der Magnus-Hirschfeld-Gesellschaft* and Head of the Society's Research Unit on the History of Sexual Science. He has produced many publications on the Berlin Institute for Sexual Science (1919–33) and on the history of the gay movement in Germany.

Franz X. Eder is a historian at the Institute for Economic and Social History, University of Vienna. He has carried out research on quantitative methods and on the history of the family and labour organisation. Current projects on the history of sexuality include sexual discourses in the German speaking countries, eighteenth to twentieth centuries. He is co-editor of *Geschichte der homosexualitäten* (Österreichische Zeitschrift für Geschichtswissenschaften 1998, no. 3); forthcoming is a book on *Sexual Cultures in Germany and Austria, 1700–2000*.

Tony Fahey is a sociologist in the Economic and Social Research Institute, Dublin. His work consists mainly of applied research on topics connected with social policy in Ireland and the European Union, but he also has an interest in the modern history of Catholicism in Ireland. His most recent book (co-authored with John FitzGerald) is *Welfare Implications of Demographic Trends* (Dublin, 1997).

Lesley A. Hall is Senior Assistant Archivist, Contemporary Medical Archives Centre, Wellcome Institute for the History of Medicine, London, and Honorary Lecturer in History of Medicine, University College London. She has published *Hidden Anxieties: Male Sexuality 1900–1950* (Oxford, 1991); (with Professor Roy Porter) *The Facts of Life: The Creation of Sexual Knowledge in Britain, 1650–1950* (New Haven CT, 1995) and numerous articles, chapters and reviews on questions of sex, gender, birth control, eugenics, VD, etc. She is currently working on a biography of British feminist sex radical Stella Browne (1880–1955), a textbook on sex, gender and social change in Britain since 1880, and (with Roger Davidson) an edited volume on the social history of venereal diseases in Europe 1870–2000.

Gert Hekma is a lecturer in gay and lesbian studies at the University of Amsterdam where he co-chairs the gender, sexuality and culture stream of courses. He has published widely in the field of the history and sociology of (homo)sexuality, is an editor of *Thamyris* and a regular contributor to *Sexualities*.

Igor S. Kon, PhD (b. 1928) is at the Institute of Ethnology and Anthropology, Russian Academy of Sciences. His publications include *Sexual Revolution in Russia* (Free Press, 1995), and in Russian: *Sexual culture in Russia*; *Tasting the Forbidden Fruit*; *Moonlight at Dawn: Faces and Masks of the Same-sex Love*; *Sociological Psychology*; *Introduction to Sexology*.

Robert A. Nye is Thomas Hart and Mary Jones Horning Professor of the Humanities and Professor of History at Oregon State University (USA). He is working on a comparative history of medical ethics. His most recent books are *Masculinity and Male Codes of Honor in Modern France* (Berkeley, 1998) and a reader entitled *Sexuality* (Oxford, 1998).

Harry Oosterhuis (b. 1958) teaches history at the University of Maastricht. He has published several articles and books on the history of Catholicism and homosexuality in the Netherlands and of homosexuality and male bonding in Germany. At present he is writing a book on the work of the German-Austrian sexologist Richard von Krafft-Ebing, focusing on the role of psychiatry and autobiography in the late nineteenth-century making of sexual identities.

Bruno P. F. Wanrooij (Rotterdam NL, 1954) is professor of Humanities and Social Sciences in the Programmes of Georgetown University and Syracuse University in Florence, Italy. His research is in the field of the history of the family and of sexuality. Besides articles and contributions to collective volumes he has published *Storia del pudore. La questione sessuale in Italia 1860–1940* (Venice, 1990).

Acknowledgements

The editors would like to thank the Forum on Sexuality at The Netherlands' Universities Institute for Co-ordination of Research in Social Sciences (SISWO), Amsterdam, for its support for the workshop conference 'Sexual Cultures of Europe 1700–1995', 21–3 June 1996, at which early versions of the chapters in this volume were discussed by all contributors, and the Wellcome Trust for providing travel funding for several participants. They extend further gratitude to the participants at the conference for the lively and useful discussion of the papers. Particular thanks are extended to Andrew Blaikie, Sam Pryke, Hugo Röling and Cornelie Usborne, who, although their papers are absent from these volumes, made invaluable contributions during discussion to the outcome of this project.

Introduction

We use the term *sexual cultures* intentionally. There has been a debate on the nature of the object and perspective of women's studies. These are nowadays generally accepted as gender, being understood as the cultural organisation of sexed roles. Sexed roles include not only feminine and masculine, but also androgynous, unfeminine and unmasculine, third-gender roles and so forth. Women's studies rejects the bipolar model of sexes current in biology, in traditional humanities and social sciences, and in society, in favour of the broader question of gender. As historians of sexuality have made a similar move from nature to culture, so sex, sexuality or sexology are no longer adequate descriptions of the object, or of the terrain, of historical research. We suggest a change from sex and sexuality to sexual culture, comparable to the change from sex to gender in women's studies, while an adequate name for the discipline could well be, instead of sexology, sexual studies, in line with the new concepts of cultural studies and gender studies. The term 'sexual cultures' covers both individual experience and collective interpretations and does not favour one or the other side.

Society has a strong influence on the shapes and definitions of sexuality. Since about 1980, sex research has underlined the social and historical forms of sexuality: the constructionist point of view as developed by Michel Foucault (Foucault 1976), Jeffrey Weeks (Weeks 1981) and many others. But if the social forms of sexuality vary from culture to culture, what does it mean for sexuality and sexual emancipation in contemporary Europe? This introduction will discuss initially the evolution of the history of sexuality and the history and variety of sexual cultures of Europe, then question the social and political implications of this diversity, and, finally, indicate how the

1

chapters in this volume will contribute to advancing our understanding of European sexual cultures.

The history of sexuality

The history of sexuality is at least as old as the history of modern sexology itself – about a hundred years. This does not mean that history was not used to question, to contrast or to legitimise societies before the late nineteenth century. On the one hand, subjects like procreation, fertility, continence, sexual intercourse, etc. were already parts of more general historical and anthropological studies. On the other hand, before the 1880s these studies dealt only with those aspects of human sexual life which were of social relevance for contemporary society. From the eighteenth century the two most important topics were the history of prostitution and of venereal diseases (Duchâtelet 1836; Rosenbaum 1839; Sanger 1858). With the emergence of the sciences of sexuality at the end of the nineteenth century, historical research focused also on all other aspects of the new object of investigation. In many cases anthropological, ethnological and especially historical studies and materials were used to compensate for the thin empirical basis on which early sexologists tried to build their hypotheses and theories.

In the years before the First World War and during the 1920s the historiography of sexuality was dominated by a specific type of analysis and description: histories of sexual manners and customs (e.g. the German studies: Dühren 1899; Fuchs 1909–16; Bauer and Scherr 1928; Hirschfeld 1930–1). Usually these works were written not by historians but by physicians, anthropologists, etc. These authors saw themselves as 'historians of culture' and took the sexual behaviour of previous societies as a criterion for the moral status and the degree of civilisation of the culture concerned. In their eyes 'sexuality' was the omnipotent and omnipresent driving force of history. Their voluminous books claimed to describe all expressions of sexual life, for example positive as well as negative sexual values and 'perverse' forms of behaviour beside 'natural' ones. By recent standards these authors interpreted historical texts and pictures in an absolutely uncritical way. They used them as a direct reflection of the social practice of former times and did not consider that these sources were produced with moral or didactic aims and implications.

In spite of the importance attributed to sexuality in the theory of Freud and his successors, psychoanalytical approaches remained more or less insignificant in the historiography of sexuality for the first half of the twentieth century. During the 'sexual revolution' of the late 1960s a new history of sexuality was established in contrast to the traditional histories of manners and customs. Then, professional historians as well as other historically interested social scientists used Freudian theory as an analytical framework for studies of sexual life and the sexual cultures of former centuries. They thought they had located the social causes of the development of sexuality during the period from the seventeenth century to the present day: middle-class attitudes towards sexual expression in human life – a field which had been designated 'sexuality' since the late eighteenth century – became the main centre of interest. Most scholars interpreted the emergence of bourgeois sexuality as a history of repression and suppression. Both developments were said to have led to the sexual troubles criticised by the 'sexual liberation movement' of the end of the 1960s.

In most studies bourgeois sexuality was depicted as having an extreme polarity (Young 1964; Marcus 1966; Ussel 1968; Pearsall 1969). On the one hand, it was claimed, there had been increasing denial and suppression of the sexual drive since the beginning of the early modern period. This process was said to have culminated in the nineteenth century in Victorianism, which brought about an extensive prudery, erecting a wall of silence around all sexual matters. According to this hypothesis, women in particular became victims of bourgeois sexual morality; the social denial of their sexual desires was considered to have rendered them frigid and unsatisfied. On the other hand, it was supposed that a dark, forbidden, but none the less widely available sexual underground for men pullulated under this prudish surface. The double standard made it possible for men to enjoy sexual pleasures despite their asexual wives, by means of mistresses, prostitutes and pornography. Repression and the double standard were also supposed to have been the main causes of the many neuroses and psychic illnesses which spread in the nineteenth century. Only through movements of liberalisation following the Second World War had people become free of these negative influences of bourgeois sexuality and thereby more and more able to satisfy their intrinsic sexual drives.

The social history of the 1970s did not greatly change the

double-standard model. However, it was indubitably the achievement of the new social historians to enlarge the research field methodologically and in content. Methodologically, they brought in quantitative studies on a large scale, especially demographic investigations into potential indicators of sexual behaviour. As to content, research was extended to the sexual life of all groups of the population – not only to specific samples and groups such as the nobility, the middle classes or so-called sexual minorities like prostitutes or gay men. For those doing this, the issues of fertility and illegitimacy during the eighteenth and nineteenth centuries became the centre of interest (Tilly 1978; Rotberg and Rabb 1980; Laslett 1980) and there were extensive discussions about the increasing suppression or dissemination of sexual freedom during the emergence of bourgeois society, the Industrial Revolution and the socio-economic changes in rural areas in particular (Mitterauer 1983).

In the mid-1970s this paradigm of the historiography of sexuality was changed by an upheaval which still determines the landscape. Although there had been similar approaches by other scholars (e.g. Shorter 1975; Flandrin 1975), Michel Foucault was the first who de-naturalised and, at the same time, historicised 'sexuality' in the first volume of his *Histoire de la sexualité* (Foucault 1976). Foucault radically questioned the seemingly solid basis of previous historiography on sexuality. According to him the idea of increasing repression of the sexual drive during the emergence of bourgeois society was not wrong in principle. But this notion ignored the fact that 'sexuality', as we think of it, was first invented or produced by the discourse of the modern human sciences. During the last three centuries more and more spheres of life came under the influence of the sexual *dispositif* which also sexualised the human search for identity and truth.

Besides Foucault, proponents of the gay and lesbian movements and of women's liberation also criticised the previous essentialist explanations of sexuality by means of social constructionist arguments (Stein 1990; Stanton 1992; Eder 1994). Their critique of the traditional history of sexuality was very strong indeed: every attempt to trace back hetero-, homo- or any other sexual desires to an inborn sexual drive had to be distrusted. Even Freudian psychoanalysis – which proceeds on the assumption that there is an active sexual drive which is modelled or repressed by society – could no longer remain the primary theory of scientific research on sexuality. Instead of the essentialist foundation of 'sexuality' (as sexual desire, orientation and identity), social and therefore also historical construction of these human qualities had to be uncovered.

This outlines the potentials as well as the dilemmas of the current history of sexuality. On the one hand, there is no way back to the formerly firm essentialist terms and theories. Most exponents of essentialist arguments have moved back to a view which still promises them good future prospects: they regard biological and depth-psychological processes as extremely complex and, therefore, research in its present state cannot progress to the real roots and causes of sexuality; thus further research is rendered a necessity. Most essentialists present themselves as open to social and cultural extensions of their assumptions and generalisations. During the last decades examples from socio-biology and psycho-biology have demonstrated that hypotheses about the physical causes of sexual behaviour – e.g. about specific homosexual regions in the brain of gay men (LeVay 1993) – may be more or less speculation but enjoy great popular success.

At the moment, however, there are no socio-sexual theories, either, able to grasp the emergence, orientation and satisfaction of sexual desire in a social constructionist and historic way. The permanent repetition of constructionist critiques of historiography orientated towards psychoanalysis and biological theories cannot occlude the fact that, at the moment, their own efforts to find a convincing explanation for the emergence of the sexual subject and sexual identity deal only with public discourses and with the categories and terms of the sciences. To work further on the deconstruction of these entities is one project; to find new theories which include the socio-psychological construction of the sexual subjects in their specific historical context is another, still unresolved one. Statements in favour of one or the other direction, as well as an attitude of 'anything goes' and pluralistic, interdisciplinary and inter-methodical approaches and works, characterise the current scene. Even the *Journal of the History of Sexuality*, which has enriched the relevant historiography since 1990, devotes itself to this unclearness:

> Now the study of human sexuality is being addressed by social historians, sociologists, anthropologists, philosophers, psychologists, literary scholars, classicists, art and film historians, and scholars in other fields from a variety of disciplinary and cross-disciplinary perspectives. It is far too early in the progression of

this new area of scholarship to establish its parameters, and, therefore *JHS* will encourage the publication of a broad range of essays, review essays, reviews, and even primary sources (with editorial commentary) on all aspects of the history of sexuality from ancient times to contemporary sexual politics. (Fout 1990: 1 f.)

Over the last two decades historians of sexuality have been confronted with a subject of investigation which has become ever more difficult to handle and to analyse. In the end one has to re-invent sexual life in its specific historical forms of drive, desire, orientation etc. without being influenced by recent images and ideas of sex and sexuality. However, historical abstraction and distance rarely seem to be so hard for scholars at the end of the twentieth century as in reference to this field of human life so intensively loaded with individual images and experiences.

Theoretical and interpretative difficulties characterise not only the object of historic investigation but the sources which are analysed. On the one hand, there is scarcely any other historiographic terrain where sources containing self-interpretations of actions, imaginations and emotions are so rare. Most of the materials which are analysed today on a large scale – for example the trial records very fashionable at the moment – mostly describe the emergence and satisfaction of sexual lust in institutional or standardised language and rarely quote the words of the persons concerned or their everyday language. Therefore the few autobiographical documents which have survived have obtained great importance for the major theories of the history of sexuality. However, by far the biggest stock of sources derives from discourses on sexuality, which include all cultural 'texts' of which we may suppose that they also determined or constructed the conceptual, categorical and symbolic world of their subjects (Eder 1996).

The history and variety of sexual cultures in Europe

The different cultures in Europe have rather diverse sexual patterns, resulting from the spatial and historical separation of the various countries. We can discern at least four historical sexual systems, more or less connected with Europe's four most important religions. This scheme is very general and serves only to indicate some sexual differences and parallels. There is much more to say about this subject which the cited literature makes abundantly clear.

The north-western part of Europe with its Protestant traditions developed severe attitudes towards non-marital sexuality, but had at the same time a strong tradition of individualism as far as religious beliefs were concerned. The nuclear family was the main social model. There was no space for any form of sexual behaviour outside the bonds of marriage: masturbation was condemned on both moral and medical grounds; prostitution was frowned upon but allowed to exist as an outlet for male desires and to prevent worse sexual perversions, and the homoeroticism of friendships and male bonding was highly valued among schoolboys, students, artists, soldiers, politicians as long as it did not lead to sexual relations.

The Catholic countries of southern Europe had comparably stringent moralities but more lenient attitudes, permitting a gap to exist between moral values and sexual practices. In Catholicism sins can be absolved. For this reason gay and straight males from northern Europe imagined they could find in southern Europe, especially in Italy, sexual freedoms which exist only on a practical, not an ideological, level. On the other hand, the typical Protestant religious individualism is absent in Catholicism. These southern cultures had and still have strong family traditions. Whether there were and are significant differences between Catholicism in the Mediterranean cultural area and in the more northerly European Catholic communities is a question which still requires more thorough analysis.

On the sexual history of the Orthodox countries of eastern Europe we have less information; their situation seems to have borne a certain resemblance to the Catholic countries. Until 1700 all kinds of non-marital sexual behaviour seem to have been rampant in Russia, notwithstanding protests by the clergy. Only after that date did the Russian Orthodox church apparently succeed in restraining certain forms of sexual behaviour, in co-operation with the czars and the institutions of the state that wanted to modernise Russian society. Among Old Believers, namely the Skoptsy and the Khlysty, quite different sexual patterns developed. Nowadays the Orthodox churches have remained very conservative since they have undergone no recent religious renewal; however, notwithstanding their traditionalism, women had always a relatively strong position (Engelstein 1992; Kon 1995).

The fourth religious system, Islam, which influenced the south-eastern realm of Europe, and nowadays extends its sway to the northern parts, is very strict on sexual behaviour according to religious law, but social reality differs sharply from ideal norms, perhaps even more so than in the Catholic world. As long as men do not depart from public male norms – taking an active role in sexuality – and as long as their sexual behaviour remains private, they will have few problems in engaging in promiscuous behaviour and neglecting religious norms. Here women are sequestered in the home, which is very much the female domain, but even there they are under male control and have few sexual options. Girls are in exceptional cases still forcibly married while boys continue to be circumcised.

Most parts of Europe have known, or still know, a system of honour and shame independent of religion and strongly influencing sexual behaviour. Honour belonged to families, not to individuals, and the family's patriarchs were responsible for the honour of their dependants. Sexual transgressions were no problem, as long as they remained hidden or if they put shame on to other families. As long as men remained in the active role, for example by seducing the wives or daughters of other men, their honour was enhanced, but the other men became shameful cowards who were not able to control their female dependants. In north-west Europe, this system of shame and honour was replaced with a system of guilt, which is usually associated with the rise of Protestantism. Sexual transgressions were no longer permitted and engendered feelings of remorse, even if they were hidden or were honourable according to the old value system. Feelings of guilt about forbidden behaviours were individualised, and did not reflect back as much on the family of the transgressor as with shameful acts. This system of honour and shame was traditionally most strongly associated with, and still persists, in many areas around the Mediterranean (Gilmore 1987).

At least three major breakthroughs in sexual patterns have taken place since 1700 affecting most European cultures and are still influential on contemporary sex-life. First of all, in the eighteenth century the Enlightenment engendered a critique of Christian (sexual) practices and values, and the French Revolution replaced these with new values and moralities which were meant to be founded on rationality. In the second place the formation of sexual psychopathy or sexology around 1900 further quasi-rationalised sexual attitudes and politics (see Oosterhuis, Chapter 9). In the third place movements for sexual reform and women's, gay and lesbian emancipation since the 1960s have broadened the spectre of sexual possibilities, at least in western Europe.

The most important results of these changes were the formation of sexual identities, new definitions of normal and abnormal sexuality (replacing older definitions of licit and illicit sexual conduct) and the development of emancipation movements, advances in methods of birth control, and the strengthening of a body politic. The support of companionate marriage and the prevention of behaviour considered abnormal have been the most important elements of this body politic.

The newer sexual moralities and habits are as unequally distributed in Europe as the older ones. So the liberalism and libertinism of the Enlightenment had the strongest impact in Catholic France, but very little on Poland, which was as Catholic as France. A century later socialism in Germany developed its own ideology in accordance with the new tenets of sexology, which was especially influential in the countries of eastern Europe. Communist ideology was based on an ideal of companionate marriage, with the possibility of divorce and birth control, and was strongly opposed to sexual 'decadence', including prostitution and homosexuality. During periods of low natality, communist regimes reinstituted constraints on contraception and abortion to achieve higher birth rates and to strengthen their national states. The communist parties and states had a very bad reputation in their treatment of homosexuals. Social democrats think along the same lines as communists and have considerable trouble in understanding undisciplined forms of sexuality. The modern women's as well as gay and lesbian movements nevertheless in general had leftist outlooks, since left-wing ideologies have at least provided a space for thinking about changes to social norms rather than adhering to existing conventional morality (Hekma, Oosterhuis and Steakley 1995). Such liberation movements have had most influence in north-western Europe (i.e. the Protestant countries), and much less in the southern and eastern parts of Europe (Greece, Portugal) (Oosterhuis, Duyvendak and Hekma 1994). In eastern Europe they have largely emerged since the fall of the Iron Curtain (Parikas and Veispak 1990). The presence of a gay movement does not, however, say much about the extent of homosexual pleasures and preferences.

The newer sexual ideologies did not overturn the older ones, but were supplementary. So Catholicism in France, however much it may have changed, still exists alongside the rationalism of the Enlightenment. And although in the Netherlands governments have been dominated by Christian parties since 1900, there were never-theless strong sexual reform and gay and lesbian emancipation movements. The ideologies confronted each other, and changed in these confrontations. The Catholic and Protestant churches in the Netherlands are an example. They defined homosexuality at the turn of the century as a sin, then they started to discuss it in medical terms. It was no longer an abomination, but an aberration. In the 1950s and 1960s Catholic and Protestant clergy and psychiatrists acknowledged the existence of a homosexual identity and began to support gay and lesbian relations, although retaining reservations as far as the sexual act was concerned. The Catholic and Protestant denominations were influenced first by medical knowledge and later by the language of sexual reform and homosexual emancipation. Remarkably, in the Netherlands the breakthrough in the Catholic and Protestant churches started before the sexual revolution came about (Oosterhuis 1992). Another interesting example of such a volte-face was the Dutch Communist Party, which was in the mid-1970s one of the last parties to be definitely anti-gay, but became within five years the most outspoken political party regarding gay rights, creating its own 'queer' group.

The divergent developments in three Catholic countries – France, Italy and Spain – are remarkable. The later the sexual reforms started, the more radically and quickly they seem to have taken place. In France there has been an ongoing reform of sexual politics since the 1950s, notwithstanding some setbacks in the 1960s. Important changes came under centrist governments in the 1970s while the socialist governments of the 1980s accelerated these changes (Mossuz-Lavau 1991). Italy holds a middle position, and since the 1960s has slowly moved forward to changes in sexual manners and politics (see Wanrooij, Chapter 5). Spain experienced a watershed about 1975 following the death of the Fascist president General Franco and witnessed a radical break with a conservative past. Under the socialist governments of the 1980s all progressive sexual reforms have been realised in Spain: gradual legalisation of means of birth control, decriminalisation of abortion, pornography and homo-sexuality. These examples indicate some general trends of sexual reformation, while the different countries still have divergent time schedules and priorities.

Changing sexual systems and lifestyles

What have been the consequences of the different sexual systems for sexual relations and lifestyles? We will discuss the changes in the sexual horizon in line with the three watersheds mentioned above. For the Catholic church, from the thirteenth century sodomy was the ultimate sin. Sodomy was an act, defined either as any sexual act outside marriage which did not lead to procreation or as anal penetration, with males, females or beasts. It had nothing to do with sexual identities. But as the church did not have an effective system of social control, it rarely came into action against sexual sins. Only with the gradual development of the confessional did the clergy obtain a form of control, but this was not very reliable and moreover very private. The same applies even more for the Protestant churches, which did not even have the institution of the confessional. The persecution of sodomy was mostly the prerogative of the state, which acted upon Christian beliefs but used quasi-rational arguments. Under this system, in which the aims of church and state coincided to a large degree, the ultimate punishment for sodomy was the death penalty. But under most regimes this penalty was rarely or never executed. So in certain circles homosexual feelings could be expressed without reserve, for example at royal courts. But in the rising city-states of Renaissance Italy, in the booming cities of Spain after the discovery of America and in the Netherlands in the eighteenth century, sodomy was persecuted more or less systematically. The same legal situation concerning sodomy could have completely opposed consequences. Whereas some men enjoyed complete and far-reaching sexual freedoms, others were killed for a single sexual transgression (Gerard and Hekma 1989).

The philosophers of the Enlightenment opposed the criminalisation and stigmatisation of most forms of sexuality. After the French Revolution the criminal law changed and sodomy was not a crime any more according to the Code Napoléon. Many countries followed suit, especially the Catholic countries, Italy, Spain, Portugal, Belgium, Bavaria, and the Protestant exception, the Netherlands. The Enlightenment was, however, remarkable not only for its rationalism but also for its difficulties in facing the emotions. Whereas heterosexual libertinism was considered a minor transgression, masturbation became a heinous practice resulting from defects in education and upbringing from early childhood. The Reason of the Enlightenment bore monsters indeed: the struggle against 'onanism' which was started by the Swiss doctor Tissot. This battle was more important in establishing an enlightened pedagogic with a new body politic than in preventing masturbation. All the proposed measures against this heinous sin were very effective in education, as they implied strategies concerning the clothing, sleeping, reading, diet and socialising of children. Preventing onanism and the fantasies that produced it proved a good starting point for all kinds of educational control (Tarczylo 1983; Stengers and Neck 1984; Porter and Hall 1995). In the same vein Socratic love, as Voltaire named same-sex love, was not something to be honoured but a social abuse to be prevented, though no longer punished (Stockinger 1979).

The Enlightenment and the French Revolution seemed to include the promise of women's freedom, but feminists would see foremost important curtailments of their rights and sexual possibilities. The unproblematic equation of male and female bodies came to an end, and scholars started to stress differences between the sexes and the superiority of the male body, both in biology and in aesthetics (Laqueur 1990). After the Enlightenment the struggle for women's rights had only just begun. Sodomy might have been decriminalised, but sexual irregularities such as masturbation and male love became a problem for the body politic. The Revolution of the eighteenth century was for most people, from sodomites and sapphists to women and onanists, a change with two faces: on one hand a promise of freedom, on the other a strengthening of social control over many forms of sexual behaviour. Prevention instead of repression of presumed social and sexual evils was a leading thread of the Enlightenment.

Prostitution in particular became a topic of social struggle and scholarly research in the second half of the nineteenth century, starting with the work of Parent Duchâtelet (Duchâtelet 1836; Corbin 1978). It was a debate over the right of men, because of their supposedly irrepressible drives, to have sexual access to certain women. In practice it came down to a total disregard of all women, prostitutes and non-prostitutes alike. The medical control of prostitution which was intended to prevent the spread of venereal diseases was a result of liberal sexual politics which mostly favoured males. It was strongly supported by doctors for reasons of public hygiene, but at the same time fiercely opposed by Christian, socialist and feminist organisations. Christians considered it the legalisation of sin, socialists capitalist abuse of lower-class women, and feminists male oppression of victimised women. At the end of the nineteenth century most European countries were restraining instead of regulating prostitution. England was the first country to abolish the limited regulation it had introduced rather late by European standards (1860s), and introduced in 1885 penalties for procuration and brothel-keeping, as well as raising the age of female consent (Walkowitz 1980). The so-called white slavery of women for prostitution was combated on a European scale by around 1900. The struggle against liberalism by new political movements had also become a struggle against toleration of whoredom. Following the decline of the bordello system and of political support for medical control of prostitutes, other sexual stumbling-blocks were invented. For venereal diseases other solutions were found, for example clinics where free treatment was offered. Moreover, with the invention of salvarsan an effective therapy was available for syphilis.

The discussion on prostitution made possible the opening of debate on other topics, such as pornography, child sexual abuse and homosexuality (Hekma 1987). In law the age of consent was raised during the nineteenth century. In France there was no age of consent until the 1830s and then it was established at eleven, changed to thirteen in the 1860s. In the Netherlands it was raised from twelve to sixteen in 1886. Childhood became something to protect carefully, as was also done in laws on child labour and the extension of compulsory education. Pornography became more widespread owing to better printing techniques and the development of photography. It was produced both for local and international markets. Worldwide efforts were undertaken to restrain the spread of lewd images and texts which led to all kinds of legal prohibitions, ranging from prohibitions against producing or exhibiting them to the interdiction of transmitting them by postal services.

The interest in homosexuality was a main starting point for the establishment of sexology. In the 1860s the German lawyer Karl Heinrich Ulrichs began to defend the rights of homosexuals and developed a biological theory to this end. According to his ideas 'uranism' was not a crime against nature but a natural phenomenon. Homosexuality was inborn. By the way, he coined in 1864 the first modern word for it, *uranism*, five years before Kertbeny introduced the *homosexual* label. Ulrichs spoke in favour of decriminalising male love in the new German criminal laws of 1870. He lost his political cause, because at the unification of Germany in 1870 the infamous article 175 of the Prussian code, rather than the more liberal Bavarian code, was enacted (Kennedy 1988). But his theory that homosexuality was biologically determined was taken over by all leading psychiatrists, such as Krafft-Ebing, Charcot, Lombroso and Tarnowsky. According to them it was perhaps innate, but also pathological. Several strategies were developed concerning male love. Some doctors began to claim to cure homosexuals of their preferences. Others proposed preventive measures.

Starting with 'sexual inversion', many of these psychiatrists went on to invent and study other sexual perversions. New terms came up: exhibitionism (Lasègue), fetishism (Alfred Binet), sadism and masochism (Krafft-Ebing), and sexuality became a new commonplace name for erotic lust while the term had been reserved earlier for sex difference. The bible of the new interest in sex was Krafft-Ebing's *Psychopathia Sexualis*, which had had a few but less successful forerunners in France. Whereas Krafft-Ebing mostly discussed sexual perversions, as one said then, Albert Moll started to study sex in general: not just abnormal practices but also heterosexuality. A new science, sexology, came into being which researched sex foremost in its biological and psychological aspects (see Oosterhuis, Chapter 9).

The new visibility of sexuality and especially of homosexuals led to some notorious scandals: Oscar Wilde in 1895 in England, Krupp in 1902 and Eulenburg in 1907 in Germany (Cohen 1993; Steakley 1975). It was definitely made clear that not only homosexual behaviour but also being homosexual was something scandalous and undesirable. The growing knowledge of homosexuality, developed by the new science of sexology, was two-sided. On the one hand, homosexuals such as Ulrichs, Hirschfeld and Carpenter used such knowledge to defend the rights of homosexuals. But on the other hand, a stronger and more influential current used this knowledge to curtail homosexuality. In retrospect we can state that the biological theories of an inborn homosexuality have done more harm to homosexuals than they have furthered homosexual emancipation. It had been a sin and a crime, and now it became also a disease. Psychotherapy, castration, brain operations, criminal prosecution, exclusion of homosexuals from the military, the high level of suicides among them, their exclusion from straight society, have all to do with their medical identification. Nevertheless, the most important currents of homosexual emancipation have been based on the same framework of biological theories. Von Kupffer was the first to oppose this medicalisation of manly love with a cultural, and male chauvinist, theory, but without much success. Many literary people followed suit, with André Gide's *Corydon* the most famous example.

Most European countries around the turn of the century faced an opening up of sexual possibilities and at the same time a strengthening of sexual codes. Literature and the arts became focal points for laxer attitudes towards sex, whereas at the same time new laws were promulgated to restrain what was seen as sexual licence. In France judges tried to stop juicy literature, in England Parliament introduced laws against brothel-keeping and homosexual conduct and tightened up existing measures against soliciting, whereas the predominance of Prussia in the new German empire meant a broadening and hardening of sex laws. Vienna in Austria became a centre for both experimentation and research into sex. Russia had authors and sexologists who started to discuss sexuality in its many variations. Finland had the unique experience of introducing the criminalisation of lesbianism. But the flood of sexual innovations and freedoms was uncurtailable, and certainly after the First World War wider sexual possibilities became more widespread. New forms of popular entertainment in music, dancing, film broadened the access to free sexual expression. The sexual reform movement instigated by such male doctors as Magnus Hirschfeld, Havelock Ellis and many others gained force, and feminist sexual reformers such as Helene Stöcker and Marie Stopes started to enjoy great popularity.

The successes of sexual reform were limited, however. For some time the Soviet Union was considered to be implementing exemplary sexual politics. But its supposedly rational attitudes to sex did not take long to show their ugly face, and soon after the communists had taken power prostitutes were persecuted, and in the early 1930s homosexuality and abortion were again criminalised. The 1930s witnessed a conservative movement regarding sex: a puritanical government in the east and the rise of right-wing movements in the middle and south of Europe that were as opposed to free sexual expression as the communists. After the Nazis came to power in 1933, Berlin immediately lost its reputation as a sexual paradise, and most sexologists, many of whom were Jewish, had to hide or to flee Germany. Republican Spain saw some efforts at sexual liberation (see Cleminson and Amezúa, Chapter 7) but Franco put an end to this for forty years. Italy faced somewhat earlier a comparable change and also soon lost its reputation as a sexual paradise. Britain had never been very liberal in sex matters and in Scandinavia they had started to introduce eugenic measures, such as castration of sex criminals, before Nazi Germany began to do so. When the sexologists had to flee Germany, there were few places to go to, and after Hitler had invaded most other countries of Europe, the last survivors had to move again beyond Europe. After the Second World War Europe had lost its sexual freedoms and its sexologists, and sexual reform started again only slowly. Sexology became an American speciality after 1945 and remains so to this day. The liberation of Europe in 1945 brought perhaps a short uproar of sexual possibilities, but sexual restraints were put in place very quickly with the Cold War.

The sexual revolution of the 1960s put an end to thirty years of increasing restraint of sexual expression. This changeover can be explained in several ways. In the first place it was part of the youth movement. In the second place there was a new technology of birth control, the pill. The treatment of venereal diseases with antibiotics also contributed to it. Furthermore, Kinsey's sociological information on the sexual habits of the Americans influenced European society on many levels. Most Americans appeared to have been involved in activities which were defined as criminal either by the Federal government or by the legislation of particular states. Even if the sexual behaviour of Europeans was different from the Americans', Kinsey's work had revealed a radical disjuncture between orthodox and conventional morality and private conduct which had universal implications. Before the advent of the sexual revolution, churches had already started to change their position and to acknowledge forms of sexual desire outside marriage. Several countries began to reconsider sex crimes and to decriminalise certain forms of sexual behaviour. This was the result of the British Wolfenden Report on prostitution and homosexuality. Movements for sexual reform and women's and homosexual emancipation started to have an impact on social life. Improved methods of and increasing access to birth control ended many fears women felt about sexuality, but it became also a strong weapon for men to induce women to have sex with them. With regard to sexual minorities, homosexuals had their first successes in the 1970s, in the USA, Britain, Scandinavia, the Netherlands, West Germany and France, mainly in the urban areas. Another remarkable result of the sexual revolution was the representation of the nude. Pornography emerged in public and became more diverse, while mass media and advertising employed increasingly eroticised imagery.

The sexual revolution implied a liberation of sexuality. But it had its reverse side: sexuality was not the pure, natural expression of desire most people thought. Violence appeared to be intimately connected with sexual life. Sexual abuse of children and women, especially in relations of dependency such as within the family, in education and within the system of medical care, was and is very general and became a social and political topic of great importance. Youth and beauty are nowadays adored in the West, and older and ugly people had better forget participation in sexual subcultures. In the 1980s there came a backlash, for example feminist attacks on pornography and an increasing concern over paedophile relations and the sexual abuse of children. Prudery in sexual language has never been overcome and the sexuality of children remains an unmentionable topic. The appearance of a new disease, AIDS, contributed to intensifying existing fears of the imagined and real dangers of sexuality. The sexual revolution liberated sexuality in many respects, and gays and lesbians especially have profited greatly from it, but new sexual disciplines and fears have been put in place. New anti-homosexual legislation was introduced in England even during the 1980s under the rubric of 'family values'.

The sexual revolution seems not to have had a major impact on sexual behaviour, as it adapted sexual morality to sexual practices that had changed long before. Some decades after the sexual revolution, in many European countries sexual morality has become very open and any sexual subject is freely debated. But now sexual behaviour lags behind the open morality. Although few restraints on sexual behaviour are left, all sociological surveys on sex show that most people do not have a rich and varied sex-life (Spira 1993; Wellings *et al.* 1994; Zessen and Sandfort 1991). There are several ways to explain this awkward situation. First, western men still believe that sex is natural and there is nothing to be learned about it. So there is no need for sex education or cultivation of sexual pleasures and no reason to develop sexual rituals. Moreover, sex is considered to be a private affair, which has made any public expression difficult. There are few public spaces devoted to courtship rituals or sexual pleasures, as there are for sportive games or religious beliefs. Because sex is not spatially or ritually institutionalised, the expression of sexual feelings makes people feel childish, or else psychiatrists define these as infantile. This has been said about any and every sexual pleasure, from masturbation to sadomasochism. Finally, there is little political or social support for expressions of pleasure (Hekma 1995).

Europe has become a complex patchwork of sexual cultures and this process of differentiation is going on. There are important differences between countries, between religions, and moreover between regions (northern and southern part of Italy), between city and countryside, between genders and generations, between social classes, and so forth. Diversity existed in the past and is not dead today. Sexual cultures have overcome the homogenising patterns of progress. Immigration from other countries and cultures has moreover diversified the sexual kaleidoscope of urban centres. Every European city nowadays has a strong presence of men and women from other European, African, Asian or American nations, or of mixed origin. They have implanted foreign cultural seeds in the urban centres and contributed to racial, cultural and sexual syncretisms. This will certainly enrich the language of lust and love.

Eastern Europe has missed many of the developments that western Europe experienced. Russia bypassed most of the sexual changes of the Enlightenment, early sexology and sexual revolution, whereas other countries such as Hungary and East Germany experienced the changes of the Enlightenment as well as those of sexology and early homosexual emancipation. But there the latest developments since the sexual revolution and the legendary start of gay and lesbian emancipation with the Stonewall riots are unknown. The modernisation of the East has been very partial. The same is true for many groups which have immigrated to Europe recently. These cultures may be contemporary, but in certain ways they face a lag of decades. That may not be too important, as it is easy to adapt the newest sexual theories and practices. But on the other hand, the minds of people change rather slowly and, when it comes to the moulding of sexual opinions and practices, a retardation of some decades is a real disadvantage. In certain respects the different cultures are synchronic, but in others anachronic.

Notwithstanding the emancipatory effects that modernisation has had in many respects, not all of it has been advantageous to everybody. The sexual revolution of the 1960s may have brought myriad liberties, but it also brought all kinds of sexual exploitation and violence to the surface, foremost incest and sexual violence against women and children, though it may well be argued that it has made these formerly concealed matters visible and discussable. Paedophiles profited less from this turnover than did gays. A reason to review European sexual cultures is to discuss the clash of western and eastern, northern and southern sexual theories and practices, and also to analyse the positive and negative effects of modernity and tradition. Modernisation brought many debates that are nowadays outdated, for example whether women should have the same rights as men or on the supposedly biological origin of homosexual orientation (LeVay 1993). There is no need to rehearse all western discussions on sexuality elsewhere.

At present we can see a very complex system of sexual cultures in Europe: sexual differences are great, with strong and influential conservative currents in many places and postmodern developments with kinky sex elsewhere. Nobody is able to predict what will happen with sexual cultures and policies in the East, how the sexual syncretism of the West will develop, and what both the homogenising and the diversifying effects of the mass media will be. Many developments seem to be irreversible, as with the struggles for women's rights and gay and lesbian emancipation. For scholars the main challenge nowadays is to throw off the shackles of traditional sexology and to put in place a science able to face the modernisation and differentiation of sexual cultures.

Overviews

In view of the problems within the recent historiography of sexuality mentioned above, the contributions to this volume and its companion volume try to give a general idea of the research which has taken place during the last decades. Furthermore they are an endeavour to probe and to enlarge the insecure terrain of human sexual life in the European past. Because of the heterogeneous state of the art, we can cover neither all European regions and countries nor all topics in the history of sexuality.

This volume presents overviews on European countries which have similar but also very different histories of sexuality: Britain, Ireland, France, Germany, Austria, Russia, the Netherlands and Italy and Spain. We should have liked to include something from the Scandinavian region, more on eastern Europe, and something on the

Balkans, but a limiting factor (which also applies to the issues covered in volume II) was the availability of scholars capable of undertaking such studies and willing and able to participate in this project at the present time.

A further limiting factor was the differing state of current historiography relating to the sexual life of specific nations. Some countries have a tradition going back at least several decades if not further of reflecting on the historical roots of their sexual cultures; others have numerous empirical studies of specific aspects if no overarching synthetic view; in others the subject has scarcely been addressed at all. Even for those countries with a developed tradition, there are still periods and areas for which there are more questions to be asked than historical evidence to be adduced.

In the case of Great Britain, remarkable continuities can be discerned. This may well be due to the early date at which modernisation and bourgeoisification of British society took place, developments already well under way during the eighteenth century, as well as to the relative political stability of the British state.

The somewhat Anglocentric tendency of Chapter 1 is to some extent modified in Chapter 2 by Fahey's analysis of Irish sexual culture, and the papers in the second volume which deal with aspects of the sexual cultures of Scotland and Wales. All of these had their own specific inflections of British culture, often arising as reaction and resistance to English cultural hegemony. An area which is touched on in these two volumes, but not perhaps as fully analysed as might be desirable, is the question of the relations between the sexual cultures of centre and periphery, between those of different ethnic or religious groups within the nation (a study of Belgium or Switzerland might be illuminating) as well as differing social class constructions.

Fahey draws attention to the relative lack of research into sexual questions in Ireland, which contrasts with the lengthy British tradition of reflecting (though often with moral opprobrium) on facets of national sexual mores. Fahey emphasises the highly and continuingly significant relationship of Catholicism to Irish national identity, and its strong influence on the state since Independence in formulating laws to regulate moral conduct. While Irish religion formed a site of resistance to British rule, one response to British cultural hegemony was to take even further the sexual tenets of high Victorian morality. Irish sexual culture since the 1960s has been liberalised along similar lines to those described by Wanrooij and Oosterhuis in Italy and the Netherlands. However, whereas other European Catholic nations have seen birth control and even abortion legalised, these remain sticking points for the Irish, who have instead destigmatised unmarried motherhood (although the availability of abortion and birth control in the United Kingdom may render the problem less acutely pressing).

Oosterhuis in his study of the Netherlands (Chapter 3) makes clear the significance of deeply rooted confessional loyalties. Interestingly, his chapter suggests that, while one might imagine the Catholic and Calvinist pillars of the Dutch state to have been rivals, the political importance of these groups with a moral agenda founded in religious beliefs was a strong counterbalance to forces of secularisation or religious indifference. Religious sensitivities which lay very largely along the same lines as regarded sexual attitudes, in spite of sectarian differences in doctrine, lay behind the increasing intervention of the Dutch state in the sphere of private morality from the later nineteenth century. Continuities between this past and the modern liberalised Netherlands, often held up as an example to less enlightened states, are shown to exist.

Another nation which has a long tradition of sexual culture manifesting considerable continuities is France. As Robert Nye elucidates in Chapter 4, while on the level of legislation the French appear to be liberal in their designation of a non-intervention zone of private morality from the early nineteenth century, there has been strong public pressure and unofficial feeling in favour of a pronatalist, strongly heterosexual norm. (We may note that this strong rhetoric of pronatalism coexisted with what were widely regarded as the most successfully contracepting marriages in Europe.) While the disjunction which often exists between other nations' perceptions of a particular sexual culture and its sense of its own emerges from this volume, Nye shows that the French themselves accept the image of their sexual sophistication and particular expertise in the amorous sphere, while demonstrating that this has been purchased at the price of a rather narrow definition of the permissible realm of the sexual.

Italy has often been wistfully perceived by the nations of northern Europe as a sunny paradise of guilt-free sensuality. Wanrooij's study of Italy (Chapter 5) indicates that this has been very largely the point of view of the economically privileged tourist (in some cases, specifically sex tourist). As might be expected from a nation which for much of the nineteenth century was regarded as a 'geographical expression' rather than a coherent nation state, the importance of differing regional cultures is emphasised. The influence of Catholicism was clearly a major factor in the development of Italian sexual culture, its moral norms being enacted by the secular post-unification state and, to some extent, Fascism.

The German-speaking areas of Europe also had considerable regional differences, and in particular urban–rural differences, although, as Eder argues in Chapter 6, many customs of peasant culture were extremely widespread throughout this area. Urbanisation took place perhaps rather later and more abruptly than in Britain or France, but Eder suggests that the apparent continuity in the urban context of peasant attitudes to sexual conduct concealed mutation and adaptation to the very different pressures of urban life, and that, by the second generation of city life, beliefs and behaviour had radically altered. The particularly dramatic developments of the twentieth century, the vaunted liberalisation of the Weimar Republic and the backlash of Nazism are seen to have had elements in common, and ambiguous implications for German sexual cultures.

Spain in particular underwent modernisation very late, and tended to perceive this as an alien imposition upon native traditions. As Amezua and Cleminson point out in Chapter 7, there is still much work to be done on the sexual cultures of the Iberian peninsula, and to what extent these modernising influences drew on long-standing attitudes. However, as an example of the contradictions which are so intricately a part of any sexual culture, we may observe the deeply anti-sex tradition of Spanish Catholicism and its misogynist tendencies, while noting the emergence of (at however subterranean and surreptitious a level) a literature of popular sex education, as described in this chapter. Many exciting questions and possibilities of further study are raised: in particular the regional differences may, on further investigation, prove interesting variations on the norm. For example, Amezua and Cleminson point to the strong anarchist tradition of Catalonia in which women played a significant part.

In Russia also, as Kon makes clear in Chapter 8, 'modernisation' and 'westernisation' have often been situated as identical, and reacted to in monolithic ways. This chapter also indicates the influence on sexual cultures of another religious tradition, that of the Orthodox church, imposed (in European terms) very late and not always with great success over persistent pagan practices, if not coherent belief-systems. Russia has perhaps undergone some of the most wrenching and abrupt societal upheavals of all the nations discussed, and yet, it is argued in this chapter, there have in fact been persistent continuities in how Russia has reacted to the processes of change. The extremely startling contradictions which Kon indicates have been a feature of Russian sexual culture are currently embodied in the wide dissemination of pornography in contrast to the lack of organised sex education.

Additionally included in this volume are two overviews of Europe-wide phenomena which have been touched on in their national manifestations in the preceding chapters. It is by now almost a cliché to say that older notions of sexual deviations as sins were replaced by concepts of disease and pathology with the development of a *scientia sexualis* identified with the emergence of medical discourses on sexuality during the second half of the nineteenth century. Harry Oosterhuis in Chapter 9 draws on his work on Richard von Krafft-Ebing, which has already revised the existing image of Krafft-Ebing as the great pathologiser (as depicted, for example, in Paul Robinson's *The Modernisation of Sex*), to present a nuanced picture of the development of sexology. While eschewing earlier uncomplicatedly Whiggish interpretations, he argues that the development was not as malign, nor as imposed from the top down, as more recent writers have suggested. It is clear to anyone who studies the subject that sexology was very much a trans-national development and in no nation did it enjoy any considerable esteem: those who pursued this unpopular topic therefore often found their strongest allies and colleagues among foreigners.

This theme is pursued in Ralf Dose's study in Chapter 10 of the World League for Sexual Reform, a body with a strongly European orientation founded by Magnus Hirschfeld, representing individuals from several European nations who considered themselves progressive and forward-thinking. He demonstrates how the existence of an international body of this kind in fact promoted the development of national groups (not necessarily pursuing similar agendas) during the 1920s and 1930s. He points out the problems of researching this body in the light of the paucity of evidence, and the archivist among the editors would like to emphasise the problems of investigations in an area in which the historical evidence is perhaps peculiarly likely to be destroyed, even without deliberate interventions (such as the Nazi destruction of Hirschfeld's Institute) or the destruction of records through war – by bombing or through salvage drives for waste paper.

These volumes, therefore, cannot be a definitive account of sexual cultures in Europe. They illuminate the state of the historiography and the historical differences between a number of contrasting European nations, and it can be seen that even neighbouring nations with apparently considerable similarities have had differing sexual cultures modulated by variations in religion, legal structures, political systems, economic factors and geographical features as well as more nebulous elements of 'national culture'. This volume, and its companion volume *Sexual Cultures in Europe: Themes in Sexuality*, establish, it is hoped, an agenda and further suggestions for future work in this area as well as an account of the current state of research.

Bibliography

Bauer, Max and Johannes Scherr (1928), *Weib, Dame, Dirne: Kultur- und Sittengeschichte der deutschen Frau*, Dresden, Aretz.

Cohen, E. (1993), *Talk on the Wilde Side: Toward a Genealogy of a Discourse on Male Sexualities*, London, Routledge.

Corbin, Alain (1978), *Les Filles de noce: misère sexuelle et prostitution, 19ᵉ siècle*, Paris, Aubier Montaigne.

Duchâtelet, A. J. B. (1836), *De la prostitution dans le ville de Paris*, Paris, Baillière.

Dühren, Eugen (=Iwan Bloch) (1899), *Der Marquis de Sade und seine Zeit: ein Beitrag zur Kultur- und Sittengeschichte des 18. Jahrhunderts*, Berlin, Barsdorf.

Eder, Franz X. (1994), 'Die Historisierung des sexuellen Subjekts: Sexualitätsgeschichte zwischen Essentialismus und sozialem Konstruktivismus', *Österreichische Zeitschrift für Geschichtswissenschaften*, 5, 3, pp. 311–27.

— (1996), 'Sexualized Subjects: Medical Discourses on Sexuality in German-speaking Countries in the Late eighteenth and in the nineteenth Century', in Institute of the History of Medicine and Social Medicine (ed.), *Civilization, Sexuality and Social Life in Historical Context: The Hidden Face of Urban Life*, Budapest, University of Budapest, pp. 17–29.

Engelstein, Laura (1992), *The Keys to Happiness: Sex and the Search for Modernity in Fin-de-siècle Russia*, Ithaca, Cornell University Press.

Flandrin, Jean-Louis (1975), *Les Amours paysannes: amour et sexualité, dans les campagnes de l'ancienne France, XVIᵉ–XIXᵉ siècle*, Paris, Gallimard/Julliard.

Foucault, Michel (1976), *Histoire de la sexualité*, vol. 1: *la volonté de savoir*, Paris, Gallimard.

Fout, John C. (1990), 'A Note from the Editor', *Journal of the History of Sexuality*, 1, 1, pp. 1 f.

Fuchs, Eduard (1909–16), *Illustrierte Sittengeschichte vom Mittelalter bis zur Gegenwart*, 3 vols and 3 additional vols, Munich, Langen.

Gerard, Kent and Gert Hekma (1989) (eds), *The Pursuit of Sodomy: Male Homosexuality in Renaissance and Enlightenment Europe*, Binghamton, Harrington Park Press.

Gilmore, David D. (ed.) (1987), *Honour and Shame and the Unity of the Mediterranean*, Washington, American Anthropological Association.

Hekma, Gert (1987), *Homoseksualiteit, een medische reputatie: de uitdoktering van de homoseksueel in negentiende-eeuws Nederland*, Amsterdam, SUA.

— (1994), 'De klemmen van de lust: De ontwikkeling van het plezier sinds de seksuele revolutie', *Etnofoor* 7, 2, pp. 5–24.

Hekma, Gert, Harry Oosterhuis and James D. Steakley (eds) (1995), *Gays and the Sexual History of the Political Left*, Binghamton, Harrington Park Press.

Hirschfeld, Magnus (1930–1), *Sittengeschichte des Weltkrieges*, 2 vols and 1 additional vol., Leipzig and Vienna, Schneider.

Kennedy, Hubert (1988), *Ulrichs: The Life and Works of Karl Heinrich Ulrichs, Pioneer of the Modern Gay Movement*, Boston, Alyson.

Kon, Igor S. (1995), *The Sexual Revolution in Russia: From the Age of the Czars to Today*, New York, Free Press.

Laqueur, Thomas (1990), *Making Sex: Body and Gender from the Greeks to Freud*, Cambridge (Mass.), Harvard University Press.

Laslett, Peter, Karla Oosterveen and Richard M. Smith (eds) (1980), *Bastardy and its Comparative History*, London, Edward Arnold.

LeVay, Simon (1993), *The Sexual Brain*, Cambridge (Mass.), MIT Press.

Marcus, Steven (1966), *The Other Victorians: A Study of Sexuality and Pornography in Mid-nineteenth Century England*, New York and London, Basic Books and Weidenfeld & Nicolson.

Mitterauer, Michael (1983), *Ledige Mütter: zur Geschichte illegitimer Geburten in Europa*, Munich, Beck.

Mossuz-Lavau, Janine (1991), *Les Lois de l'amour: les politiques de la sexualité en France (1950–1990)*, Paris, Payot.

Oosterhuis, Harry (1992), *De smalle marges van de roomse moraal: homoseksualiteit in katholiek Nederland 1900–1970*, Amsterdam, Het Spinhuis.

Oosterhuis, Harry, Jan W. Duyvendak and Gert Hekma (1994), 'The European Post-war Gay and Lesbian Movement', *Homologie* 14, 4, pp. 22–8.

Parikas, Udo and Teet Veispak (eds) (1990), *Sexual Minorities and Society: The Changing Attitudes toward Homosexuality in 20th Century Europe. Papers Presented to the International Conference in Tallinn May 28–30, 1990*, Tallinn, Institute of History.

Pearsall, Ronald (1969), *The Worm in the Bud: The World of Victorian Sexuality*, New York, Macmillan.

Porter, Roy and Lesley A. Hall (1995), *The Facts of Life: The Creation of Sexual Knowledge in Britain, 1650–1950*, New Haven and London, Yale University Press.

Robinson, Paul (1976), *The Modernisation of Sex: Havelock Ellis, Alfred Kinsey, William Masters and Virginia Johnson*, London and New York, Harper & Row.

Rosenbaum, Julius (1839), *Geschichte der Lustseuche im Alterthume*, Halle, Lippert.

Rotberg, Robert I. and Theodore K. Rabb (eds) (1980), *Marriage and Fertility: Studies in Interdisciplinary History*, Princeton, Princeton University Press.

Sanger, William (1858), *History of Prostitution: Its Extent, Causes and Effects Throughout the World*, New York, Harper.

Shorter, Edward (1975), *The Making of the Modern Family*, New York, Basic Books.

Spira, Alfred and Nathalie Bajos (1993), *Les Comportements sexuels en France*, Paris, La Documentation Française.

Stanton, Domna C. (ed.) (1992), *Discourses of Sexuality: From Aristotle to AIDS*, Ann Arbor, Michigan University Press.

Steakley, James D. (1975), *The Homosexual Emancipation Movement in Germany*, New York, Arno Press.

Stein, Edward (ed.) (1990), *Forms of Desire: Sexual Orientation and the Social Constructivist Controversy*, New York and London, Garland.

Stengers, Jean and Anne van Neck (1984), *Histoire d'une grande peur: la masturbation*, Brussels, Editions de l'Université de Bruxelles.

Stockinger, Jacob (1979), 'Homosexuality and the French Enlightenment', in G. Stambolian and E. Marks (eds), *Homosexualities and French Literature*, Ithaca and London, Cornell University Press, pp. 161–85.

Tarczylo, Theodore (1983), *Sexe et liberté au siècle des Lumières*, Paris, Presses de la Renaissance.

Tilly, Charles (ed.) (1978), *Historical Studies of Changing Fertility*, Princeton, Princeton University Press.

Ussel, Jos van (1968), *Geschiedenis van het seksuele probleem*, Meppel, Boom.

Walkowitz, Judith (1980), *Prostitution and Victorian Society: Women, Class, and the State*, Cambridge and New York, Cambridge University Press.

Weeks, Jeffrey (1981), *Sex, Politics and Society: The Regulation of Sexuality since 1800*, London and New York, Longman.

Wellings, Kaye, Julia Field, Anne M. Johnson and Jane Wadsworth (1994), *Sexual Behaviour in Britain: The National Survey of Sexual Attitudes and Lifestyles*, London, Penguin.

Young, Wayne (1964), *Eros Denied: Sex in Western Society*, New York, Weidenfeld & Nicolson.

Zessen, Gert van and Theo Sandfort (eds) (1991), *Seksualiteit in Nederland: seksueel gedrag, risico en preventie van Aids*, Amsterdam and Lisse, Swets & Zeitlinger.

National histories

1

Sexual cultures in Britain: some persisting themes

Lesley A. Hall

There are a number of clichés about British sexual culture: that the British have hot-water bottles instead of a sex-life, that they are subject to 'periodical fits of morality' and conversely that they don't care what people do as long as they don't do it in the street and frighten the horses. The persistent ascription of disapproved sexual manifestations to other nations, in particular the French, should perhaps be mentioned – sodomy was even more stigmatised by being attributed to even further distant nationalities, Italians, Turks or less specific 'Orientals'. However, this was not entirely unique to Britain, since all nations seem to ascribe venereal disease to foreigners, while what the English called French letters the French called *capote anglais*.

A rich historiographical tradition fails to confirm completely any of the above clichés, and illustrates a characteristic anomaly: Britain is supposed to be particularly sexually repressed (a British monarch gave the Victorian age its eponym), and yet this culture generated the word and concept of malthusianism, several standard sexological texts, at least one marital-advice manual of international renown, and this developed debate in the history of sexuality. Rather than repeating traditional charges, this chapter explores this persistently ambiguous quality in the sexual culture generated by a complex society containing a plethora of social and economic groups with very differing ideologies. Too often historians have given exaggerated attention to a single strand.

An important element in the policing and regulation of sexuality in Britain has been its complex and decentralised legal system. There was a significant common-law element based on judicial precedent as opposed to statute law, although not all courts operated on this basis. Separate ecclesiastical courts retained significant areas of jurisdiction over moral conduct well into the nineteenth century. A major factor in British sexual culture has been the reluctance, with significant exceptions, of the central state to intervene in the sexual sphere. For example, the sale of sexual services has never been illegal in itself (nor has the use of birth control), nor has it been regulated except for a twenty-year period in specific geographical locations. None the less prostitution could not be practised with impunity, and advocating birth control could lead to prosecution.

The counterpart to this official apathy has been the importance of initiatives devolved to the local level and the role played by voluntary associations of many different kinds, often working in tandem with policing authorities interested in maintaining good social order and reducing the amount of unacceptable public behaviour. In the eighteenth century there were societies for the reformation of manners and morals as well as philanthropic institutions reclaiming prostitutes, rescuing foundling children and treating the venereally diseased. During the nineteenth century there were societies to suppress vice and to rescue prostitutes, associations aiming either to repeal or to extend the Contagious Diseases Acts of the 1860s, the Malthusian League arguing for birth control and, in the later nineteenth century, the social purity societies working for moral regeneration. The twentieth century has seen social hygiene societies, organisations promoting the study of sexual questions, associations for the establishment of birth control clinics, pressure groups lobbying for legalising (and re-criminalising) abortion and decriminalising homosexuality, societies aiming to eradicate filth from television and sex education from schools, as well as the bodies dealing with various aspects of the AIDS epidemic which have emerged since the 1980s.

This account deals largely with England, which was very far from being a homogeneous society. Apart from the considerable differences between social classes, there were major variations in acceptable sexual mores by region, not only between England and Wales, Scotland and Ireland, but between the metropolis and the provinces, towns and rural areas, industrial and agrarian regions, the north and the south, and even between adjacent districts, as local studies have amply demonstrated.

The conventional view of the eighteenth century has been of a sexually liberated paradise preceding the repressions of the Victorian era. Tim Hitchcock, in his recent monograph on *English Sexualities 1700–1800*, contrasts the untypical though literate male elite group on which attention has often focused (and which he suggests was characterised by uneasy male bonding in the face of severe sexual anxieties) with the contemporary associations for the reformation of morals largely composed of the 'middling sort'. While these bodies vociferously deprecated aristocratic vice, their activities largely centred on enforcing decency in the public sphere by policing plebeian behaviour, especially prostitution, and also the increasing sodomite subculture, through alliances with local mechanisms of community control.

Hitchcock delineates a series of moral panics around the middle of the eighteenth century, concerning a variety of sexual matters, from clandestine marriage to bawdy houses, occurring in a context of political and economic instability and accelerating social change. Similar moral panics have occurred at other periods in British history and often in similar contexts, and have equally tended to obsession with some almost chimerical manifestation. Bawds and brothels were fairly insignificant factors in British prostitution but it was bawds against whom legislation was enacted. The white slavery panics of the early twentieth century similarly were less concerned to grapple with the genuine problems around prostitution and venereal disease than to eradicate the semi-mythical abduction of innocent girls from places of public amusement by procurers (often demonised as sinister alien figures).

Contemporary with this moral panic, several philanthropic institutions were founded: the Lock Hospital for venereal diseases, the Foundling Hospital for abandoned children, and the Magdalen Hospital for prostitutes wishing to quit their way of life. These ran partly counter to societal stigmatisation – for example, most hospitals regarded patients with VD as unfit objects of philanthropy – but were also deeply implicated in contemporary discourses. The Magdalen Hospital increasingly focused on victims of seduction rather than habitual prostitutes. This persistent skewing of debates on prostitution to concentrate on (the probably rather small percentage of) victims who could be regarded as uncomplicatedly 'innocent' recurred in W. T. Stead's 1885 'Maiden Tribute of Modern Babylon' articles (Judith Walkowitz has analysed their quasi-pornographic narrative structure of innocence defiled in *City of Dreadful Delight*) and early twentieth-century white slavery panics.

Philanthropic institutions encouraged prostitute women to present themselves as both victim and repentant. However, for many women in both rural and urban settings, at this and later periods, commercial exploitation of sex did not follow seduction by a social superior but was an occasional survival strategy: the majority of prostitutes were aged between sixteen and twenty-five and of the poorer classes, supplementing inadequate wages or seasonal declines in trade. Most were independent operators rather than brothel inmates, a tradition which seems to have persisted. This loose structure may have derived from the lack of state regulation but may also have militated against introducing Continental models of licensing, since institutions did not exist around which such a model could be based.

Hitchcock plausibly argues that by the end of the eighteenth century sexual practices had become less varied and far more phallocentric, with a greater orientation towards heterosexual penetration rather than non-insertive practices. In 1700 a varied repertoire of sexual behaviour was mediated through community pressures. Women were perceived as sexual to an almost dangerous degree, and early eighteenth-century prostitutes were envisaged as aggressive and out-of-control lustful sinners, disorderly women, not passive and potentially pathetic victims of seduction. Because heterosexual practice was less focused on a penetrative, penis-in-vagina model, there was some creative leeway for same-gender interactions, which became foreclosed during the century as definitions and categories hardened and became more oppressive and exclusive.

A proliferating literature condemning onanism, and recommending procreative conjugal sex, tended to stigmatise any practices which resembled masturbation or could not be subsumed to reproductive purposes. Belief in the benign nature of reproductive sex, however, received a severe blow from the gloomy prognostications of the Reverend Thomas Malthus that population would always tend to outstrip its means of subsistence. This fed into what was already becoming a rather dark vision of sex: imperative, phallic and threatened in men, passive and victimised in women, with a fetishistic importance laid on physical virginity. While apparently privileging the male, this model was capable of provoking intense, if well-hidden, anxieties, as can be deduced from the flourishing quack industry in remedies for male sexual debility (often advertised along-side spurious cures for venereal disease).

Sodomy, again, followed a traditional British pattern of periods of toleration interspersed with vicious persecution and moral panics. The change during the eighteenth century, from the image of the foppish but still, even hyper-, masculine bisexual libertine to that of the effeminate sodomite, was influenced by the hardening of cate-gories already mentioned, concurrent with the emergence of a visible homosexual subculture in large cities such as London.

Changes in heterosexual relations presumably also arose from the move to a more urbanised society. Other factors were increasing degrees of privacy (typified by a growing separation between families and their servants), a rising standard of civility which deprecated public bawdiness, an emerging middle class with a fetish for respectability and, Hitchcock persuasively suggests, the supersession of female-influenced oral traditions by a largely male-dominated literate discourse with the rise of print culture.

In spite of proto-Victorian elements already in place by 1800, in many ways a 'long eighteenth century' endured well beyond the accession of the young Queen in 1837. For much of the aristocracy, even though some individuals were profoundly influenced by morally reforming movements, the Victorian era as experienced by the middle classes hardly existed. One need only consider the lifestyle of Victoria's son, the Prince of Wales, later Edward VII, and the circles he moved in, though possibly aristocratic libertinism did become more privatised and discreet. There was also, Michael Mason has suggested in *The Making of Victorian Sexuality*, a less socially elite libertine underculture during the nineteenth century, which was largely excluded from public discussions on sexual topics and therefore is problematic for the historian to reconstruct.

A cult of moral seriousness had emerged well before 1800, although there was also a 'radical underworld', republican and anti-religious, which employed libertine discourses and scurrilous obscene satire for politically revolutionary purposes. It was from this sub-culture that the earliest neo-Malthusian writings emerged: only within a milieu in which a knowledge of contraceptive devices (the purlieu of prostitutes and libertines) existed could a challenge to Malthus's iron law be made through applying human ingenuity to thwarting the outcome of intercourse. This alliance between political radicalism and unconventional sexual morality, which nurtured such neo-Malthusian propagandists as Francis Place and Richard Carlile, was already disintegrating during the 1820s. Political radicalism was becoming increasingly allied with respectability, while libertine satire mutated into cynically commercial pornography.

There continued to be a flourishing market for the revelations of vice among the aristocracy, such as the published proceedings of *crim. con.* (criminal conversation) cases: husbands suing their wives' seducers for damages. This was a necessary legal preliminary to obtaining a divorce by private Act of Parliament, the only way of dissolving marriage in Britain at that time and confined to the rich and powerful (and of course only to men). Interest in these and other scandals was largely prurient rather than subversive, although political uses were made of the marital strife between George IV and his wife Caroline of Brunswick.

The wider effect on society of the change of monarch in 1837 was considerable. The mad George III had been succeeded (after a long regency) by his son George IV, who was widely regarded as a debauchee, as were his brothers, who rushed to discard their mistresses, marry appropriate brides and beget presumptive heirs to the throne on the death of the heir, Princess Charlotte. The sole result was the Princess Victoria, daughter of the Duke of Kent, who succeeded her uncle William IV in 1837. The marriage of this young and virtuous queen to Prince Albert of Saxe-Coburg-Gotha established a royal domestic circle very different from the courts of her predecessors. The new image of the monarchy was one with which middle-class respectability could identify. Victoria herself, however, was far from a Victorian: all the evidence suggests that she was quite the reverse of the model Victorian wife depicted by William Acton, interested in sex only to gratify her husband and in order to achieve motherhood. Victoria's eager acceptance of the use of chloroform during confinement was a significant factor in making obstetric analgesia popular and acceptable.

The Victorian era, its sexual beliefs and its behaviour have been extensively analysed. The existence of 'other Victorians', who did not conform to the image of repressed sexuality, has been common knowledge since Steven Marcus's work of that name, but Victorian 'repression' was not entirely mythical, even though significant shifts and variations occurred throughout Victoria's long reign: Michael Mason in particular, in his two volumes on Victorian sexuality and sexual attitudes, has drawn attention to these. Received ideas about Victorian sexual 'hypocrisy' may result from the elision of characteristics of very different groups or widely separated historical moments. It was not necessarily the married man who held family prayers every morning who was keeping a mistress or habitually resorting to prostitutes. Certainly there was a good deal of moral contortion, epitomised in William Gladstone, several times Prime Minister, famed for his attempts to rescue pretty prostitutes and his practice of self-flagellation. Charles Dickens is known to have led a double life. The most famous flagellant of Victorian England, however, the poet Algernon Swinburne, had no pretensions to respectability.

Attempts to prove that Victorians enjoyed pleasurable sexual lives have focused largely on the Victorian married woman. Less attention has been given to the inhibitions and anxieties prevalent over a wide social range of Victorian males, which suggest that they were hardly likely to evoke or encourage sexual appetite in their wives. Fears of seminal loss through masturbation or the disease of 'spermatorrhoea' also applied to too copious 'spending' of vital spermatic fluids within marriage.

There was an increasing degree of censorship. Bodies such as the Society for the Suppression of Vice took an active part in prosecuting the vendors of obscene material, and their efforts were supported by the passing of Lord Campbell's Act in 1857. In the case of literary texts writers' own self-censorship was encouraged by the commercially crucial circulating libraries' very strict moral codes. Nevertheless there was by no means a total silence on sexual matters in mid-Victorian Britain. Even respectable newspapers published a good deal of sensational and even salacious material. Heated debates about prostitution took place in the columns of *The Times* itself, in which there was a lengthy correspondence in 1858 about high-class prostitution and its alleged contribution to the delayed marriages of middle- and upper-class men. This included letters purporting to be written by actual 'unfortunates' themselves.

Both prostitution and the related question of venereal diseases were much discussed. Earlier the subject had been considered largely in a religious light, but by the 1850s the terms of debate were increasingly being set by medical, particularly public health, discourses in the Chadwickian era of sanitary reform − although the rescue ethos continued. It is not clear whether social changes such as urbanisation, geographical mobility and seasonality of labour actually created a greater amount of prostitution, or whether the anxieties these generated produced perceptions of vice pullulating in rapidly expanding cities. Michael Mason, in *The Making of Victorian Sexuality*, has made a plausible case for the gross exaggeration of the extent of prostitution by contemporaries, usually middle-class observers who assumed that any working-class girl seen in places of public amusement was either a prostitute or well on her way to becoming one. The relevant section of Mayhew's *London Labour and the London Poor* failed to differentiate the unmarried in monogamous unions from professional harlots, although certain occupational groups in the metropolis were notorious for their lack of attention to formal marriage ties. William Acton, in his famous study *Prostitution*, contended that street-walking was often a transitory stage in a young woman's life and that she might readily move back into respectability: Walkowitz, in *Prostitution and Victorian Society*, suggests that prostitutes in Portsmouth and Southampton did not, prior to the Contagious Diseases Acts, form a distinct and stigmatised group among the working-class communities in which they lived. Such mobility was favoured by the informal and unstructured nature of prostitution in Britain.

In the 1860s, as a result of anxieties about the health of the Army and Navy stimulated by the revelations of the Crimean War, the government passed a series of Contagious Diseases Acts regulating prostitution in designated port and garrison towns. Within these areas prostitutes could be picked up and examined for venereal disease, and if infected, incarcerated in lock hospitals until (supposedly) cured. The model of regulated prostitution on Continental lines appealed strongly to some and there were calls for the wider extension of the Acts. There were also, however, strong feelings against them: religious, class (the women involved were almost entirely working-class), feminist and civil libertarian. Thus the Contagious Diseases Acts reveal the often polarised nature of British public opinion on sexual matters. Even the medical profession was divided as to their efficacy, Sir John Simon, one of the leading sanitarians of the day, being a convinced opponent of what was seen by many as a logical development of existing public health practices.

Such polarisation of views can also be discerned in contemporary writings. William Acton's famous *Functions and Disorders of the Reproductive Organs* (1857) is often regarded as the archetypal

Victorian discourse on sexual functioning in its depiction of women as largely sexless, and of men as in almost constant danger of debilitating seminal overspending. However, it was almost exactly contemporaneous with the very different *Elements of Social Science* by George Drysdale (first published as *Physical, Sexual and Natural Religion* in 1854), which regarded sexual activity as benign and health-giving but its reproductive consequences as potentially deleterious for economic reasons: Drysdale's answer was contraception. Yet, like Acton, he believed in the dangers of masturbation and spermatorrhoea. The eminent and influential physician Sir James Paget, on the contrary, disbelieved prevalent convictions of the perils of self-abuse, while none the less describing the practice as 'filthiness'. As for ideas of female sexlessness (which Drysdale contradicted), the furore generated by Isaac Baker Brown's clitoridectomies in the 1860s, and over ovariotomy and its effect on female sexual functioning, revealed very diverse and often conflicting opinions among the British medical profession.

However, what most of the medical profession did oppose was contraception. Any mention of the subject in the medical press was largely a reaction to occurrences in lay circles, such as the press furore over Viscount Amberley's address to the Dialectical Society in 1868 recommending small families, and the 1877 trial for obscenity of Charles Bradlaugh and Annie Besant for publishing a small, inexpensive tract on birth control. The radical Leeds doctor Henry Allbutt was struck off the Medical Register in 1886 after recommending contraception in a cheap manual of health advice to women: the medical press argued that, while he was at liberty to discuss the subject with other doctors, such information was not to be disseminated at sixpence a time to the working classes.

Similar arguments about appropriate audience surfaced when Havelock Ellis, himself a doctor, published *Sexual Inversion* (1897), which was prosecuted for obscenity. The medical press claimed that the subject should be discussed by medical men (medical women, at that time a bare handful, were not mentioned) but that such a book might fall into the wrong hands (though it was at least not cheap). Earlier, J. Addington Symonds (Ellis's collaborator, whose name had been taken off the published version at the request of his executors) had avoided similar difficulties by privately printing his two pioneering works on homosexuality, *A Problem in Greek Ethics* and *A*

Problem in Modern Ethics, in small editions for personal dissemination to potential sympathisers who might influence law reform. The *British Medical Journal* reviewer of Edward Carpenter's *The Intermediate Sex* in 1909 complained of its cheapness and accessibility to a lay public.

This was a subset of a persistent concern by one group of people for the morals of other people, in particular other people with not much money. One set of laws for the rich and another for the poor, or at least the less privileged social classes, has been a recurrent theme. On the one hand, the rich and privileged have often been able to evade or bend laws falling heavily on the poor. On the other, legal remedies for desperate situations (such as divorce) were beyond the pockets of many. Or at least it has been believed that this was so: during the 1920s it was assumed that the better-off had access to birth control knowledge unavailable to the working-class woman, although enquiries received by Marie Stopes suggest that ignorance about contraception was rife throughout the social spectrum.

Anxieties about censorship have always tended to focus on materials available to the masses. Rich connoisseurs of pornography have usually been able to pursue their hobby with relative impunity, buying limited editions produced by specialist dealers. Vigilance societies, however, policed the materials available to a wider public: in the 1850s concern focused on hawkers at country fairs, in the 1930s on American 'pulp' magazines in Woolworths, and more recently on the potentially demoralising effects of video and the Internet. Another persisting theme has been the spurious nature of the erotic goods palmed off on the poorer consumer: Mayhew mentioned the sale of 'sealed packets' which did not contain the lubricious materials expected, turn-of-the-century 'French postcards' depicted nude statues, and recent reporters have commented on how unarousing expensive telephone sex-lines are.

While it was reported that the London clubs were denuded, at the time of the Oscar Wilde trial, by the flight abroad of socially elite homosexuals, homosexual members of powerful and influential networks were a good deal less imperilled than their social inferiors and could count on the influence of friends in high places. In some cases police were specifically ordered to ignore certain individuals. A similar case was abortion: the Abortion Law Reform Association actually issued a pamphlet with the title *Law for the Rich*. There had probably always been practitioners willing to procure abortion for those prepared to pay. The precedent established in 1938 by the Bourne case of the acceptability of psychiatric grounds for abortion continued to favour those who had money and knew the ropes. Poorer women still resorted to back-street operators or self-abortion.

There appears to have been a change in British sexual culture around 1880. The campaign against the Contagious Diseases Acts was proving successful, and the Acts were suspended in 1883, repealed in 1886. In 1885 a Criminal Law Amendment Act was passed, which, as a result of Stead's famous revelations about child prostitution in his articles on 'The Maiden Tribute of Modern Babylon', raised the age of consent from thirteen to sixteen. It was this Act which included the infamous Labouchère Amendment. While sodomy had ceased to be a capital crime in 1861, though still penalised by life imprisonment, this Act broadened the definition of homosexual crime to include even consensual acts between adult men in private, while reducing the penalty to two years (as opposed to the higher sentence imposed on acts often legally defined as 'attempted sodomy').

The forces of moral reform were on a high. The social purity movement emerging from the opposition to the Contagious Diseases Acts, however, attracted into its ranks individuals concerned with medico-moral policing formerly on the opposite side. Thus, while there was a strong groundswell of feeling in favour of morally reforming society, opinions as to how this should be done differed considerably. Many who had fought against the Contagious Diseases Acts, including Josephine Butler, the leader of the Ladies' National Association for the Repeal of the Acts, felt that moral purity should not be enforced but brought about through education and reform of existing abuses in society. Others, however, wanted more policing of prostitution and male homosexuality, increasing censorship, etc. The movement was very complex. The hounding and imprisonment under the Obscene Publications Act of Vizetelly, the elderly publisher of English translations of Zola, under the aegis of the purity movement, seems monstrous, but there were real and practical attempts to ameliorate sexual harassment and abuse of women and children within a legal system dominated by men at every level. A dichotomy is sometimes alleged between social purity and medical discourse, but social purity was influenced by public health ideology and many doctors were supporters.

Another dichotomy is often set up between social purity and the movement for 'sex reform' based on the new sexology, important founding works of which in Britain were Geddes and Thomson's *The Evolution of Sex*, Edward Carpenter's *Love's Coming of Age*, and Havelock Ellis's multi-volume *Studies in the Psychology of Sex*. Both these movements considered sex to be a serious matter, in opposition to a less articulate but none the less pervasive and influential conventional view of sex, which Michael Mason has usefully identified in *The Making of Victorian Sexual Attitudes* as 'classic moralism'. This assumed that sex was not for serious discussion, though in certain contexts it might be the subject of jest, and relied on uninterrogated 'common-sense' assumptions about 'human nature' under which phenomena such as the 'double standard' of morality were due to innate unchangeable factors. Such a set of barely spoken assumptions can be traced far less readily than the discourses of either social purity or sex reform, but they surfaced in parliamentary debates on prostitution and the age of consent, in judicial pronouncements and in some sections of the press.

Thus both social purity and sex reform were fighting this morally conventional conservatism, and closer observation of both groups reveals common sympathies and even alliances. They were both, on the whole, in favour of the emancipation of women, opposed to prostitution, in favour of sexual enlightenment for the young, and saw venereal diseases as a major social problem, though the actual remedies proposed might differ widely. There were specific areas of conflict: for example over questions of marriage and divorce, homosexuality and censorship. But rather than entrenched camps in dire opposition, these were rather fuzzy groups overlapping at a number of points. The social purity camp did tend to assume that the problem was defined and the answers known, whereas the sexologists felt that the matter was not quite so easy and that the state of knowledge of sexual matters was so inadequate and so deeply informed by uninstructed prejudices that a great deal of groundwork needed doing before any programme of action could be adumbrated.

It has often been claimed that an oppressive medical discourse of homosexuality was emerging in the 1890s. While the biological model of the congenital invert advanced in the works of Ellis and Carpenter could certainly prove problematic, these works, like those of J. A. Symonds, were protests against the state of affairs initiated by the Labouchère Amendment (a piece of legislation whose origins and intentions are profoundly obscure and have resisted the attempts of historians to elucidate). The media circus of the trial of Oscar Wilde was far more influential in constituting popular and even medical attitudes. Wilde was front-page news, and the expression 'an unspeakable of the Oscar Wilde sort' was probably a good deal more representative of the general public's vague notions about homosexuality than Ellis's and Carpenter's 'inverts', 'intermediates' and 'uranians'. Textbooks of medical jurisprudence reveal little acquaintance with these writers several decades into the twentieth century, continuing to cite the cases of Boulton and Park (1871) and Wilde. These textbooks indicate that the general level of understanding of homosexuality by doctors, even forensic specialists, was often lamentable, and even ludicrous. (They also demonstrate rather prurient interest in female homosexuality, which, not being illegal, had no forensic implications – it did not even constitute grounds for divorce.)

Sexology in Britain had a very tenuous connection with medicine. Ellis was certainly a qualified doctor but did not practise and had a rather low professional standing, holding the Licentiate of the Society of Apothecaries, a somewhat looked-down upon medical qualification: he is probably one of very few LMSSAs ever to have been awarded the prestigious Fellowship of the Royal College of Physicians, an accolade he received shortly before his death, in recognition of his great work for sexual enlightenment (over forty years after the prosecution of *Sexual Inversion*). The roots of his work in sexology lay, like Carpenter's, in a British tradition of ethical socialist reform encompassing a range of moral issues excluded from stricter Marxist definitions. This tradition of idealistic resistance to industrialised capitalist society was associated with pacifism, animal rights, ecology, alternative medicine, vegetarianism, a somewhat pantheistic nature-worship and feminism. Carpenter, in particular, had no hesitation in interweaving recent discoveries in medicine and science with theosophical concepts.

The British medical profession, while its leaders might feel that sex was a subject that medics, rather than the laity, should deal with, was quite happy to delegate the actual messy task of taking an interest in it to those few individuals who did so. Acton as approved expert was succeeded by Havelock Ellis, greeted as a sound English voice on a subject largely identified with Continentals. Meanwhile doctors in Britain were not even routinely taught anything about venereal diseases, which constituted one of the major public health problems of the day.

There were attempts to engender public action about this pressing problem from the 1890s, with concerned parties seeking official investigation into the extent of the diseases. The government, intimidated by the Contagious Diseases Acts debacle, especially renewed agitation over the persistence of similar regulation in India, ignored all recommendations for paying any attention to the VD problem. However, increasing pressure from certain sections within the medical profession, moral and social reformers and informed opinion generally, plus (and perhaps most importantly) the scientific advances of the Wassermann test for syphilis and the therapeutically effective salvarsan treatment, led to the appointment of a Royal Commission on Venereal Diseases in 1913. This reported in 1916, having heard copious evidence from a vast range of witnesses, on the prevalence of sexually transmitted diseases – at least 10 per cent of the male population was infected with syphilis and even more with gonorrhoea – on the inadequacy of existing medical provisions, and on what was to be done.

Obeisance was given to the need for better public education on the subject, starting in a non-specific way with the young, but the principal action taken was medical. It became an offence for any but qualified medical doctors to administer treatment for VD, and a network of free, confidential centres for expert treatment was established. These were to avoid deterring the diseased from seeking treatment: secrecy was paramount, opening times were (in theory) such that patients would not have to take time off work to attend, and (again in theory) clinics were to be administered so as not to upset their already ashamed and vulnerable constituency. The system was a great success: within a few years a million patients a year were attending, and the rate of venereal disease in the population declined steeply. In spite of the many problems faced by venereologists and their clinics (for example, their continuing pariah status within hospitals), the British system was a remarkable triumph.

However, while the clinic system was part of national public health administration, the educational provision was delegated to a voluntary body, the National Council for Combating Venereal Disease, later renamed the British Social Hygiene Council. Initially this received a block grant from the government, but subsequently funding was devolved to local authorities, many of whom were reluctant to contribute. Later its functions were taken over by the Central Council for Health Education, another non-governmental body. The persisting problems of sex education in Britain were still operating in the 1990s, as medical agendas of STD control in the era of AIDS and the reduction of teenage pregnancies clashed at the highest levels with agendas of moral education in 'family values'.

In spite of the very real problem of venereal disease in the decade before the First World War, it received a good deal less attention than the issue of 'white slavery'. This was the subject not only of campaigns by social purity organisations, and much fulmination in the press, but of parliamentary debate and legislation. The moral panic and the hasty legislative action taken (1912) may be contrasted with the refusal of the government to contemplate action on venereal disease, the deliberate ignoring of the subject by the press (the publication of the word 'syphilis' in 1913 was a major breakthrough), and the failure to implement the recommendations of the Royal Commission on Marriage and Divorce.

Changes in the law of divorce in Britain moved slowly. In 1857 a law had been passed removing matrimonial causes from ecclesiastical courts, although for a long time the only divorce court in England was in London (Scotland had a different legal system under which divorce was much easier to obtain: it was, however, the subject of strong social disapproval), and the expenses involved remained considerable. Even so a significant percentage of divorces was obtained by members of the lower middle and working classes, as well as numerous judicial separations, which were dealt with by magistrates. The great inequity of the 1857 Act was in the sphere of gender: a husband could divorce a wife for a single act of adultery, but a wife could not divorce a husband for simple adultery, however repeated or prolonged, but had to prove an additional matrimonial offence such as cruelty, desertion or incest. Collusion or condonement meant that a divorce would not be granted, as the action continued to be defined on adversarial lines with 'innocent' and 'guilty' parties.

The Royal Commission which sat between 1909 and 1912 recommended that divorce should be more readily available and its terms more equitable between the sexes, but nothing happened. There was a good deal of opposition to making the dissolution of marriage any easier. Finally in 1923 (after the social upheavals of the

First World War had generated a torrent of divorce) a new Act made adultery the sole grounds for divorce in either sex. Like the previous law, it followed an adversarial model: mutual adultery meant no divorce, and mutual consent was regarded as collusion, similarly voiding the case. None the less, there arose an accepted set of conventions whereby a husband would provide his wife with suitable evidence for her to divorce him. Humorist and politician A. P. Herbert's Private Member's Act in 1937 extended the grounds to include cruelty, desertion, insanity and sodomy, while retaining the adversarial framework. Further legislation made divorce more widely available across all social classes, but it was not until 1969 that the concepts of innocent and guilty were dropped and divorce by mutual consent became possible; it also became possible to divorce a non-consenting spouse who had not committed a matrimonial offence. The issue continues to remain controversial, especially at times when politicians agitate for the resuscitation of 'family values'.

It was no coincidence that a new divorce law was finally passed in the aftermath of the First World War. This had caused immense upheavals in British society, in particular in the role of women, who had undertaken a wide variety of war work and were finally awarded the limited parliamentary franchise in 1918. How deep these changes were is still debated: certainly in many ways life settled back to normal when the war was over. While the 1920s are sometimes seen as an epoch of madly Charlestoning jazz babies and flappers, this represented a small if flamboyant section of the population. Sex was, following the deliberate silences of the late Victorian and Edwardian era, becoming speakable once more. In many ways the apparent liberation of the 1920s was a coming to fruition of ideas which had been around for much longer, possibly even temporarily stifled by the war.

A major theme in prewar discussion of sex had been eugenics, a theory, named and advocated by Charles Darwin's cousin Sir Francis Galton, that it was possible to improve human stock by breeding from desirable specimens and preventing, or at least discouraging, the less desirable from reproducing. Eugenics and 'racial hygiene' provided many with an acceptable way of talking about sex. However, the Eugenics Education Society, founded in 1907, was extremely reluctant to associate itself with contemporary movements deemed unrespectable. Thus, although some advocates of birth control pointed out the eugenic potential of contraception, the

Eugenics Society maintained profound silence on the subject until the mid-1920s. Their vision was of middle-class meritocrats living in conventional bourgeois marriage, although other thinkers of the day (for example H. G. Wells) suggested that rather more radical sexual and reproductive arrangements could have eugenic merits. Eugenics was an ambiguous discourse which could be deployed to shore up or to undermine the societal status quo.

The eugenic discourse, with its emphasis on the importance of (fit) women fulfilling a maternal role, was contemporary with the rise of an increasingly militant movement demanding suffrage for women, although the relationship was not one of simple opposition or reaction but of diverse and sometimes overlapping responses to economic and social changes in the new century. Women demanded the vote in order to effect radical improvements in the lives of women and children, and the campaign for women's emancipation was never narrowly concerned with achieving the parliamentary vote (women could already vote in local elections). Christabel Pankhurst, leader of the militant Women's Social and Political Union, demanded 'Votes for Women and Chastity for Men', to eradicate what she claimed was an overwhelming epidemic of venereal diseases among British males. Other women, however, for example the group around the short-lived periodical *The Freewoman*, were tentatively exploring rather more positive sexual alternatives.

Influenced by both feminism and eugenics, Marie Stopes published early in 1918 what was to become an important text in the sexual discourses of the 1920s, *Married Love*. Drawing on authorities such as Havelock Ellis, Edward Carpenter and August Forel, Stopes promulgated a newly eroticised marriage. It was very much a middle-class model of conjugality, but path-breaking in the importance it gave to the wife's sexual arousal and satisfaction and in its recommendations as to how this was to be achieved. Earlier manuals might have conceded that sex should be mutually pleasurable and instructed husbands to be considerate but had forborne to provide details. The volume was a bestseller and highly influential.

Stopes was also associated with birth control; in fact her flamboyant personality has often occluded the many other workers in this vigorous struggle. Her greatest contribution was as a publicist (although she did open the first birth control clinic in the British Empire in London in 1921) through her books, her journalism and her much-publicised 1923 libel suit against a Roman Catholic doctor for claiming that she was experimenting on poor women. Others set up clinics, lobbied Parliament and local authorities, and engaged in research into the best available methods as well as in propaganda. This combined effort achieved the concession by the government in 1930 that birth control advice might be given in local authority welfare clinics, but in many areas this was in fact contracted out to the National Birth Control, later Family Planning, Association, a voluntary body.

The apparent liberalisation of sexual attitudes in the interwar period did not go very far. Stopes and other writers bound sex and marriage tightly together (though their own lives manifested a less rigorous connection). Literary censorship was still rife. Publishers refused to accept works which they feared might be prosecuted, and writers continued to exercise varying degrees of self-censorship. There were a number of trials, perhaps most notably of Radclyffe Hall's novel on lesbianism, *The Well of Loneliness* (1928). In spite of Hall's status as a serious literary figure, and support from many noted writers, thinkers and scientists, the book was condemned as obscene following a sensationalist newspaper attack. There was an increasing body of opinion opposing the prosecution of serious works on sexual subjects, but their voices were not listened to in either this case or others which took place during the 1930s.

The case of obscenity which was fought and won achieved this result by appealing to the common sense of the British jury rather than by relying on protests by opinion-makers. This was the 1942 trial of gynaecologist and psychiatrist Eustace Chesser for publishing the marriage manual *Love without Fear*. Instead of pleading guilty and paying a fine in the magistrate's court, Chesser took the risk of trial by jury. Although concerns were expressed about the book getting into the wrong hands, he was acquitted (but did tone down in subsequent editions some passages found particularly objectionable). This commonsensical tolerance of the average juror seems also to have occurred in homosexuality trials, and there were complaints by the police and members of the legal profession that juries either couldn't understand what the crime was or else didn't think it mattered. However, the stigma of appearing in court, even if acquitted, was an ordeal of exposure for a persecuted minority, and it was widely recognised that the state of the law led to a great deal of blackmail.

The existing system of venereal disease clinics was incorporated into the National Health Service (1948), although it was under-resourced, partly because of the old stigma and partly because of a belief that the discovery of antibiotics meant that venereal diseases, which responded to them almost miraculously, were vanishing. In spite of the growing acceptability of birth control, and indeed the recommendation of the properly spaced family by the Royal Commission on the Population, no provision was made for contraception under the NHS except when serious ill health contra-indicated pregnancy, and the Family Planning Association continued to be responsible for providing clinics, and even training doctors. The government was prepared to support the FPA, and similarly the Marriage Guidance Council, with grants for their work in sustaining marriage, but not to undertake such work itself. This possibly liberated both the FPA and the MGC to work in a more creative way than they could have done as state institutions, but at the expense of under-funding, reliance on volunteer workers, fears of withdrawal of grants, etc.

The 1950s are often seen as conservative and retrograde, with an ideology of almost stultifying 'separate spheres' domesticity. They certainly saw more intensive policing of homosexuality and a clamp-down on street prostitution, as well as a number of high-profile obscenity prosecutions. However, the increase in numbers of women entering the workforce suggests that ideology and behaviour were rather different things. The roots of the developments of the 1960s can be seen during this preceding decade. There were changes in sexual mores, as illegitimacy and premarital pregnancy soared beyond prewar levels, and apparently declining venereal diseases increased once more. Birth control was becoming increasingly acceptable, by the end of the decade even available to the unmarried. Several Private Members' Bills to reform the abortion law were debated in Parliament. The Wolfenden Committee on Homosexuality and Prostitution, which reported in 1957, laid the foundations for reforming legislation to come. An Act of 1959 altered the law on obscenity so that the tendency of the work as a whole could be considered rather than whether selected passages were liable to deprave and corrupt.

The 1960 trial of Penguin Books for publishing the unexpurgated edition of D. H. Lawrence's *Lady Chatterley's Lover* (first published abroad in 1926) was a test case involving a galaxy of defence witnesses representing the great and the good. As in Chesser's case, the common sense judgements of the jury prevailed over the moral opprobrium of the prosecuting counsel. The early 1960s saw the advent of the contraceptive pill. The Labour government of 1964–70 passed laws decriminalising homosexual activity in private between men over twenty-one; gave parliamentary time to David Steel's Abortion Law Reform Bill, making abortion available under the NHS on medical, psychiatric and social grounds; enabled local authorities to subsidise birth control services (although it was not until 1974 under a Tory government that birth control was finally fully incorporated into the NHS); and drastically revised matrimonial law as mentioned above.

Many of these developments, however, have had ambiguous results. The passing of the 1967 Abortion Act generated an increasingly vociferous anti-abortion movement which made a number of attempts, none of them successful, to overturn or limit the Act, though it has not yet committed the excesses seen in the USA. However, although the Act has undergone only minor modification, since the 1980s birth control and abortion services have been silently eroded through the imposition of restrictions by local health authorities as a short-term and short-sighted cost-cutting exercise. The decriminalisation of homosexuality facilitated the emergence of a gay movement, but the restricted legality of gay male behaviour, ambiguous definitions of 'public' and 'private', and the high age of gay consent, compared with the heterosexual age of consent of sixteen, generated intrusive police activity. (The age of gay male consent was lowered to eighteen in 1994; the recently elected Labour government voted in 1998 for a reduction to sixteen, but this was blocked by the House of Lords, the upper chamber of the British Parliament.) One of the most notorious examples of continuing prejudice and over-enthusiastic policing was Operation Spanner, initiated in 1987, leading to the 1990 prosecution and conviction in the Central Criminal Court of a group of men who had been involved in consensual, though extreme, sadomasochism. The advent of AIDS saw the resurgence of moral panics along predictable well-established routes. Other areas demonstrate the continuing persistence of prejudice. In cases of rape court judgements still tend to perpetuate the double standard and outworn assumptions about both male and female sexuality. Censorship is far from a dead issue. And recently there have been reports of localised vigilante action against prostitutes.

There are many aspects of British sexual culture that for lack of space have not been discussed, for example persistent transvestite themes in popular entertainment, the subculture of commercial exploitation of the sexually taboo, from cures for sexual disorders in the nineteenth century to the prostitutes' cards of more recent years, the recurrent strain of nursery tweeness in British erotic life which surfaces every year in the small ads on St Valentine's Day ('Pooh wuvs Piglet vewwy vewwy much'). The enormous topic of the role of the Empire in forming sexual attitudes and affecting sexual behaviour has barely been touched on. The exposure of vast numbers of British men (mostly: though, by the mid nineteenth century, growing numbers of women) to different sexual cultures, and the sexual opportunities (again, almost entirely for men) within them, must have had its influence on sexual cultures at home.

From this brief overview, certain characteristics of British sexual culture can be discerned: continuing tension between a desire to police others, the attitude that it doesn't matter what people do if they don't frighten the horses, moral panics (often drummed up by the media for commercial reasons) and the quiet persistence of a serious commitment to a humane agenda of sexual enlightenment and personal responsibility.

Bibliography

Benn, J. Miriam (1992), *The Predicaments of Love*, London, Pluto Press.

Bland, Lucy (1995), *Banishing the Beast: English Feminism and Sexual Morality 1880–1914*, London, Penguin.

Brandon, Ruth (1990), *The New Women and the Old Men: Love, Sex and the Woman Question*, London, Secker & Warburg.

Bristow, Edward (1977), *Vice and Vigilance: Purity Movements in Britain since 1700*, Dublin, Gill and Macmillan.

Brookes, Barbara (1988), *Abortion in England, 1900–1967*, London, Croom Helm.

Davenport-Hines, Richard (1990), *Sex, Death, and Punishment: Attitudes to Sex and Sexuality in Britain since the Renaissance*, London, Collins.

David, Hugh (1997), *On Queer Street: A Social History of British Homosexuality 1895–1995*, London, HarperCollins.

Dyhouse, Carol (1989), *Feminism and the Family in England 1880–1939*, Oxford, Basil Blackwell.

Ferris, Paul (1993), *Sex and the British: A Twentieth Century History*, London, Michael Joseph.

Foucault, Michel (1981), *The History of Sexuality Volume I: An Introduction*, trans. Robert Hurley, Harmondsworth, Penguin Books.

Grant, Linda (1993), *Sexing the Millennium: A Political History of the Sexual Revolution*, London, HarperCollins.

Grosskurth, Phyllis (1980), *Havelock Ellis: A Biography*, London, Allen Lane.

Hall, Lesley A. (1991), *Hidden Anxieties: Male Sexuality 1900–1950*, Cambridge, Polity Press.

— (1992), 'Forbidden by God, Despised by Men: Masturbation, Medical Warnings, Moral Panic and Manhood in Britain, 1850–1950', *Journal of the History of Sexuality*, 2, Jan.

— (1993a), '"The Cinderella of Medicine": Sexually Transmitted Diseases in Great Britain in the Nineteenth and Twentieth Centuries', *Genitourinary Medicine*, 69, Aug., pp. 314–19.

— (1993b), 'Uniting Science and Sensibility: Marie Stopes and the Narratives of Marriage in the 1920s', in Angela Ingram and Daphne Patai (eds), *Rediscovering Forgotten Radicals: British Women Writers 1889–1939*, Chapel Hill, University of North Carolina Press, pp. 118–36.

— (1994), '"The English have Hot-water Bottles": The Morganatic Marriage between the British Medical Profession and Sexology since William Acton', in Roy Porter and Mikulas Teich (eds), *Sexual Knowledge, Sexual Science: The History of Attitudes to Sexuality*, Cambridge, Cambridge University Press, pp. 350–66.

— (1995), '"Disinterested Enthusiasm for Sexual Misconduct": The British Society for the Study of Sex Psychology, 1913–1947', *Journal of Contemporary History*, 30, pp. 665–86.

— (1996), 'Impotent Ghosts from No-man's Land, Flappers' Boyfriends, or Crypto-patriarchs? Men, Sex and Social Change in 1920s Britain', *Social History*, 21, pp. 54–70.

— (1997a), 'Les Mutations de malthusianisme: l'evolution de la perception politique et morale du *birth control* en Grande-Bretagne', in Francis Ronsin, Hervé le Bras and Elisabeth Zucker-Rouvillois (eds), *Demographie et politique*, Dijon, Editions Universitaire de Dijon.

— (1997b), 'Heroes or Villains? Reconsidering British fin de siècle Sexology and its Impact', in Lynne Segal (ed.), *New Sexual Agendas*, London, Macmillan, pp. 1–16.

— (1998), 'Sex, Science, and Suffrage', in Maroula Joannou and June Purvis (eds), *The Women's Suffrage Movement: New Feminist Perspectives*, Manchester, Manchester University Press.

— (forthcoming), '"A Suitable Job for a Woman?" Women Doctors and Birth Control before 1950', in Larry Conrad and Anne Hardy (eds), *Women and Modern Medicine*, Amsterdam, Rodopi.

Hall, Ruth (1977), *Marie Stopes: A Biography*, London, André Deutsch.

Hammerton, A. James (1992), *Cruelty and Companionship: Conflict in Nineteenth Century Married Life*, London, Routledge.

Higgins, Patrick (1996), *Heterosexual Dictatorship: Male Homosexuality in Post-war Britain*, London, Fourth Estate.

Hitchcock, Tim (1997), *English Sexualities, 1700–1800*, London, Macmillan.

Holton, Sandra Stanley (1996), *Suffrage Days: Stories from the Women's Suffrage Movement*, London, Routledge.

Hynes, Samuel (1968), *The Edwardian Turn of Mind*, Princeton, Princeton University Press.

— (1990), *A War Imagined: The First World War and English Culture*, London, Bodley Head.

Humphries, Steve (1988), *A Secret World of Sex. Forbidden Fruit: The British Experience 1900–1950*, London, Sidgwick & Jackson.

Jeffrey-Poulter, Stephen (1991), *Peers, Queers and Commons: The Struggle for Gay Law Reform from 1950 to the Present*, London, Routledge.

Jeffreys, Sheila (1985), *The Spinster and Her Enemies: Feminism and Sexuality 1880–1930*, London, Pandora Press.

Leathard, Audrey (1980), *The Fight for Family Planning*, London, Macmillan.

Ledbetter, Rosina (1976), *A History of the Malthusian League, 1877–1927*, Columbus (Ohio), Ohio State University Press.

Lewis, Jane, David Clark and David H. J. Morgan (1992), *'Whom God Hath Joined Together': The Work of Marriage Guidance*, London, Routledge.

McCalman, Ian D. (1988), *Radical Underworld: Prophets, Revolutionaries and Pornographers in London, 1795–1840*, Cambridge, Cambridge University Press.

McLaren, Angus (1978), *Birth Control in Nineteenth Century England*, London, Croom Helm.

— (1993), *A Prescription for Murder: The Victorian Serial Killings of Dr Thomas Neil Cream*, Chicago, University of Chicago Press.

— (1997), *The Trials of Masculinity: Policing Sexual Boundaries 1870–1930*, Chicago, University of Chicago Press.

Marcus, Steven (1966), *The Other Victorians: A Study of Sexuality and Pornography in Mid-nineteenth Century England*, New York and London, Basic Books and Weidenfeld & Nicolson.

Mason, Michael (1994a), *The Making of Victorian Sexuality*, Oxford, Oxford University Press.

— (1994b), *The Making of Victorian Sexual Attitudes*, Oxford, Oxford University Press.

Mort, Frank (1987), *Dangerous Sexualities: Medico-moral Politics in England since 1830*, London and New York, Routledge & Kegan Paul.

Moscucci, Ornella (1990), *The Science of Woman: Gynaecology and Gender in England 1800–1929*, Cambridge, Cambridge University Press.

Peel, John (ed.) (1997), *Marie Stopes, Eugenics, and the English Birth Control Movement*, London, Galton Institute.

Poovey, Mary (1989), *Uneven Developments*, London, Virago.

Porter, Roy and Lesley A. Hall (1995), *The Facts of Life: The Creation of Sexual Knowledge in Britain 1650–1950*, New Haven and London, Yale University Press.

Pugh, Martin (1992), *Women and the Women's Movement in Britain 1914–1959*, London, Macmillan.

Roper, Michael and John Tosh (eds) (1991), *Manful Assertions: Masculinities in Britain since 1800*, London, Routledge.

Rose, June (1992), *Marie Stopes and the Sexual Revolution*, London, Faber & Faber.

Rowbotham, Sheila (1997), *A Century of Women: The History of Women in Britain and the United States*, New York, Viking.

Rowbotham, Sheila and Jeffrey Weeks (1977), *Socialism and the New Life: The Personal and Sexual Politics of Edward Carpenter and Havelock Ellis*, London, Pluto Press.

Russett, Cynthia Eagle (1989), *Sexual Science: The Victorian Construction of Womanhood*, Cambridge (Mass.) and London, Harvard University Press.

Seccombe, Wally (1995), *Weathering the Storm: Working-class Families from the Industrial Revolution to the Fertility Decline*, London, Verso.

Shanley, Mary Lyndon (1989), *Feminism, Marriage, and the Law in Victorian England, 1850–1895*, Princeton, Princeton University Press.

Soloway, Richard A. (1982), *Birth Control and the Population Question in England, 1870–1930*, Chapel Hill and London, University of North Carolina Press.

—— (1990), *Demography and Degeneration: Eugenics and the Declining Birthrate in Twentieth Century Britain*, Chapel Hill, University of North Carolina Press.

Stanley, Liz (1995), *Sex Surveyed 1949–1994: From Mass Observation's 'Little Kinsey' to the National Survey and the Hite Reports*, London, Taylor & Francis.

Sutherland, John (1982), *Offensive Literature: Decensorship in Britain 1960–1982*, London, Junction Books.

Szreter, Simon (1996), *Fertility, Class and Gender in Britain 1860–1940*, Cambridge, Cambridge University Press.

Thomas, Donald (1969), *A Long Time Burning: The History of Literary Censorship in England*, London, Routledge & Kegan Paul.

Walkowitz, Judith R. (1980), *Prostitution and Victorian Society: Women, Class, and the State*, Cambridge and New York, Cambridge University Press.

—— (1992), *City of Dreadful Delight: Narratives of Sexual Danger in Late-Victorian London*, London, Virago Press.

Weeks, Jeffrey (1977), *Coming Out: Homosexual Politics in Britain, from the Nineteenth Century to the Present*, London, Melbourne and New York, Quartet Books.

—— (1981), *Sex, Politics and Society: The Regulation of Sexuality since 1800*, London and New York, Longman.

Wilson, Elizabeth (1980), *Only Half-way to Paradise: Women in Postwar Britain 1945–1968*, London, Tavistock.

2

Religion and sexual culture in Ireland

Tony Fahey

Until recent decades the social construction of sexuality in the Republic of Ireland took place in a cultural framework which was dominated by Catholic social and moral teaching. Sexual culture had become increasingly aligned with religious culture under the umbrella of Catholic nationalism from the mid nineteenth century onwards. This alignment was consolidated in the decades immediately after national independence in 1921 and persisted more or less unchallenged until the watershed decade of the 1960s.

Changes in sexual culture in Ireland since the 1960s have been quite dramatic and have broken the hold of Catholic moral teaching over sexual life. Urbanisation and industrialisation, the declining economic importance of agriculture, the expansion of second- and third-level education, the rise of feminism, the growing cultural influence of the urban middle classes and the more unambiguous embrace of international English-language culture have contributed to this development. At the same time Catholic religious affiliation has held up quite strongly, despite sharp declines in the 1990s. Indicators of religious practice such as weekly church attendance are still exceptionally high by the standards of other European countries.

The overall thrust of recent developments is thus that conceptions of sexuality have moved outside the religious frame, but the religious frame remains strong in many areas of life. The result, in part, is a new tension between religion and sexuality, and a widespread sense of sexuality as having escaped from a religious straitjacket. At the same time one might remark how contained that tension appears to be – many new patterns of sexual behaviour have spread quite easily without undermining religious affiliation among many Catholics, even though they are nominally in conflict with Catholic teaching. Part of the resolution to this paradox is that religious culture in Ireland has subtly adopted to sexual culture in new ways. While Catholic belief rejects much of the secular frame within which sexual culture is now cast, it finds pointers to a new Christian ethic of sexual life in other aspects of the same culture. Thus sexual and religious culture have become de-aligned from each other, but that de-alignment is by no means total. It has been tempered by the capacity of religious culture to accommodate, as well as by the ability among many Catholics to find certain strands of continuity between their religious outlooks and the sexual values of the new cultural regime.

The aim of this chapter is to examine how sexual culture in Ireland has evolved during this transition from a sacralised to a partly secularised cultural environment. In doing so, it is hampered by the lack of any tradition of research into sexual issues in Ireland. Anthropological studies, most of which have focused on rural communities, have often referred to the sexually repressive nature of Irish culture but few have attempted to explore that repressiveness in any depth (for partial exceptions, see Messenger 1969; Scheper-Hughes 1979). None has examined the transformations which have occurred in recent decades, and there have been no studies of present-day sexual culture or of individual-level sexual behaviour or attitudes. This chapter cannot make good that research deficit but it can outline some of the broad features of sexual culture in Ireland, describe the major changes which have occurred in recent years and assess how those changes have related to the religious environment.

This chapter focuses mainly on the Republic of Ireland and for that reason, in speaking of religion, it refers largely to Catholicism. In the 1991 Census of Population, Catholics accounted for almost 92 per cent of the population of the Republic, and religious minorities (mainly Protestant) accounted for only 4 per cent. The remaining 4 per cent (those who stated they had no religion or did not reply to the religion question in the census) represent an increase in the non-affiliated over recent years and it is likely that a substantial proportion are former Catholics. Denominational differences in sexual cultures have been evident at certain periods in such things as differential fertility rates, but denominational differences are not prominent in public debates about sexuality in Ireland, nor are they evident as differentiating factors in day-to-day sexual conduct.

Religion and sexuality – the alignment period

We first turn to the alignment of sexual and religious cultures which dominated the period from the mid nineteenth to the mid twentieth century in Ireland. Demographic indicators provide the most concrete evidence of sexual culture in this period, though state legislation and policy also provide a reflection of popular attitudes in this area.

The demographic perspective

From the mid nineteenth century to the 1960s, Ireland presented an extreme instance of sexual behaviour patterns which demographers suggest were characteristic of western Europe from the late Middle Ages to the late nineteenth century. These patterns had three out-standing components – extensive marriage avoidance (i.e. late age of marriage, high proportions never marrying), strict sanctions against sex outside of marriage, and unrestrained fertility within marriage. Marriage avoidance seems to have been less prevalent in Ireland in the early nineteenth century than in many other parts of Europe, and this may have been one of the factors contributing to the rapid population growth which occurred between 1800 and 1840. Following the great Famine of the late 1840s, however, Ireland entered a century-long period of demographic decline in which emigration was high, rates of natural increase were modest and total population fell.

Marriage avoidance was a key part of this post-Famine population pattern. It spread during the late nineteenth century and peaked in the period around 1900–40, at which time it reached levels that were unprecedented either in Irish or in broader European history. Average age at marriage in the 1920s rose to thirty-five for men and twenty-nine for women. Permanent non-marriage also greatly exceeded the traditional European norm of 10 to 15 per cent of each age cohort. Among those aged forty-five to fifty-four in Ireland in the 1930s, for example, 29 per cent of men and 24 per cent of women had never married. For those who did marry, fertility rates in the nineteenth century appear to have been among the highest recorded in modern European history (Ó Gráda 1991; Coale and Watkins 1986). Though marital fertility rates declined after 1880, they were still high in the early twentieth century and thenceforth declined at an exceptionally slow pace until the 1980s. Since the early 1980s, fertility has fallen more quickly and has converged towards the

European average. It still lies at the upper edge of the European range but is no longer the extreme outlier that it was in the past.

Fertility outside of marriage was low for much of this period – it hovered just above 2.5 per cent of all births throughout the first half of the twentieth century, and dipped to 1.6 per cent in 1961. To the extent that we can take low non-marital fertility as an index of low levels of sexual activity outside of marriage, the Irish were the most virginal as well as the most marriage-averse of peoples in this period. Even if we accept that practices such as birth concealment, 'shot-gun' weddings and emigration among pregnant single women kept the recorded non-marital fertility artificially low, we are still left with an exceptionally high incidence of ostensible virginity among Irish adults.

Catholicism in Ireland

The revival and expansion of Catholicism and the Catholic church was a major feature of nineteenth-century Irish history, affecting politics, culture and social structure. In 1800 the Catholic church in Ireland was in a weakened state following the anti-Catholic penal laws of the eighteenth century. By 1900 parish and diocesan structures in the Catholic church had been thoroughly restored, the number of priests had doubled, membership of religious orders (especially the new female orders) had soared, and popular affiliation and religious practice had been fully revitalised and brought into line with orthodoxy. By 1900 also, mass attendance and regular devotional practice had come to be seen as the necessary and outward signs of being a Catholic and became a routine part of Irish Catholic life throughout the country and in all social classes, even in the cities (Fahey 1992).

Yet another important feature of the success of the Catholic church in Ireland was the degree to which it became embedded into the system of social services developed under the British administration in the nineteenth century. This was especially so in education. By the early decades of the twentieth century, the colonial regime had created an education system which at primary and secondary levels gave unparalleled ownership, access and local control to the churches, while the burden of financial and central administrative responsibility was carried by the state. This pattern of denominational control was repeated to a more limited extent in areas such as hospitals, the care of orphaned and homeless children, the 'rescue of fallen women' and a limited range of services for the poor and for unemployed women. Church provision in these areas sometimes evoked a hostile, competitive response from the British administration, but for the most part partnership of some sort was the preferred option, with the result that most areas of social services became a joint venture between 'voluntary' church effort and state funding and administration.

As separatist sentiment gathered force in the nineteenth century, the modern nationalist identification of Irishness with Catholicism took hold and was expressed politically in an alliance between the Catholic church and the constitutional nationalist political movement. Although the Catholic hierarchy frequently condemned the physical force tradition in nationalism which finally succeeded in winning national independence, the church's broader nationalist sympathies helped secure its position in the new state created after independence in 1921 and consolidated its role in education and social services (for a good recent review of the Catholic church's place in twentieth-century Ireland, see Keogh 1996). The Catholic church was accorded a 'special position' in Irish society in the Constitution of 1937. After independence, most of the Protestant population was contained in the six counties which stayed in the United Kingdom as Northern Ireland. In the remaining twenty-six counties, Protestants dwindled from 10 per cent of the population before independence to less than 5 per cent in the 1960s, so that religious homogeneity in the newly independent state increased steadily over this period (Sexton and O'Leary 1996).

Despite signs of decline, Catholicism has survived as a strong social force right up to the 1990s in Ireland. Vocations to the priesthood and religious life have fallen dramatically since the peaks attained in the 1960s but other indicators of religious affiliation remain strong. In the 1991 Census of Population only 2 per cent of the population described themselves as having 'no religion'. Survey sources show that weekly mass attendance, which in the early 1970s had been practised by more than 90 per cent of Catholics in Ireland, had fallen almost to 80 per cent by the late 1980s and to below 65 per cent by 1995 (Corish 1996). Yet, despite the sharp drop in recent years, attendance rates at weekly church services in Ireland are still remarkably high by European standards, where the average is generally between 10 and 30 per cent (Whelan and Fahey 1994).

57

The Irish Catholic church has been rocked by a number of sex scandals in the late 1990s, most damagingly in regard to child sexual abuse. These scandals have dented the church's social prestige but have by no means undermined it entirely. It continues to play a large role in education, health care and other social services, alongside its usual liturgical role in the religious life of believers. That role is still widely accepted and is highly valued by many. While some multi-denominational and non-denominational schools have been developed, there is little public demand for a reduction of church influence in these areas.

Connections between religious and sexual culture

The emergence of Catholic cultural hegemony from the mid nineteenth to the mid twentieth century coincided with the extreme marriage avoidance and high celibacy rates which characterised the same period, so that there is a presumption of a causal connection between the two. While such a connection is highly plausible, it is not at all clear how strong it was or in what direction the causal influence ran: did Irish Catholics embrace Catholicism and its teachings on sex because these confirmed and supported what they tended to do for other reasons, or were the Irish a 'priest-ridden people' who were led by the Catholic church into accepting a religiously determined view of how they should conduct their lives?

Those who tend to downplay the independent causal force of Catholicism point to the social, economic and political conditions which they see as the real determinants of behaviour and as part of the conditions which made Catholicism attractive to Irish people. These include the psychological after-effects of the Famine (to which the vigour and confidence of the Catholic church could be seen as an antidote); the dominance of agriculture in the economy; the sympathy between Catholicism and small-farm family values; the lack of diversity in the class structure which arose from the decline of the proto-industrial rural proletariat and the eventual elimination of the landlord class through land reform; the weakness of modernising urban culture; the loss of the Irish language as a mark of cultural identity (for which Catholicism provided a substitute); the significance of the Catholic church in nationalist political mobilisation, and so on (see e.g. Kennedy 1973).

More specific matters such as marriage avoidance can be related also to structural conditions, in this view, especially to the structure of economic opportunity. One school of thought, for example, interprets marriage avoidance less as a culturally determined practice than as a rational individual response to prevailing economic circumstances. According to this view, marriage was not essential to economic security in the economic conditions of late nineteenth-century Ireland, and may even have been a threat to individuals' living standards. As a result celibacy represented a 'sensible' option for many Irish people, and for Irish men in particular, and so was nothing more than what one would expect on the basis of rational economic choice (Kennedy 1973; Guinnane 1991). These arguments would suggest that Catholic teaching may simply have provided some reinforcement for behaviour that was primarily determined by economic interests.

Those who argue for the independent causal influence of religion point not only towards the general causal force of cultural ideas but also towards the organisational strengths of the Catholic church and the leadership skills of the hierarchy and clergy which gave it independent sources of power in Irish society (see e.g. Inglis 1989). This approach suggests that there was nothing inevitable about the strength which the Catholic church acquired in Ireland nor about popular acceptance of its teaching on matters connected with family life. These outcomes, rather, were the product of a conscious ecclesiastical project which the Catholic church brought to a triumphant outcome by virtue of its sheer effectiveness in building a social power base.

The question of the Catholic church's influence is further complicated by the fact that many of the beliefs and attitudes about domestic life which it preached were not that distinctively Catholic. For example, the repressive attitude towards sex which was such a feature of Irish Catholicism had much in common with prevailing standards in Victorian Britain, in secular as well as religious circles. Indeed its prominence in Irish Catholicism arose at least in part from the tendency among Irish Catholics to compete for respectability in terms defined by metropolitan British culture, and to congratulate themselves when they outdid their colonial masters on those standards. It was not so much that Catholicism differed from other Christian denominations in what it preached in these areas but rather, as the Catholic church often told itself, that it preached the same message much more effectively.

Catholic discourse on sex

In any event, whatever the precise causal links between Catholicism and sexual behaviour in Ireland in the first half of the twentieth century, there is no doubt that Catholic teaching provided much of the imagery and language in which relationships between the sexes and with the human body were spoken and thought about by the majority of the Irish population. The Catholic church focused very much on family and sexuality as the core concerns of its moral teaching, and Irish people accepted that focus as legitimate. The church's central message rested on the classic Christian opposition between the spirit as the expression of goodness and truth, and the flesh as the source of temptation and sin. In this world-view sex was seen as one of the core domains of the flesh, both because of its sheer physicality and for its urgent, ever-present tendency to invade and corrupt the spirit. The struggle with sexual temptation, for the individual believer in his or her daily life and for the church as a whole, was a battle between darkness and light, and the Catholic church in Ireland deployed enormous energy to ensure that the forces of light won in this particular theatre of war. Even the thought or temptation to stray – 'occasions of sin' such as 'company keeping', immodest dancing or suggestive literature – had to be carefully policed.

These concerns produced what now seems like a bizarre obsession among the Catholic clergy and hierarchy with real or imagined threats to strict ascetic standards in matters of sexuality – things such as unsupervised dances, immoral music (e.g. jazz), 'company keeping' among young people, corrupting literature, and so on (Whyte 1980, pp. 24 ff.).

It is also true that some Catholic commentators implicitly pointed to the lack of legitimate sexual outlets for Irish adults as itself a source of concern. This was typically expressed by reference to the widespread reluctance to marry and the consequences that this attitude had for the moral and personal well-being of those who remained single. This 'unnatural and unwholesome phenomenon', as one prominent Catholic bishop called it, was understandable to the extent that it was rooted in shortages of employment and economic opportunity, but it was worrisome from the church's point of view to the extent that it arose from selfishness: 'for instance, the woman who does not want to give up her independence or her job, the man who does not want the burden of supporting a home' (Minority Report, Commission on Emigration and Other Population Problems, 1948–54, p. 356). However, concerns of this kind did not amount to a view that sex was necessary for a healthy life. Rather, they reflected the belief that marriage was a necessary means to provide for and contain the sexual impulses of those who might otherwise be led into sin. In public discourse about sexual morality at this time, the dominant concern was that there was too much rather than too little expression of sexuality in Irish life.

Catholic moral legislation

Many of these concerns relied for their effect on informal social sanctions. Under the government of the newly independent state in Ireland, however, the Catholic hierarchy had the opportunity to press its concerns on legislators. The result was that Ireland acquired a certain amount of new moral legislation in the late 1920s and 1930s, some of it the result of clerical prompting but much of it simply reflecting the prevailing Catholic ethos. A new censorship law in 1929 not only provided for the control of erotic literature but also defined as obscene any literature which provided information on or advocated 'unnatural' birth control methods. Legislation in 1935 banned the sale and importation of artificial contraceptives (a ban which lasted until it was struck down by the Supreme Court as an unconstitutional infringement of the right to marital privacy in 1973). The Public Dance Halls Act in the same year aimed to eliminate the threat to morals represented by unsupervised dances. The Constitution adopted in 1937 strongly reflected Catholic social teaching in its provisions on marriage and the family (among other things it prohibited the legalisation of divorce). While these were the principal landmarks in the crusade for moral legislation, there were many other smaller instances of Catholic influence on government regarding moral matters. At their Easter meeting in 1944, for example, the Catholic bishops decided that the new sanitary tampons called 'Tampax' could harmfully stimulate girls at an impressionable age and lead to the use of contraceptives. They therefore delegated the Archbishop of Dublin to request the Department of Local Government and Public Health to ban their sale and, more indicative still, the Department duly complied (Barrington 1987, p. 149).

Secularisation of sexual culture

The liberalising trend

Sexual behaviour in Ireland has shared in many aspects of the western sexual revolution of the post-1960s period. This was evidenced, for example, in the growth in non-marital fertility. From a low of less than 2 per cent of all births in the early 1960s, non-marital births rose to almost one in four births in 1996. Marriage thus lost much of its previous hegemony as a gateway to sex and reproduction, and sex outside of marriage has been normalised to a degree that would have been unthinkable a generation ago.

Survey data on attitudes towards sexual morality reinforce this impression of rapid change. Thus, for example, in a national survey carried out in 1973–4, 71 per cent of those surveyed felt that premarital sex was always wrong (Table 1). Strong generational differences were then emerging in that younger adults (those aged eighteen to thirty) were more liberal, but, even in that age group, 44 per cent felt that premarital sex was always wrong. Twenty years later, in 1994, the overall proportion who felt that premarital sex was always wrong had dropped to 32 per cent and among those aged eighteen to thirty it had dropped to 8 per cent. Generational differences were still present, but it is clear from a comparison of age-cohorts in Table 1 that middle-aged and older people in 1994 had

Table 1   Agreement that premarital sex is 'always wrong', 1973–4 and 1994 (%)

	1973–4	1994
By age-group:		
18–30	44	8
31–50	74	22
51+	87	58
All	71	32
By attendance at religious services:		
weekly or more	n.a.	43
1–3 times per month	n.a.	9
less than monthly	n.a.	5
All	71	32

Sources: Nic Ghiolla Phádraig 1976; ISSP 1994

become more liberal on this question than they had been when they were twenty years younger. A cross-classification of attitudes to premarital sex with attendance at religious services (Table 1 again) shows that, while weekly churchgoers in 1994 were more disapproving of premarital sex than those who attended less often or not at all, even among the former the proportion who thought that premarital sex was always wrong was only 43 per cent. Thus a small majority of regular churchgoers had swung around to the new thinking.

Changes in popular attitudes and behaviour were paralleled by changes in law and social provision. The increasingly liberal Supreme Court of the 1960s and 1970s provided much of the early impetus towards change in the law, most notably in its *McGee* judgement in 1973 which struck down the legal ban on contraceptives as unconstitutional. Censorship was relaxed in the 1960s, social supports for unmarried mothers were introduced in the 1970s, membership of the EEC in 1973 brought a new wave of legislation to eliminate formal discrimination against women in the labour market, legal discrimination against children born outside of marriage was abolished in 1987 and homosexuality was decriminalised in the early 1990s. The new cultural order which these changes represented was most strikingly symbolised by the election of Mary Robinson as president in 1989, since she was an avowed feminist with a long-standing involvement as a campaigner for the liberal agenda.

A conservative counter-attack against this liberalising tide began with a campaign in the early 1980s for the insertion of an anti-abortion clause into the Constitution. Though abortion was illegal and there was no significant lobby in favour of liberalising the law, the concern of those who initiated the campaign was that existing anti-abortion legislation might one day be overturned either by a liberal Supreme Court in Ireland (along the lines of the *McGee* judgement on contraception or the *Roe* v. *Wade* judgement on abortion in the United States) or as a result of legislation enacted in Europe. The campaign led to a constitutional referendum in 1983, in which a two-to-one majority voted to accept a constitutional amendment guaranteeing the right to life of the unborn. However, the famous 'X' case in 1992, involving a fourteen-year-old girl who had become pregnant as a result of a statutory rape and who had threatened suicide if she was not allowed to travel to England for an

abortion, led to a controversial Supreme Court ruling on circumstances under which abortion should be allowed under the 1983
amendment. This inflamed the abortion issue again and necessitated
further referendums in 1992 on questions related to foreign
abortions (see Girvin 1994 for a full account of these tangled events).
At the time of writing, it is declared government policy to have a
further national referendum in the foreseeable future on detailed
legislation on abortion.

Conservative forces scored another resounding victory in 1986
when a government-sponsored referendum to remove the ban on
divorce from the Constitution was defeated by a two-to-one majority
of the popular vote. At the same time public opinion polls regularly
showed that a majority of voters were in favour of removing the ban,
thus reflecting a great ambivalence among Irish people towards
divorce. In a second run at the same question in November 1995 the
government of the day carried through a pro-divorce amendment to
the Constitution. However, the margin of victory could scarcely have
been tighter (the vote was 50.3 per cent in favour and 49.7 per cent
against the amendment), indicating that the Irish electorate was still
far from enthusiastic about the idea of making divorce widely
available in Ireland.

Catholic perspectives on the new sexual culture

It would oversimplify matters to present the cultural conflicts about
sexuality in Ireland since the 1960s as a struggle between the
conservative impulse of Catholicism and the liberalising influences of
secular culture. The actual picture is more nuanced, if only because
mainstream Catholic attitudes themselves changed quite extensively
and became more diverse. This transformation is well exemplified by
the church's changed approach to unmarried parenthood and, by
implication, to premarital sex. Traditionally, unmarried mothers had
been harshly treated in Catholic teaching and practice, reflecting the
broader view of parenthood outside of marriage as the shameful consequence of sexual laxity. By the late 1960s this repressive approach
was coming to be seen as unchristian and led to internal criticism
within the church. In addition the passage of the 1967 Abortion Act
in Britain opened up new options for Irish women with unwanted
pregnancies. The availability of abortion in England led to a view in
Catholic circles that, compared with abortion, unmarried motherhood

was very much the lesser of two evils and should be treated much more supportively on that account. Furthermore, the 'shot-gun marriage' solution also came to be seen as dubious, not only because marriages formed in such a way had a high risk of instability but also because the pressure on the couple often compromised the validity of the marriage in canon law, thus giving rise to subsequent nullity proceedings in church tribunals.

For all these reasons the Catholic church, paradoxically, became one of the institutions in Ireland which contributed to the de-stigmatisation of unmarried motherhood. Pastoral policy also changed in the 1970s so that face-saving marriages among young pregnant women were actively discouraged. The church began to promote the view that the couple should marry after the birth of the child if they still wished to rather than before. These changes took much of the force out of the church's traditional hostility towards premarital sex – it was impossible to promote a supportive attitude towards unmarried mothers and at the same time sustain the traditional total condemnation of sex before marriage. Indeed, it dissipated much of the traditional Catholic obsession with sexual purity as a key aspect of the moral life.

The consequence of these internal developments in Catholicism was that no major social force in post-1960s Ireland persisted with undiluted traditional attitudes to sexuality. The centre of gravity in public discussion of sexuality shifted in a liberal direction, inside the Catholic church as well as outside it. To the extent that a strict conservative position survived in Catholicism, it became the preserve of fringe lay groups rather than of the mainstream church. It is significant in this regard that much of the Catholic political activism on questions such as divorce and abortion from the early 1980s onwards was generated by radical conservatives rather than by the clergy or hierarchy.

The new accommodation

These trends meant that in many ways Catholic teaching accommodated the new morality of sexual life which the sexual revolution helped promote. The extent of that accommodation undoubtedly says something about the internal loss of confidence in the traditional Catholic position which assailed the Catholic church in the Vatican II era. But it also says something about the nature of the sexual revolution, since there were aspects of the new sexual morality which appealed to certain aspects of the Christian ethic and which, for those who were so inclined, could be dressed in a Christian garb. While many Christians might speak about the sexual revolution as a slide into indulgence and immorality, others saw ethical progress in the shedding of hypocrisy and the search for a more humane approach to sexuality which the new order brought with it.

Again we can look to survey data to provide an illustration of some of the nuances of this transition. We have already seen that disapproval of premarital sex in Ireland collapsed from the early 1970s to the early 1990s, especially among younger people and to a great extent also among weekly churchgoers. The story is quite different for attitudes in another area of sexual morality – sex outside marriage among married persons. The 1994 survey mentioned earlier, which investigated this issue, showed some variation by age-group and churchgoing in the directions more or less as one would expect – the old and weekly churchgoers showed the highest levels of disapproval of sex outside marriage (Table 2). However, these variations are slight and are less striking than the very high levels of disapproval even among the most accepting groups. Eighty-seven per cent of those aged eighteen to thirty and 78 per cent of those who attended church less than monthly thought that sex outside

Table 2   Attitudes towards sex outside marriage, 1994 (%)

	Always or nearly aways wrong	Not wrong
By age-group:		
18–30	87	3
31–50	83	2
51+	95	1
All	87	2
By attendance at religious services:		
weekly or more	92	1
1–3 times per month	87	1
less than monthly/never	78	4
All	87	2

Source: ISSP 1994

marriage among married people was either always wrong or nearly always wrong. It would therefore appear that in 1994 disapproval of sex outside marriage was still the overwhelming norm in Ireland, and was nearly as much so among irreligious groups as among those with strong Catholic affiliation.

The strong contrast in attitudes to premarital sex and marital infidelity indicates that, while certain traditional moral strictures had all but lost their force, others survived in what outwardly might seem like their traditional form. However, the different ways in which these attitudes related to indicators of religious affiliation showed that, even where sexual codes remained restrictive, their moral basis had lost much of its traditional religious character. One did not need to be a practising Catholic to disapprove of marital infidelity, and being a practising Catholic did not necessarily mean that one disapproved of that great evil of the traditional Catholic imagination, premarital sex. It was as if, for Catholics as much as non-Catholics, the moral basis for judgements about sexual behaviour had moved off traditional Catholic grounds and found new foundations.

To provide a broad-brush characterisation of those new foundations, one can look to the culture of ethical individualism and its influence on Catholic attitudes. The emphasis which ethical individualism places on individual rights and self-expression has led this culture to throw off the repressive strand of the Christian tradition and extol sexual freedom as a valuable means to self-realisation. It rejects the valuation of sex by reference to its procreative function and the downgrading of the relational and recreational aspects of sex. While these developments are liberal and permissive in many ways, they also entail a strong ethical and regulatory dimension. This dimension turns on the principle of negotiation as the basis on which sexual relations between persons should be built. Immorality in sexual life is defined by reference less to substantive rules than to the procedures of fair and balanced negotiation and to the trust which negotiated agreements rely on. Marital infidelity is thus disapproved of because it is a deceit and breaches a commitment freely given, while premarital sex is acceptable on the assumption that both partners want it and have agreed to engage in it (the increased acceptance of homosexuality could be accounted for on the same basis).

If deceit is regarded as a wrong in this new view, an even greater wrong is the abuse of power. The abuse of power in sexual life, particularly the physical power of men over women and adults over children, gives rise to forced sex. Forced sex has been identified as the great evil of sexual life by the new sexual ethics and has become the target of the most urgent and most strongly felt moral and legal crusade. The legal outcomes of this approach can be seen in changes in the law on rape (including rape within marriage), domestic violence, sexual harassment and child abuse. These new measures contrast with the absence of effective regulation in these areas in the past. In some cases (such as rape and violence within marriage), traditional Catholic teaching is now criticised as being part of the problem rather than of the solution, in that it resisted any attempt to regulate the abuse of power within families in order to protect the authority of the father.

This new regulatory approach affected Catholicism in two ways. One was its educative influence on Catholic thinking. The new ethic of negotiation was consistent with certain interpretations of the Christian message and thus carried great moral force for many Catholics. For those who thought in these terms, the new morality was virtually impossible to resist on religious grounds and amounted to a persuasive secular influence on religious sexual ethics. The second effect was the negative impact of the new approach on the credibility of Catholic authority in sexual matters. The male-centred, patriarchal traditions of the church came to be seen as part of the system which had tolerated shocking levels of harshness and abuse in sexual life, especially where women and children were concerned. In this view the traditional Christian approach was not simply incorrect, it also had the potential to shelter and perhaps even cultivate evil. Scandals about child sexual abuse and other forms of sexual corruption in the church seemed to confirm this view and threw the church into a defensive, apologetic mode as far as sexual morality was concerned. Its capacity to provide confident moral leadership in sexual matters was severely weakened as a result.

Conclusion

Catholicism flourished and expanded in the course of the nineteenth century in Ireland and emerged as the semi-official religion of the national state in the post-independence period. As part of this process, it came to provide the dominant cultural framework within which sexuality was thought about, talked about and regulated. The

Catholic approach to sexual matters echoed that of Victorian Protestantism, but the completeness of its hold within the monocultural context of post-independent Ireland was scarcely matched elsewhere.

Despite the depth of its hold in Ireland, Catholicism proved to be ineffective as a bulwark against the liberalising tide of the post-1960s sexual revolution. Sexual practices and attitudes have changed dramatically ova the past thirty years in Ireland, and many Catholics have abandoned their religious affiliation in the move towards a new sexual outlook. However, as far as religious affiliation is concerned, the principal effect of the sexual revolution was to seep through Irish Catholicism rather than sweep it aside. It altered the nature and tone of the Catholic approach to sexual life, partly by undermining official Catholic teaching on sexual matters among very many otherwise faithful Catholics, and partly by loosening and softening traditional Catholic certainties about sexual questions. Recent highly publicised sexual scandals among the Catholic clergy, ranging from 'normal' sexual indiscretions to child abuse, have added a new and as yet only partially absorbed dimension to this evolution.

In the past, religion in Ireland expressed much of its moral authority through intense regulation of the sexual lives of believers. Today the moral foundations of sexual life have been largely secularised, in Ireland as elsewhere and, it would seem, among practising Catholics as much as among non-believers. This does not mean that Catholicism has lost its role in Irish people's lives but it does entail a drastic narrowing of that role. How long and how steadily Catholicism can retain its footing on the narrower moral ground it now holds is an open question.

Bibliography

Barrington, R. (1987), *Health, Medicine and Politics in Ireland 1900–1970*, Dublin, Institute of Public Administration.

Coale, A. J. and S. C. Watkins (eds) (1986), *The Decline of Fertility in Europe*, Princeton, Princeton University Press.

Commission on Emigration and Other Population Problems (1948–54), *Reports*, Dublin, Stationery Office.

Corish, M. (1996), 'Aspects of Religious Change in Ireland', in E. G. Cassidy (ed.), *Faith and Culture in an Irish Context*, Dublin, Veritas Publications.

Fahey, T. (1992), 'Catholicism and Industrial Society in Ireland', in J. H. Goldthorpe and C. T. Whelan (eds), *The Development of Industrial Society in Ireland*, Oxford, Oxford University Press.

Girvin, B. (1994), 'Moral Politics and the Irish Abortion Referendums, 1992', *Parliamentary Affairs*, 47, 2.

Guinnane, T. (1991), 'Re-thinking the Western European Marriage Pattern: The Decision to Marry in Ireland at the Turn of the Twentieth Century', *Journal of Family History*, 16, 1, pp. 47–64.

Inglis, T. (1987), *Moral Monopoly: The Catholic Church in Modern Irish Society*, Dublin, Gill & Macmillan.

ISSP (1994), *International Social Survey Project: Data File for Ireland Survey 1994*, Dublin, Economic and Social Research Institute.

Kennedy, R. E. (1973), *The Irish: Emigration, Marriage and Fertility*, Berkeley, University of California Press.

Keogh, D. (1996), 'The Role of the Catholic Church in the Republic of Ireland 1922–1995', in Forum for Peace and Reconciliation (ed.), *Building Trust in Ireland: Studies Commissioned by the Forum for Peace and Reconciliation*. Belfast, Blackstaff Press.

Messenger, John C. (1969), *Inis Beag: Isle of Ireland*, New York, Holt, Rhinehart and Winston.

Nic Ghiolla Phádraig, M. (1976), *Survey of Religious Beliefs and Practices in Ireland. Vol. 3: Moral Attitudes*, Dublin, Research and Development Commission.

Ó Gráda, C. (1991), 'New Evidence of the Fertility Transition in Ireland, 1880-1911',.*Demography* 28, 4.

Scheper-Hughes, N. (1979), *Saints, Scholars and Schizophrenics. Mental Illness in Rural Ireland*, Berkeley, University of California Press.

Sexton, J. and R. O'Leary (1996), 'Factors Affecting Population Decline in Minority Religious Communities in the Republic of Ireland', in Forum for Peace and Reconciliation (ed.), *Building Trust in Ireland: Studies Commissioned by the Forum for Peace and Reconciliation*, Belfast, Blackstaff Press.

Whelan, C. T. and T. Fahey (1994), 'Marriage and Family', in C. T. Whelan (ed.), *Values and Social Change in Ireland*, Dublin, Gill & Macmillan.

Whyte, J. (1980), *Church and State in Modern Ireland 1923–1979*, Dublin, Gill and Macmillan.

3

The Netherlands: neither prudish nor hedonistic

Harry Oosterhuis

Translated by Ton Brouwers and James Steakley

The history of sexuality in the Netherlands of the late nineteenth and twentieth centuries differs to some extent from that in other western European countries. Although there may be some discrepancy between dominant morality and actual social conduct, it is commonly argued that, between the late nineteenth century and the 1960s, Christian norms and values have influenced sexual thinking and behaviour more strongly in the Netherlands than in other countries. Despite the ongoing trend towards secularisation that started in the late nineteenth century, in particular among the members of the more liberal Dutch Reformed Church, until the 1960s the Netherlands counted not only as a bourgeois society but also as a typical Christian nation.

The disproportionately large influence of the views of Catholic and orthodox Calvinist groups in Dutch society is to be understood in light of *pillarisation*: the close interconnection of religious ideology and socio-political organisation which for the greater part of the twentieth century covered all areas of Dutch social life, cut across social class and united groups of people from all walks of life in a common world-view. Following the example of Christian groups, the Dutch social democrats and liberals also constituted specific blocs, but these were not as all-embracing as the various Christian pillars. Although the formation of confessional blocs does not represent a singularly Dutch phenomenon, in the field of public morality they have manifested themselves more prominently in the Netherlands than elsewhere: they succeeded in imposing their restrictive sexual morality on the Dutch population at large. Simultaneously, the pillarisation of Dutch society contributed to a more radical sexual revolution in the 1960s – a revolution which has also had a more permanent influence in the Netherlands than in other western nations. Dutch society, it seems, has made an about-turn in only a short timespan: from puritan to liberal. Whereas the country was known as quite conservative and law-abiding in the 1950s, Dutch liberalism and tolerance have become proverbial since the second half of the 1960s. Abroad the Netherlands has gained the reputation of being either a sexual paradise or a Sodom and Gomorrah.

In this chapter I will focus on pillarisation as a peculiarly twentieth-century Dutch phenomenon and on its relevance for the historical significance of the sexual 'revolution' in the Netherlands. I will argue that the seemingly sudden and radical changes in sexual ideology during the 1960s can be understood also as merely an acceleration, as part of a long-term historical development.

Whereas sodomy and prostitution were punishable in the Calvinist Dutch Republic and there had been fierce persecutions of sodomites during the eighteenth century, the French occupation at the beginning of the nineteenth century entailed a separation of sin and crime and a decriminalisation of several sexual offences. The *Code Pénal*, introduced by the French in 1811, and the new Dutch criminal code of 1886, were based on liberal principles. One of the basic principles of classic liberalism is the assurance of individual freedom *vis-à-vis* the state through the fundamental separation of, on the one hand, public sphere from private sphere, and, on the other, law from morality. Sexuality belonged to the private domain, and, in so far as there was no force, violence or public indecency at stake, the state was not supposed to interfere in the sexual life of its citizens. Laws involving public morals were mainly aimed at preventing sexual expression in the public domain and at protecting minors and individuals in relationships of dependence from aggressive or unsolicited sexuality.

Although the liberal bourgeoisie set the tone of Dutch social and political life and the framework of a liberal democratic state was established during the second half of the nineteenth century, the state and several social groups none the less became increasingly interested in and preoccupied with various forms of sexuality. Presented as a matter of public hygiene, a civilising effort was undertaken against the alleged immorality of the lower classes and all other forms of publicly expressed sexuality, such as prostitution and male homosexual behaviour. The criminal pursuit of moral offences was systematised, and doctors began simultaneously to frame sexual conduct in the public sphere as a health issue. Thus, under the aegis of preventive medicine, sexuality entered the socio-political domain. The state's involvement with sexuality grew stronger towards the end of the nineteenth century when Catholics and orthodox Calvinists, who felt excluded from the elitist liberal establishment, initiated an emancipation offensive and gained substantial political influence. In the first two decades of the twentieth century the religiously based communities took over political power from the liberals, partly as a result of the extension of suffrage. For almost five decades, from 1918 to 1967, the religiously based political parties held a majority in Parliament, and between 1918 and 1994 they were uninterruptedly represented in the Dutch government as well. The emancipation of orthodox Calvinists and Catholics resulted in Dutch society's characteristic pillarisation along religious-ideological lines. With their emphasis on morals and family values, they tried to define themselves against the 'godless' liberals and socialists. As the social presence of the church had been negatively affected by the growing influence of science on the one hand and, successively, the rise of liberalism and socialism on the other, these parties focused their attention more than ever on morality. This emphasis grew even stronger towards the close of the nineteenth century when they were confronted with a number of specific developments in this field which they – as militant Christians – deemed undesirable.

The late nineteenth-century morality offensive of the Dutch religiously based groups, just like the purity movements in other western European countries, was a response not only to the emergence of a commercialised, urban entertainment culture and changes in modern literature allowing for more open depiction of sexuality than heretofore, but also to changes in prostitution, the treatment of venereal diseases, birth control and homosexuality. The orthodox Protestant leadership, which saw itself supported by feminists and socialists alike, initiated the struggle against the medical regulation of prostitution. Medical surveillance of prostitutes, aimed at preventing venereal diseases from spreading, which was supported by liberal (moderate Protestant) governments, was seen by orthodox Calvinists as an inadmissible vindication of vice and by feminists and socialists as consent to male bourgeois exploitation of working-class women. Around the turn of the century this permissive liberal attitude towards prostitution, which was backed by members of the medical establishment, was reversed.

The religious groups also reacted strongly against two new developments in the realm of birth control: the rise of neo-Malthusianism and the increased use of contraceptives. The Neo-Malthusian Society (Nieuw-Malthusiaanse Bond, NMB), founded in 1881 by progressive liberals in support of birth control, was vigorously resisted by Christian purity leagues. Although the NMB favoured birth control for socio-economic and hygienic reasons, while leaving the dominant marriage and family ideology more or less unassailed, its antagonists argued that contraception separated procreation from sexuality and charged it with promoting licentious behaviour and abortion. The religious groups were equally critical of new views on sexually deviant behaviour, homosexuality in particular. Around the turn of the century liberal medical practitioners no longer repudiated homosexuality in terms of sin or crime, but moved away from the traditional Christian, moral frame of reference by resorting to medico-biological explanations. Religious groups considered this scientific approach a justification of sin. In doing so they were not altogether wrong, though, for the Dutch Scientific Humanitarian Committee (Nederlandsch Wetenschappelijk Humanitair Komitee, NWHK), a homosexual emancipation movement founded in 1912 following the German example of Magnus Hirschfeld, based its reasoning on medical explanations of homosexuality: it was congenital, and thus had to be accepted as a natural phenomenon.

The moral laws of 1911 represent a milestone in the twentieth-century history of sexuality in the Netherlands. Initiated by confessional politicians, an extension and tightening of the existing moral laws was brought about. These included regulations against prostitution, pornography, birth control, abortion and homosexuality. Sexual 'acts' between adults and minors of the same sex became punishable by law, while sixteen had been established by law as the age of consent for heterosexual relations; in contrast to Britain and Germany, homosexuality between adults was never criminalised in the Netherlands, except during the German occupation. Liberal principles regarding the inviolability of the private sphere and the separation of law and morality were partly pushed aside.

More important than the actual suits and sentences was the fact that the new moral laws set the tone for a social climate of repression in sexual matters, in particular because they facilitated preventive control and could be tightened locally by special police ordinances. Although efforts to prohibit sexual emancipation movements like the NMB and NWHK failed, these movements were forced on to the defensive and into keeping a low public profile. Furthermore, the moral laws provided an opportunity for the confessional leadership to mobilise its constituency to organise against and actively fight immorality at large. Numerous grassroots initiatives sprang up to defend Christian moral values against developments which threatened to undermine marriage, family and public morality. Whereas liberals considered sexuality a private matter and socialists saw it as secondary to socio-economic problems, the confessionals viewed sexual morality as a cornerstone of their public image. All sexuality outside of marriage was not only deemed sinful but also seen as a threat to the existing social order. Licentious activity was a subject with broad public appeal that could well serve to illustrate the potential dangers of the outside, non-Christian world as well as to overcome internal social divisions (the confessional blocs consisted of members of all social classes). For Catholic leaders in particular, sexual issues presented a battleground for unifying their forces and closing their ranks.

Dutch Catholicism and orthodox Protestantism derived their force and stability from the anchoring of their religious and social philosophies in a wide variety of social organisations. The confessionals left their mark in particular on what could be termed the social middle ground where the private and public spheres met: welfare, education, health and social care. Given the relatively large number of Catholic and Protestant organisations that were founded in the 1930s to provide counselling in domestic and marital matters, and the central role of sexuality in discussions on (mental) health, it is only natural that the control of sexuality through intervention in the nuclear family – by priests and ministers, and later on also by physicians and social workers – was considered crucial.

The exceptional demographic pattern of Dutch society from the late nineteenth century until 1965 reveals the degree to which the confessionals – the Catholics in particular – succeeded in imposing their moral ideology on the population. The decline of the birth rate, which began in the industrialised western nations around 1875, was more gradual in the Netherlands than in surrounding countries; while in most European countries the birth rate had already decreased to less than twenty per thousand inhabitants by

1950, the Netherlands did not reach this level until 1965. Although the belated industrialisation of the Netherlands (which did not occur on a grand scale until the 1950s) offers a partial explanation of this relatively high birth rate, it is none the less primarily the result of the disproportionate influence of Christian views on Dutch social and political life. Although the threat of overpopulation was publicly debated, notably in the years right after the Second World War, birth control was, for moral reasons, hardly a subject of discussion, at least not until the 1960s. Liberals and socialists were reticent in this area because they depended on the confessional parties to form coalition governments. Even though the state was not actively seeking to influence marriage and family life, its policies indirectly resulted in a high birth rate. There were legal restrictions on the distribution of birth control devices; married women were discouraged from working outside the home to reduce the danger of childlessness and 'unhealthy family relationships'; and in 1941, particularly because of Catholic insistence, a child allowance was introduced.

Despite high birth rates and the public appeal and rhetorical zeal of the Christian moralists, the official church view of sexuality lagged behind the actual sexual practices of the Dutch. As conventional forms of social control and religious socialisation lost ground because of industrialisation and urbanisation, the confessionals had to alter their strategy. They became increasingly worried about the loss of faith among their constituencies and about moral decay in general, and, therefore, it seemed imperative to have Christian norms affirmed again and again from above. In this way the conflict between religious ideology and social reality grew stronger, which in turn caused new problems and encouraged individuals to find solutions on their own, outside of official doctrine. After all, the repressive moral system could not guarantee that forbidden forms of sexual interaction were not practised. Although the church repudiated birth control categorically and permitted the rhythm method only in exceptional cases based on sound reasons, it was already commonly practised among Catholics – as was *coitus interruptus* before the Second World War. Moreover, it was not infrequently tolerated by the clergy. Statistical material on 'shotgun' marriages shows that having premarital sex was common also among Christians.

It seems likely, then, that the morality offensive of the confessional parties resulted not so much in more chastity among the population but rather in an intensification of attention to sexuality and a guilt-ridden perception of it. In this light it is understandable that experts from the religiously based blocs – including, in addition to members of the clergy, Christian doctors, psychiatrists, psychologists and educational specialists – displayed much interest in sexual problems. Pillarisation was not only a structure for protecting traditional religious values but also a way to ensure that modern accomplishments and new organisational methods in education, health care, social care, science, technology and mass media would serve the interests of Christian communities. Although pillarisation was primarily aimed at conserving traditional religious values, it went hand in hand with the modernisation of the ways and means of social organisation. This explains why the intellectual elites of the confessional blocs were left some freedom of movement outside of the church's area of patronage. As sexuality became a subject that could be more openly discussed, it was harder to maintain the gap between ideology and reality. After 1945 in particular, traditional moral views came under pressure as a result of the professionalisation of health care and the expanding welfare state. Increasingly, this caused internal conflicts in the various blocs between conservative and progressive forces. The net result of the religious preoccupation with sexuality is that in the postwar period Christian leadership and expertise – as paradoxical as it may seem – contributed significantly to reforming sexual morality in the Netherlands.

Conflict between preservation and renewal is characteristic of the Dutch social climate during the 1940s and 1950s. In order to turn back the allegedly unsettling effects of German occupation and rapid postwar industrialisation, churches, politicians and professional caretakers worked hard for the preservation and healing of family life. The slogan was 'Family Recovery brings Population Recovery'. The desire for security and stability was fed by the need for cooperation on the road to material recovery and by the threat of communism. The result was a moral climate characterised by discipline and austerity. The anxiety about an alleged moral decline represented, in fact, a final flaring up of the prewar morality offensive. Traditional sexual morality was undermined in the 1950s by the rapid industrialisation and urbanisation of the Netherlands. More prosperity and the expansion of the welfare state created more individual independence and greater mobility for a growing number of people. The rapid diffusion of television after 1955 broke down the moral isolation of large segments of the population. The widening of the options in terms of leisure and consumption created more space for self-expression and led to the emergence of an autonomous youth culture. Various pillarised organisations, in particular those in health care, welfare and the media, gradually took a more independent stance against religious authority. In co-operation with the more progressive members of the clergy, Christian intellectuals tried to adjust the dominant, conservative morality to a changed social situation.

In the field of marriage, family and sexuality, the traditional keepers of morality – clergy and members of the medical establishment – had to give way to new experts, including psychiatrists, psychologists, education specialists and social workers. In contrast to conventional Christian morality and medico-biological thinking, these new experts relied on modern social sciences, especially psychology and education, but later also on sociology. The professionalisation and scientification of social care provided a new frame of reference: what had initially been defined in terms of morality was now seen as a (mental) health issue. Normalisation and integration based on psycho-social strategies took the place of sanctions and prohibitions, whereas sexual norms were formulated in relation to general human standards involving health, well-being and personal growth. The emphasis shifted from a moral and biological approach to a more psychological one: sexuality was no longer seen solely in terms of procreation but also as an autonomous means of communication, as expression and confirmation of a love bond, initially only within marriage but gradually also outside of it.

The shift from a procreation morality to a relationship ethics, not only in expert discourse but increasingly in religious discourse on sexuality as well, resulted in the early 1960s in a more flexible attitude towards birth control, premarital sex and homosexuality. It became possible to have a positive view of heterosexuality or to either vindicate or accept homosexuality, if at least it was expressed in a responsible and meaningful way in a steady relationship. By combining personal development with self-restraint and individual responsibility, this new Christian-humanistic set of norms and values offered a middle way between the denial of sexual urges and unbridled hedonism. Sexuality was still a sensitive issue but it was revalued and seen as a source of personal and relational enrichment. In this respect the ideological distance between, on the one hand, the reform-minded confessionals of the 1950s and, on the other hand, the sexual emancipation movements of those days, such as the Dutch Organisation for Sexual Reform (NVSH) and the Organisation for the Emancipation of Homosexuals (COC), was not as substantial as it may seem at first glance. The mainstream among the sexual reformists also viewed sexuality as a positive force that contributes to personal growth through relational bonds. Inside as well as outside of Christian circles, sexual reform was more successful and permanent when the romanticised ideal of a steady one-to-one relationship based on love was within reach and there was no real threat to the basic concept of monogamous marriage.

Precisely because the confessional experts based their response to social changes on their specific set of beliefs, which also helped them to translate these changes for their constituency, they caused a change in mentality which during the 1960s affected church authorities as well as Dutch society at large. In this way the confessional intellectuals helped set the stage for the sexual 'revolution' of the 1960s. Within the organisational structures that were meant to certify a Catholic or Calvinist identity, ideas gained currency that quickly turned out to be hardly distinguishable from those of Dutch Reformed or unaffiliated Dutch people. This suggests that a new, broadly shared humanistic set of values had replaced the various belief systems of the separate pillars. It is one of the ironies of history that the reform euphoria of the 1960s was most passionately felt among the new generation of Catholics and Protestants.

The decade between 1965 and 1975 represents a cultural and ideological watershed in postwar Dutch history. Material security and physical safety had been more or less a given for those who came of age in the 1960s, and this was expressed in a new set of values. The protest generation of the 1960s had higher demands regarding the quality of life, focusing on non-material values like personal growth and emancipation, values that were hardly even recognised by existing pillarised political organisations. One of the fields in which the cultural renewal of the 1960s manifested itself most strongly was that of marriage, family and sexuality. In the early 1960s one taboo after the other was broken, especially in the arts and media. The talks on sexuality and relationships by the Catholic psychiatrist C. J. B. J. Trimbos for the Catholic radio network had considerable influence. Television, which entered the living room of the average Dutch household in the 1960s, played an even more stimulating role than radio. In 1963, the year when the pill was introduced, the popular Bishop Bekkers declared on television that birth control was a matter of a married couple's individual conscience, thus distancing himself from the official Roman Catholic view. In a short period of time a wide variety of information on sexuality flooded the market, from candid sex education booklets, complete with pictures of various 'positions', to all sorts of pornography. The media reported extensively on the sexual underground, for instance the gay scene, group sex experiments, partner-swapping, and 'erotic panoramas'. Several controversial acquittals involving pornographic issues in the years around 1970 cleared the way for a strikingly permissive attitude. Porno shops and sex theatres enriched Dutch towns.

The force of the sexual revolution was significantly enhanced by developments in birth control technology, especially the introduction of the pill in 1963. Until the early 1960s contraception was a major taboo in the Netherlands, but in 1965 the government put the issue on the political agenda. The liberalisation of laws and the introduction of the pill in the package covered by medical insurance (1971) – so that it quickly found its way to family doctors – made sure that contraceptives were readily available, while a pragmatic approach to sex education certified their effective use. One sign of the effective use of contraceptives by young people in particular was that the number of 'shotgun' marriages and babies born out of wedlock, which had risen since the mid-1950s, began to drop starting in 1969. If up to the mid-1960s the number of illegitimate births was relatively low in comparison to the neighbouring countries Belgium and Germany because of the strength of Christian morality in the Netherlands, after the onset of the sexual revolution it was low in comparison because of the rapid diffusion of contraceptives, among both religious and secular groups of the Dutch population.

Around 1970 there was a general consensus among Dutch politicians about the desirability of family planning and, by implication, the necessity of free access to contraceptives. Although Rome condemned the use of contraceptives in the 1968 encyclical letter *Humanae Vitae*, most Dutch Catholics, just like the Protestants (with the exception of the orthodox Calvinists), had no scruples about putting aside the official views of their church. The wide availability of effective contraceptives facilitated successful family planning.

During the 1970s the Netherlands was the world's leader in terms of the quantity of contraceptives used. Whereas before 1965 the Netherlands was among the European countries with the highest birth rates, in the late 1960s the Dutch followed closely in the footsteps of countries with low birth rates, like Denmark and Sweden. Between 1960 and 1975 the birth rate – the number of live-born children per thousand inhabitants – dropped from 20.9 to 13.0, and in the period between 1955 and 1981 the average number of children in each household declined from 3.0 to 1.6.

Precisely because of the availability of effective contraceptives, unwanted pregnancy became harder to accept. Therefore, abortion could emerge from the realm of silence and secrecy. In the early 1960s it was openly debated by doctors and members of the legal profession, but already by the late 1960s more and more out-patient help was provided, leading to a rapid shift in the mindset from 'no, except' to 'yes, except'. However, this did not lead to an increase in the number of abortions. The demand for abortions even dropped after 1971, when the first Dutch abortion clinic opened its doors, and had stabilised at a low level by 1974. The increase in premarital sex did not cause a rise in abortions. Together with a decline in illegitimate births and 'shotgun' marriages, this indicates a wide-spread use of contraceptives. Abortion was considered not as a replacement for contraception, but rather, and probably even more so than in earlier decades, as a last resort. Although article 251 of the criminal code, which prohibited abortion, was given such a broad interpretation during the 1970s that ending a pregnancy was no longer a pressing issue, this medical procedure was still a controversial political and ethical matter. Not until 1981 did the Dutch Parliament vote in favour of an amendment which permitted abortion on medical and social grounds, provided that a consultation between doctor and woman takes place and a required three-to-five-day reflection period is observed. However, this did not go far enough for the women's movement, which viewed the right to abortion as a touchstone of woman's autonomy.

The ensuing heated debate on abortion, in which both supporters and opponents referred to the rights of the individual (of the woman as well as the unborn child), presents a clear example of the politici-sation of sexuality that was caused by the sexual revolution. Already before the second feminist wave had declared the politics of the personal, the fusion of Marxism and psychoanalysis by such German thinkers as Herbert Marcuse and Wilhelm Reich offered a theoretical framework for understanding individual and psychological phenomena as an integral part of socio-political relationships. Not surprisingly, the societies for sexual reform and for the integration of homosexuality (NVSH and COC) also tied their aims of sexual emancipation to a more general social reform. In the mid-1960s the COC stepped out of its hiding place and publicly argued for the social integration of homosexuality through a process of mutual adjustments in both society and the homosexual minority. But when it became clear in the 1970s that this process was not advancing swiftly, the gay and lesbian movement radicalised: the activities of separatist groups like Paarse September, the Flikkerfront and the Rooie Flikkers were inspired by the aim to confront and provoke the general public. The gay movement was enriched by a flowering subculture: from the 1960s Amsterdam was not only a magic kingdom for hippies but also a Mecca for homosexuals.

During the second half of the 1960s the NVSH became a potent social force. By this time the society for sexual reform had over two hundred thousand members and more than sixty consultation offices for family planning across the country. It also published its own information booklets and broadcast its own programmes on television. In contrast to the NMB, which focused only on birth control, the NVSH, founded in 1946, also aimed at ending repressive moral legislation, improving scientific knowledge of sexuality and developing a more open and positive approach to sex education. The right to a more satisfactory sexual life was seen as a condition for improving society at large. The NVSH's basic view was that a healthy and fulfilling sexual lifestyle was an intrinsic part of the process towards personal growth and that neither the state nor society had the right to determine the dominant norm in the area of sexuality; instead, it had become a matter of personal choice and individual responsibility. However, the substantial growth of the NVSH (from over 26,000 members in 1946 to 202,000 in 1966) was attributable not to its alternative sexual ideology but rather to its successful efforts to distribute contraceptives and pragmatic information. During the 1960s there was a marked division of interest between an inspired avant-garde which favoured radical sexual liberation and a more conservative following which primarily valued practical information about sexuality. Once contraceptives became widely available, the NVSH saw its membership quickly decline again.

Although legislation and the actual application of moral laws lagged behind social developments, in 1970 the government demonstrated that it recognised the need for sexual reform. After legal impediments against the distribution of contraceptives had gone, in 1971, divorce was made simpler and easier. In the same year, article 248bis, which discriminated against homosexuals, was dropped. In legal and ethical debates, recourse to 'public decency' as the basic norm was no longer taken for granted; instead, new criteria prevailed, involving basic individual rights, the harmfulness of certain forms of sexuality, and the unequal power relations in sexual bonds. Thus, in 1981, rape in marriage became a crime.

In many ways the sexual revolution in the Netherlands was spectacular and had a lasting impact, partly because it was enacted and discussed publicly, thanks to the presence and attention of the modern media. Possibly the openness and heatedness of the debates were a response to the more restrictive climate of the preceding period. During the 1960s sex became visible and debatable, and particularly in Amsterdam the sexual revolution was characterised by radical experimentation. Yet has all this also substantially altered the sexual conduct and views of the average Dutch person?

Opinion polls conducted in the 1960s and 1970s clearly indicated the dissolution, except among small minorities of orthodox Calvinists or Catholics, of the traditional, strongly Christian repressive morality which permitted only marital sex aimed at procreation. The decade between 1965 and 1975 marked a turn in the norms on sexuality, marriage and family within the church, politics, health care and social care, as well as in public opinion. A 'sexual enthusiasm', the idea that sexual liberation was essential to the individual's well-being, could be felt everywhere. Sexuality became associated less with shame and aversion; opinion polls taken between 1965 and 1981 indicated an increasingly liberal attitude, in particular with respect to contraceptives, masturbation, premarital sex and cohabitation. With respect to homosexuality, abortion and prostitution, the Netherlands, alongside Denmark, was the most tolerant European country in those years. Clearly, the clock could no longer be set back with regard to countless issues, for instance the disconnection of reproduction and sexuality, and the emancipation of young people, women and outsiders like homosexuals – groups which perhaps have benefited most from the permissive society.

However, it remains to be seen whether the results of opinion polls on sexuality correspond well with the sexual revolution viewed as a liberation of desire. The ongoing liberalisation, notably regarding premarital sex and contraception, has not caused the Dutch to submit *en bloc* to a hedonistic, consumer-like attitude towards sex. Although some people have engaged in experiments with partner-swapping or group sex, tolerance for extramarital or promiscuous sex seems to have grown only slightly. Increasingly, in fact, such 'aberrations' of the sexual revolution have been met with scepticism and rejection. For most Dutch in all age groups, mere physical attraction alone is not, unlike a tight affective bond, adequate justification for sexual contact. For the majority of the Dutch population, sex remains more or less exclusively tied to a monogamous love bond, whether sealed by marriage or not. The tolerance of premarital sex, for instance, is dependent on the presence of a love bond or marriage perspective.

It seems, then, that the sexual revolution has not seriously affected the close tie between sexuality and the exclusionary romantic love ideal. The distrustful and restrained attitude towards sexuality was replaced by a positive evaluation of sexuality within affective bonds. In the 1960s and 1970s the Netherlands predominantly became a couple-oriented society: people primarily found meaning in family life and in relationships. Yet the ways in which marriage and partnerships were actually enacted did change significantly. Compared with the decades preceding the 1950s, there is more equality between partners, there is more space for negotiation and personal growth, stereotypical gender roles have been broken down and mutual demands of sexual partners tend to be higher. But with the strong emotional and erotic nature of modern (marital) relationships, the potential for all sorts of psychological tensions that make them more fragile and less durable has increased, as is indicated by the growth in the number of divorces. The more or less self-evident, enduring marital engagement has been replaced by a pattern of 'serial monogamy'; most Dutch remain quite monogamous, in their premarital sexual engagements as well.

Support for the findings of opinion polls can be found in demographic data which show that the popularity of marriage reached a high at the end of the 1960s. During the 1950s and 1960s more and more people married at a younger age, and the percentage of unmarried individuals declined. Between 1950 and 1975 the average age of men and women at marriage decreased. Until the 1970s the percentage of those who were married among people in their twenties and thirties went up. Only after 1971, as alternative forms of living gained popularity, did marriage frequency start to decrease, while the lowering of the average age at marriage began to slow down. The change in ways of living together during the 1970s manifested itself particularly in the growing number of unmarried couples sharing a household, (younger) singles and one-parent families, rather than a growth in communes and communal living experiments.

What was seen as either a shocking moral decline or a hopeful breaking of taboos in the 1960s may be considered, in hindsight, as no more than an acceleration in a long-term development of changing sexual attitudes and behaviour. The change in mentality since the 1960s was preceded by a gradual, long-term behavioural evolution. Over the course of the twentieth century a decreasing number of young people postponed sex until after marriage, while the age of first sexual contact gradually declined. During the 1950s sexual conduct already failed to fall in line with official morality, even though it was not publicly legitimised. The sexual revolution can be seen as a catching up of public morality with actual behaviour. Moreover, what is at issue, it seems, is not so much a sudden and radical liberation of repressed sexuality as a shift in emphasis concerning the meaning and evaluation of sexuality.

The sexual revolution of the 1960s in the Netherlands was characterised by two changes: first, sexuality became visible and debatable, it could be openly discussed, and, second, there was a turn in the signification and evaluation of sexuality: whereas before the emphasis was on sexuality as an amoral drive which threatened culture at large, from the 1960s onward the positive influence of gratifying sexual relationships on health and well-being was stressed. The sexual conduct of individuals used to be determined by social status, hierarchy, social responsibility, economic interests and fixed gender roles, but in modern western society personal emotion and desire have gained primacy in sexual matters. The historical roots of the sexual revolution can be found in the link of sexuality and the romantic love ideal as it was conceptualised around 1800 and became part of social reality during the nineteenth century. In the long run, this connection undermined the traditionally restrictive pattern of sexuality based on social and familial demands and economic interests. Particularly in (marital) relationships based on freedom and mutual attraction and affection, it became possible to attach a positive and autonomous meaning to sexuality. The emancipation of sexuality did not result so much in a liberation of sexual desire as in a different way of containing such desire. While the traditional repressive morality needed few yet strict and unambiguous prohibitions, based as it was on force and control imposed from outside (which of course could not guarantee the prevention of forbidden sexual practices), the new, more flexible ethics was geared towards individual growth and demanded more subtle rules of engagement that depended on people's talent for negotiation and empathy. Changed social circumstances have been tied to new modes of social interaction that require a great degree of flexibility, self-awareness, individual responsibility and self-control.

The sexual revolution was in many ways ambiguous. Instead of liberation it created a host of new problems, on a personal as well as on a political and social level. Once sexuality had turned into an ordinary subject of public debate, all its troubles and difficulties could also come out into the open. The shift from the traditional do's and don't's to a more individualised psychological frame of reference did not necessarily mean that sexuality was experienced more freely at the personal level. Now that sexual expression was left to individual choice and responsibility and there was room for personal growth and emancipation, many people did not know what to do with the increased liberties; they had doubts and felt insecure and confused. New norms concerning erotic attractiveness and sexual achievement could make individuals feel as unfree and unhappy as under the old taboos. The new view of sexuality may have caused fewer feelings of guilt, yet they were replaced by other emotional problems: fear of not living up to the new norms, fear of feeling inadequate or being not attractive enough, fear of being abnormal, fear of losing one's partner and of failing to achieve a satisfactory balance between unimpeded sexual fantasies and the limitations of everyday life. Sexual liberation not only invoked new sexual norms about optimal sexual functioning, but as sexuality grew more important for personal identity and the continuity of relationships, problems in these areas also gained prominence and were more intensely experienced at the individual level. Counselling on sexual issues boomed right after the onset of the alleged sexual revolution – this is one of its paradoxes. As a source of personal and relational growth, sexuality remained a sensitive issue. And, obviously, 'good' sex was not just there, but needed practice and experience.

The feminist argument that sexuality is far from innocent because it can be used for manipulative and egotistical purposes indicated that many sexual reformers had miscalculated the complex and ambivalent nature of sexual desire and the large differences in male and female sexual experience. Therefore, the ongoing reform of moral legislation was a controversial point in the 1980s. Proposals to change legislation concerning pornography, sexual violence and the age of consent for sexual activity gave rise to heated debates and were met by resistance from both Christian and feminist circles. The women's movement considered rape, sexual child abuse, prostitution and incest as evidence of the fact that liberated sexuality is often male, aggressive and violent; as such, it poses a threat to women and children. As a consequence of the heightened awareness of the dangerous sides of liberated sexuality, a large part of the Dutch population turned back to somewhat more conservative attitudes.

The emergence of AIDS in the 1980s also cast a chill over the sexual revolution. In the early 1980s the hedonistic gay subculture – quite possibly the only place where the fundamental principles of the sexual revolution were consistently practised – was first struck by the epidemic, after, in fact, the number of infections involving venereal diseases had already risen drastically in the 1970s. It should be pointed out, though, that in the Netherlands, in contrast to Britain and the United States, the new disease did not unleash a moral backlash against the accomplishments of the sexual revolution. Obviously the time of carefree promiscuity – if ever it existed – is over; the epidemic has led to more caution and a revalorisation of committed relationships, but as yet there is no sign in the Netherlands of a return to a repressive sexual morality, except regarding paedophilia. It can be argued that AIDS has in fact contributed to even more openness about sexuality in general and about homosexuality in particular, in terms of both its pleasures and its pains.

In the Netherlands, even more than in other western countries, sexuality has become visible and discussable since the 1960s. There are many ways in which consumer culture tries to appeal to sexual desire. We are constantly exposed to ideals and information about our sexual functioning. Advertising, fashion, lifestyle magazines, pop music, movies and the entertainment business stimulate our sexual emotions and represent erotic attraction as a significant determinant of happiness. Therapeutic discourse treats us as sexual beings, and the media suggest to us that optimal sexual functioning is an imperative for personal growth. The educational system, social services and governmental information teach us what responsible and healthy sexuality entails. The media devote much attention to all kinds of sexual variation, from homosexuality to sadomasochism, and from fetishism to exhibitionism. In Amsterdam in particular there is a wide choice available for satisfying all sorts of sexual needs, and 'kinky parties' are well attended. Both in government and among the general public a tolerant attitude prevails. It remains to be seen, however, whether modern society can truly provide its members with the means for forming and satisfying the sexual needs which it constantly invokes and incites. At times it seems as if sexual liberties are propagated rather than practised. Where formerly morality lagged behind actual behaviour, now it appears that liberal views do not lead to a rich or versatile sexual life. For the majority of the populace, sexual practice is limited to steady partners and sexual activity shows little variation. In that respect the Dutch are hardly very different from other western nations.

An array of culturally determined assumptions still prevent a varied, multifaceted sexual culture from developing, not only in the Netherlands but in the entire western world. First, the difference between the ways in which men and women experience sexuality presents an obstacle to sexual equality; at present it overfreights heterosexual relationships with discussions about liberties and sexual violence. Second, the debate on sexuality is marked by a polarisation between 'good' sex, conductive of individual freedom and personal growth, and 'bad' sex, characterised by inequality and force. Third, the connection of sexuality and love prevents individuals from seeking sexual experimentation outside their relationship. At the same time sexuality is perhaps overestimated in relationships, and this burdens love relationships with changeable and unpredictable sexual desires. Fourth, the idea that sex properly belongs to the invisible private sphere discourages the formation of a public sexuality. Finally, and perhaps most importantly, the formation of a new sexual culture is prevented by the deeply rooted assumption that sex is 'natural' and that therefore it cannot be learned or cultivated.

The drive model is central to both traditional Christian-bourgeois morality and various liberalisation ideologies of the sexual revolution. This means that sexuality is considered a part of human nature that has an autonomous existence regardless of society.

Before the 1960s it was the dominant idea that sexual urges posed a continuous threat to the moral order because of their explosive and barely controllable nature; therefore, they had to be strictly repressed by outside regulation and control. Since then the emphasis has shifted towards a positive evaluation of sexual desire as the heart of the self. Yet the social-critical elements of the sexual revolution have been hastily overlooked. Since the 1970s the common understanding of sexual liberation has stressed personal awareness and individual growth within the existing social order. Because every individual harbours sexual desire, according to the new morality, he or she has the right to sexual gratification, as long as certain rules are met. Although sexuality has unmistakably entered the public arena since the 1960s, it has concurrently – and paradoxically – become a more personal, private and psychological affair. The ever more negative responses that can be witnessed today in the Netherlands to the expression of various sexualities in public are an indication of how difficult it is to break these ingrained patterns and views.

Bibliography

Akkerman, T. and S. Stuurman (eds) (1985), *De zondige riviera van het katholicisme: een lokale studie over feminisme en ontzuiling 1950–1975*, Amsterdam, SUA.

Berkel, D. A. M. van (1990), *Moederschap tussen zielzorg en psychohygiëne: katholieke deskundigen over voortplanting en opvoeding 1945–1970*, Assen and Maastricht, Van Gorcum.

Bolt, A. (1989), 'Jeugd en seksualiteit in Nederland: een vergelijking tussen enquête-materiaal uit 1968 en 1981', *Tijdschrift voor Seksuologie*, 13, 4, pp. 266–75.

Brongersma, E. (1980), 'Seksualteit en wetgeving', in J. Frenken (ed.), *Seksuologie: een interdisciplinaire benadering*, Deventer, Van Loghum Slaterus, pp. 36–59.

Glasbergen, P. and R. Zandanel (1976), *Bevolkingsgroei en welvaartsstaat*, Assen and Amsterdam, Van Gorcum.

Heeren, H. J. (1985), *Bevolkingsgroei en bevolkingsbeleid in Nederland*, Amsterdam, Uitgeverij Kobra.

Hekma, G. (1987), *Homoseksualiteit, een medische reputatie: de uitdoktering van de homoseksueel in negentiende-eeuws Nederland*, Amsterdam, SUA.

— (1994), 'De klemmen van de lust: de ontwikkeling van het plezier sinds de seksuele revolutie', *Etnofoor*, 7, 2, pp. 5–24.

Hekma, G. *et al.* (eds) (1990), *Het verlies van de onschuld: seksualiteit in Nederland*, Groningen, Wolters-Noordhoff.

Hofstee, E. W. (1981), *Korte demografische geschiedenis van Nederland van 1800 tot heden*, Haarlem, Fibula-Van Dishoeck.

Ketting, E. (1983), 'De nieuwe seksuele beheersingsmoraal', *Tijdschrift voor Seksuologie*, 3, pp. 93–109.

Kooy, G. A. (1975), *Seksualiteit, huwelijk en gezin in Nederland*, Deventer, Van Loghum Slaterus.

— (1976), *Jongeren en seksualiteit: sociologische analyse van een revolutionaire evolutie*, Deventer, Van Loghum Slaterus.

Kooy, G.A. *et al.* (1983), *Sex in Nederland: het meest recente onderzoek naar houding en gedrag van de Nederlandse bevolking*, Utrecht and Antwerp, Het Spectrum.

Mooij, A. (1993), *Geslachtsziekten en besmettingsangst: een historisch-sociologische studie 1850–1990*, Amsterdam, Boom.

Nabrink, G. (1978), *Seksuele hervorming in Nederland: achtergronden en geschiedenis van de Nieuw-Malthusiaanse Bond (NMB) en de Nederlandse Vereniging voor Seksuele Hervorming (NVSH), 1881–1971*, Nijmegen, SUN.

Noordhoff, J. D. *et al.* (1969), *Sex in Nederland*, Utrecht and Antwerp, Het Spectrum.

Oosterhuis, H. (1992), *Homoseksualiteit in katholiek Nederland: een sociale geschiedenis, 1900–1970*, Amsterdam, SUA.

Röling, H. Q. (1987), *'De tragedie van het geslachtsleven': Johannes Rutgers (1850–1924) en de Nieuw-Malthusiaanse Bond*, Amsterdam, Van Gennep.

Schnabel, P. (1973), 'Seksualiteit in de welvaartsstaat', *Sociologische Gids*, 3, pp. 189–206.

Stuurman, S. (1983), *Verzuiling, kapitalisme en patriarchaat: aspecten van de ontwikkeling van de moderne staat in Nederland*, Nijmegen, SUN.

Tielman, R. (1982), *Homoseksualiteit in Nederland: Studie van een emancipatiebeweging*, Meppel, Boom.

Top, W. (1988), *Fijn en frisch: seksuele voorlichting onder Gereformeerden 1900–1965*, Amsterdam, VU Uitgeverij.

Warmerdam, H. and P. Koenders (1987), *Cultuur en ontspanning. Het COC 1946–1966*, Utrecht, Veen.

Zessen, G. van and T. Sandfort (eds) (1991), *Seksualiteit in Nederland: seksueel gedrag, risico en preventie van Aids*, Amsterdam and Lisse, Swets & Zeitlinger.

4

Sex and sexuality in France since 1800

Robert A. Nye

As the French themselves have discovered to their profit, their country has long been the object of the erotic fantasies of foreigners. For much of its modern history France has also been a welcome refuge for political dissidents and exiles, so that 'liberty' possesses a semantic richness in France it does not dispose of elsewhere. The French have themselves been complicit in the production of stereotypes about their own sexuality, especially in the twentieth century, because it makes France, and Paris in particular, an appealing and attractive tourist destination for young lovers, newlyweds and couples who hope to relight the fires of youthful love.

However, if we leave aside the confection of stereotypes, there seems little doubt that France has a richly deserved reputation as the land of 'amour' much celebrated in song, literature, the graphic arts and popular culture. Chivalric and courtly love blossomed first in France, European romanticism took its inspiration from French novelists, poets and painters, and French was for a century and a half the preponderant language of European pornography. To this day, visitors from abroad remark on the open expression of affection between French couples, and the French, for their part, appear to find hypocrisy in sexual matters common everywhere they go, especially in America (Lamont 1992). Consider that there is no English-language equivalent for the French phrase *'c'est l'amour'*, which in French, it should be said, carries a dark fatalistic meaning acknowledging the possibility that lovers do not always live happily ever after.

At times this reputation threatens to obscure a tradition of criticism of romantic ideals in France second to none, nourishing, as it has, writers like Emile Zola, Marcel Proust and, most notably, Gustave Flaubert, whose great novel *Madame Bovary* brings the spiritual side of love most decidedly down to earth (Singer 1987). France has also had its share of sexual radicals who have opposed the regnant ideal in thought and in action. Among others the Marquis de Sade, Charles Fourier, Colette, André Gide, Jean Genet and, in our times, Michel Foucault are representatives of this tradition. However, these wilful deviants from the culture of 'amour' are best understood as *monstres sacrés* whose exceptionalism has helped obscure a full understanding of the historical process in which French sexual culture has come to link love exclusively to heterosexual sexuality and to the courtship rituals in which heterosexuality historically developed.

In light of the extraordinary hegemony of 'amour', the historian of French sexuality has, in my view, three principal tasks: first, to write an account of 'French sex' that tries to include non-heterosexual, non-marital sexuality; second, to explain how hetero-sexual sexuality and the forms of love that nourished it took an ideological form that was obsessively maintained; and, finally, to explain the relation between the two.

I take 'sexual culture' here to include both sexual behaviour and the discourse about it generated in society. I think we can assume a kind of reciprocity between the two, much as Michel Foucault does in the portrait of sexuality he sketches in his *History of Sexuality* (volume I). For Foucault 'sexuality' is part of a linguistic and repre-sentational economy of discourses that virtually constitutes 'sex', including the 'forms of power' and the 'channels' it takes as it 'pen-etrates and controls everyday pleasure – all this entailing effects that may be those of refusal, blockage, and invalidation, but also incitement and intensification' (Foucault 1980a: 11). 'Sex', in Foucault's usage, is a blend of prescriptive ideals about 'good' and 'bad' sex acts that are incorporated into sexual experience as pleasure or aversion; but sex is also the 'truth' of the sexual body, whether male, female or a 'deviant' form that falls somewhere between or outside them.

As is well known, the conception of power adopted by Foucault minimises its legal forms and expressions in favour of those of scientific and medical norms. He first applied this insight to crime in his book on the invention of the prison, *Surveiller et punir*, but devel-oped it most completely in his writing on sexuality. It is Foucault's point that governmental authority and statutory law are singularly ineffective in regulating sex because they attempt only to repress its publicly forbidden forms; hence his scorn for the 'repressive hypothesis' of 'Victorian' sexuality. We shall learn far more about sex, he suggests, if we explore the ways that society has taken up the 'truths' of science and medicine, transforming them into cultural norms for sexual life that embrace the entire range of human sexual experience.

It is my contention that Foucault's insight about the power of cultural norms derives largely from his experience as a gay man in a society that has minimally repressed private homosexual behaviour but has virtually sacralised heterosexual love (Nye 1996). This sacralisation has occurred, I will argue, in large part because heterosexuality is the inevitable path to procreation and healthy population growth. Since the mid nineteenth century, when the first statistics on the precipitous decline in births became known, French elites have considered the 'depopulation' problem to be a uniquely French 'pathology' in the range of social problems that plagued all industrial societies (Nye 1984; Pick 1989). Following several years of negative population growth in the last decades of the nineteenth century, the need to stimulate births became a public obsession, made more desperate still by huge casualties in twentieth-century wars. In the years before the Second World War France was virtually the only nation in the industrial world with an utterly stagnant population. A vigorous natalist (pro-birth) movement resulted out of these concerns about 'depopulation' which has become, as Hervé LeBras has written, 'the chief means for affirming the social link between all the French, a sort of laic religion which permits them to evince their attachment to the nation' (LeBras 1991: 14).

An irony of this anxious concern is the fact that the French political elite could not intervene massively in social or family life to promote procreation on account of a preceding and equally sacrosanct principle of tolerance for private consensual behaviour, enshrined in the Napoleonic Code as a sharp legal distinction between public and private spheres. With respect to sexuality, only its dangerous public manifestations – rape, child molestation, outrage to public sentiments – were punishable (Copley 1989; Sibalis 1996). As reflected in public opinion polls, the principle that the state has no business 'regulating [sexual] rules of conduct. Private life is private' (*Nouvelle Observateur*, no. 1179, 12–18 June 1987, pp. 79–80) is respected to this day.

However, as Foucault reminds us, the impotence of the law in matters of private sexuality was more than counterbalanced by the appearance in French society of a discourse of cultural norms supported by the authority of science and medicine. In this domain of representations, positive ideals of motherhood, fertile love-making and healthy family life circulated together with negative conceptions of masturbation, homosexuality, perversions and other forms of 'egoistic' or 'sterile' sexuality that were characterised as the 'shame' of *honnêtes gens*. There are various ways of documenting this interpretation; in what follows I will present a chronological account that emphasises these continuities from the mid nineteenth century to the present. I lack the space for much comparative argument, but my aim will be to emphasise the relative uniqueness of France in this combination of legal tolerance with censorious norms, and the obsessive linkage of love with procreation.

The foundations for these modern developments were laid during France's long Catholic past. By the early Middle Ages the church had reluctantly embraced marriage and procreation, but it continued to reject non-marital or non-reproductive sexuality. The church had already begun to lose the initiative in these matters by the eighteenth century to a monarchy driven by the logic of mercantilism, which took a keen interest in the health and numbers of the population as a category of national wealth (Foucault 1980b). The Revolutionary and Napoleonic wars demonstrated that wars are no longer, in the words of Michel Foucault, 'waged in the name of a sovereign who must be defended; they are waged on behalf of the existence of everyone'. The need for more 'power over life' worked to focus the attention of policy-makers on the 'normalising' power of sex, wherein 'The mechanisms of power are addressed to the body, to life, to what causes it to proliferate, to what reinforces the species, its stamina, its ability to dominate, or its capacity for being used' (Foucault 1980a: 137, 146).

These developments coincided with the perfection (by P.-J.-G. Cabanis) and popularisation (by J. J. Virey) in France of a new anatomo-physiological science focusing on human reproduction, wherein a woman's 'reproductive function determined her [social] role and reciprocally' (Fraisse 1989: 99). Scientists and doctors studied the contributions of both sexes to procreation assiduously, and articulated a conception of sexual complementarity as a 'harmony of corresponding inequalities' based on the 'natural' differences between the sexes (Fraisse 1989: 94). The passion of sexual attraction and fertility depended, in this conception, on a strongly marked physical and characterological dimorphism: masculine men and feminine women. Sterility thus came to be closely associated with anatomo-physiological ambiguity and its presumed sexual indifference (Nye 1993).

The socio-political situation of post-Revolutionary France strengthened these conceptions in various ways. The new civil code reinvented old-regime patriarchy by legitimating the principle of 'masculine management' of family assets, encouraging a man to maintain a tight control over both his material and biological capital, and to think about inheritance literally as a mode of self-perpetuation. Family and blood were so strongly associated in this system that adoption was unthinkable and a wife's bastard a grave legal and cultural threat to her husband's patrimony. A man's own infidelities were, however, excused in the code by differentially severe punishments for adultery and by a ban (until the twentieth century) on paternity suits (Knibiehler 1987).

The high premium placed on the careful management of biological capital exacted a high price, however, in the form of an early and rapid decline of the birth rate. It is not known whether the French had better access to birth-control methods than other Europeans, but they used the methods at their disposal so effectively that the population grew only sluggishly from the 1840s on (McLaren 1990; Bardet and LeBras 1988). The concerns felt at the highest levels about the 'birth dearth' were magnified tenfold following French defeat in the Franco-Prussian War of 1870, which dramatised the geo-political implications of stagnant population growth. For the reasons outlined above, not to mention the notable hypocrisy of their own minuscule families, French government leaders offered little legislative relief, but they lent their encouragement to an astonishing array of voluntary organisations engaged in exposing and fighting against the putative causes of infertility (Offen 1984). Population experts and medical men often held leadership positions in these organisations, so it is not surprising that their discourse favoured biological metaphors of pathology and norm with respect to the survival of the French 'race' (Nye 1993; Tomlinson 1985).

In the search for the causes of infertility the usual suspects were rounded up: egoism, a failure of the will, secularisation, a host of 'moral' causes, including everything from pornography and prostitution to alcoholism, and fertility-sapping diseases like tuberculosis and syphilis (Cole 1996; Pedersen 1996). Whatever else they counted as decisive causes, however, the overwhelming majority of commentators identified deficits in masculinity and femininity as important components of the problem. They usually meant by this some departure from the 'normal' gender roles 'nature' had decreed for each sex, but increasingly the depopulation debate became freighted with scientific and medical language that focused on sexual identity and function.

A model for charting the variations of sex identity and function already existed in French medicine in the form of the science of teratology (the study of monsters), the invention of the French biologist Isidore Geoffrey de Saint-Hilaire (Daston and Park 1985; Herdt 1994). Teratologists identified a continuous spectrum of 'intermediary' forms of male and female on which could be plotted corresponding strengths and orientation of 'genital' drives. The hermaphrodites who occupied the centre of the spectrum between normally endowed males and females were both anatomically ambiguous and deficient in sexual capacity, true monsters of sterility.

This spectrum of sexual identity was the foundation on which French doctors and sexologists constructed the sexual perversions in the last decades of the nineteenth century. In this they differed somewhat from other European sexologists whose model for a 'third sex' was less an *intermediary* variation than a distinct and complex type of its own (Hekma 1994; Bleys 1995; Rosario 1996). In France deviant sexuality, indeed sexuality in general, was invariably located with respect to the reproductive capacity of normally constituted males and females. That is, it was an ensemble of physical signs and correlative functions that explained sexual aim and object.

The conflation of sex, sexuality and reproductive capacity in French medicine was an equation taken deeply to heart in prewar French society. As war tensions rose with Germany, the attentions of the elite were focused obsessively on deviations from the 'normal' affiliations of sexual difference, heterosexuality and fertility. Indeed the French were second to none in the era 1880–1910, when the sexual perversions were being catalogued and described by the first European pioneers. Alfred Binet, Jean-Martin Charcot and Valentin Magnan, Benjamin Ball and many others provided clinical accounts of inversion, fetishism, exhibitionism, bestiality, sadism and other phenomena. French experts differed from students of sexuality elsewhere by resisting the notion that sexuality could be conceived as a force or drive independent of an individual's sex or sex organs, for which Freud provided the classic arguments in his 1905 book *Three Essays on the Theory of Sexuality*, and by generally disparaging the quality of non-heterosexual, non-intromissive sex (Davidson 1987; Nye 1993). Freud argued on behalf of an organic drive, the libido, which was not programmed for any particular combination of sexual aim and object but gained its orientation in the course of an individual's life experience. For French sexologists, however, sexual aim and object were naturally embodied in sexed individuals, making 'normal' male A wish to insert his genitals in 'normal' female B and for her to wish to be penetrated genitally by same. Thus, while sexological reformers elsewhere often defended the sexual vigour and masculinity of homosexuals or inverts, French sexologists expressed their defence of beleaguered gallic heterosexuality by formulating contemptuous descriptions of homosexual sexuality as hypotrophic and degraded, and above all as 'effeminate' (Rosario 1996). They contrasted it, as in this formulation by the French Freudian Angelo Hesnard, with 'the rich synthesis of impressions and actions that characterises the natural sexual union' (Hesnard 1933: 303; Hanna 1996).

The French had their dissenters from this characterisation of the effeminate homosexual, but they were at best marginal to the mainstream medical discourse and had more impact in literary than in clinical circles. The eccentric French-educated critic Marc-André Raffalovich wrote a controversial study on what he called 'unisexualité' that was published in 1896 in which he argued that such men were seldom effeminate and in any case constituted a kind of intermediate sex that could not be construed to be abnormal (Raffalovich 1896; Rosario 1997). André Gide's famous defence of pederasty, *Corydon*, published in 1925, also disputed the medical discourse on inversion, but it met with fierce resistance from medical critics and enjoyed only a modest literary success (Hanna 1996).

The comparatively harsher tone of sexology in France is often overlooked in view of the regime of legal tolerance that prevailed there, and that was the envy of European sex reformers elsewhere engaged in struggles against legislation forbidding even private and consensual homosexual sexual relations. This is not to say that there was no regulation of unconventional sexuality in France. From the eighteenth century onwards, with perhaps some slackening between 1815 and 1848, the *police des moeurs* patrolled the parks and urinals on the lookout for homosexual activity that might be prosecuted under the law forbidding 'outrages to public morals' (Thompson 1996). Expert medical testimony on the dangerous instability of homosexuals often helped to bring in convictions of homosexual men even where other evidence was lacking, simply on the basis of signs that they had engaged in sodomitical relations (Peniston 1996). Judging from the increased size and activity of the vice squad, police vigilance intensified after 1870 (Berlière 1992). The bourgeois norms of the Third Republic, it appears, operated most effectively when the guardians of order could confidently employ scientifically legitimated physicalistic stereotypes to identify and marginalise class, political and sexual enemies (Nye 1984; Thompson 1996).

Between the French Revolution and the end of the Second World War prostitution was tightly controlled by a medico-administrative regime of *maisons de tolérances*. In the late 1880s the 'closed' system of state-inspected brothels had to compete with increased numbers of streetwalkers, and this, in turn, not only eroded the clear-cut lines between prostitutes and 'honest' women but gave the police far more work to do (Harsin 1985; Corbin 1990). In an era when there was no cure for syphilis and when 'syphilophobia' was at an all-time high, a medical discourse of sexuality enjoyed unusual visibility in both elite and popular culture. The first vigorous government campaigns against venereal disease, which endured through the 1930s, began in this era, ensuring that the vast public understood that the 'dangers' of non-marital sexuality threatened more than just the immortal soul (Carol 1995).

The censorship of the book and periodic press was equally energetic. The *Enfer* of the Bibliothèque Nationale became a promiscuous mix of pornography and serious works on sexual aberration. So long as they were not written in Latin (as were the relevant sections of the first edition of Richard von Krafft-Ebing's *Psychopathia Sexualis*), medical texts dealing directly with sexuality were subject to censorship and segregation in bookstores and libraries. French remained the language of European pornography throughout the nineteenth and early twentieth centuries, but the government censors and public prosecutors did their best to erect a *cordon sanitaire* around the domestic mass market (Hunt 1993; Stora-Lamarre 1990; Ory 1997).

Law, censorship and police surveillance do not produce sexuality so much as attempt to contain it or channel it in desired directions, but they alert us to the phobias and tensions that rack society, and they showcase the prescriptive ideals that contemporaries hoped would relieve them. As was true throughout the West in this era, these phobias and these ideals were often expressed within the same frame of reference. Thus, the literature of the *fin de siècle* simultaneously celebrated and dreaded the appearance of the 'new' independent woman (and the feminist movement she heralded), and the written and artistic representations of female beauty dwelled on allure, but of the 'fatal' kind. Femininity was often portrayed in a hyperbolic mode as a weapon in the war of the sexes; characterisations of women as seductresses, vampires and sexually inexhaustible were common, especially in modernist literature and art. Yet, for all the polysemy in 'woman', women themselves were held in the discourse of the era to have been cut from the same pattern. Thus, as a recent historian of the 'femme fatale' has written, 'Men were, in their respective ways, different from one another, while confronting them was this unique type, this synthesis, woman' (Dottin-Orsini 1993: 29).

The contradictions that lay at the heart of this imagery flourished especially in characterisations of prostitutes, who were alternately portrayed as seductive *gamins* or diseased man-eaters (Bernheimer 1989; Lipton 1987; Matlock 1994). One has to think only of the transformation of Emile Zola's Nana from a 'magnificent animal' glowing with health and sexual vitality into a rotting, syphilitic symbol of the decline of the nation itself. Prostitution as a social 'problem' was similarly coded: high-minded reformist texts on prostitution served up cautionary tales *and* eroticised images for male and female readers alike (Harsin 1985).

This extraordinary ambivalence appeared at its most extreme in male society and in the forms of male sociability. Nineteenth-century male singing clubs raised their voices to the pleasures of the flesh, usually of the debauched, non-marital kind, but their lyrics also expressed the physical and moral dangers of dangerous liaisons and the security of married life (Gauthier 1992). Similarly the walls of the *salles de garde* of medical interns were splashed with buxom nudes and their meal-time songs garnished by tales of sexual conquest, but death's heads and skeletons also appeared, as did anguished references to the pox (Balloul 1993). Indeed, at the turn of the century, and on the very threshold of a 'cure' for syphilis, France experienced a veritable 'syphilophobia' in which the once-unmentionable disease became a common topic in literature, the theatre and public discourse generally.

One 'solution' to this anxious ambivalence and to the other secular problems in French society lay in the eroticisation of marriage and the celebration of marital love. This does not mean that the 'double standard' suddenly disappeared in society or in the law, or that marital infidelities were treated with more even-handedness than before. The infamous *droit de cuissage*, which made lascivious employers practically invulnerable to prosecution from sexually exploited female workers, continued as before, and no substantial changes were made in the one-sided legal procedures for adultery, separation and (after 1884) divorce (Louis 1994). However, a substantial part of the progressive and 'feminist' campaign in favour of the reinstatement of divorce was an opposition to old-fashioned arranged marriages; advocates touted 'love matches' instead, not just because they respected the wishes of each partner but because such unions were more companionable and invariably more *fertile* (Guerrand and Ronsin 1993; Phillips 1988).

It is not likely that the eroticisation of bourgeois married life did much to change patterns of sexual or marital behaviour in the working classes. Amongst the popular classes of Paris and other large cities in France, casual unions remained frequent. Young women without means had little leverage to compel their partners to marry, unlike their middle-class sisters whose dowries provided incentives and guarantees for prospective mates (Battagliola 1995). On the other hand it appears that working-class milieux were generally more accepting of all forms of marginal sexuality. Homosexual men were at least tolerated, and there seems to have been a large proportion of stable lesbian relationships within the large community of both regulated and unregulated prostitutes in Paris, and, of course, more fleeting same-sex unions in the nation's prisons (Peniston 1996; Sautman 1996).

As with the legislation on divorce, a distinctly natalist outlook also inspired much of the earliest welfare-state legislation in France concerning women and children. In this domain, unmarried and poor women with infants qualified for varying degrees of local and state support beginning in the 1870s and 1880s, including housing and maternity care. But for the politicians and bureaucrats who passed and administered these new measures, the motive was less some high-minded or sentimental concern with women than their obsession with the precious offspring they produced (Fuchs 1992; Accampo, Fuchs and Stewart 1995). Indeed, though many of the developments in medicine and public hygiene in the era between 1890 and 1945 centred on a variety of improvements in maternal health and neonatal care, the dominant political discourse of the era makes it perfectly evident that the mother's role was chiefly that of a reproductive vessel and nurturer. As Dr Adolphe Pinard, the celebrated developer of the 'puericulture' movement, put it, 'A mother's milk belongs to the child.' In this devil's bargain, poor women gained help and financial support in return for having their bodies treated as birthing machines by a state worried about national decline (Schneider 1990; Carol 1995). Indeed the only things inhibiting the development of a full-bore programme of eugenics were the fear of putting impediments in the path of any birth, however humble, and the long-standing respect for the privacy of the couple.

In the long run the long-standing obsession with fertility in France produced a variety of other effects that probably did as much as the foregoing to shape an erotics of conjugality. Beginning in the 1890s, for instance, the French couture industry began to design clothing for mature and married women based loosely on fashions reserved formerly for *demi-mondaines*, revealing cleavage and body shape to an extent unthinkable in the days of *grandmère*. Following the First World War fashions underwent a true revolution, reaching all levels of society, bringing hems up and slimming body shape. Sexual dimorphism in dress began, as Philippe Perrot has remarked, the first stages of a long evolution towards unisexual style (Perrot 1981). But though the new image of the *garçonne* was deplored by social conservatives, there was reluctant agreement within the natalist and medical communities that the new fashions favoured better diet and exercise and put a highly desirable emphasis on physical appeal (Roberts 1994). However, if fashion made some concessions to the rhythms of modern life and taste, a refurbished model of sex difference and complementarity maintained a stranglehold over virtually all cultural representations of the sexes, social roles in marriage, and love.

Stereotypical linkages of femininity with maternity, and paternity with happy family life, were obsessively repeated in the natalist writings of the interwar period and appeared widely in popular publications and advertising (Huss 1990; Koos 1996). Following the disruptions of the First World War, doctors, sexologists and psychiatrists made every effort to 'reconstruct' the norms of sex difference along more or less traditional lines. During the war male shell-shock victims had displayed symptoms of hysteria usually associated with women, and women performing war work seemed to act and dress like the men they had replaced on assembly lines. Such alarming gender reversals were given a positive ideological twist in the development of a set of new therapeutic norms favouring a relaxation of the double standard. In this new psycho-social schemata men were more chaste, less authoritarian and were discouraged from infantilising their wives; women were encouraged to 'develop their "maternal instinct" fully without being exploited by the patriarchal double standard that took advantage of [their] sensuous nature as well as their natural passivity' (Dean 1992: 80). These new standards were urged by groups like the Ligue Nationale Française d'Hygiène Mentale and by the Association d'Etudes Sexologiques of Dr Edouard Toulouse precisely because they were believed to foster, in the words of Dr Robert Chable, a marital sexual life 'in its true hygienic and social role as a procreative function not as an instrument of debauch' (Dean 1992: 92–5). Presumably, a wife could borrow some of the love-making techniques of a courtesan without becoming a simple object of her husband's sexual lust.

The state did not leave the work of moral regeneration entirely to private initiative in these anxious times. Laws passed soon after the war punished the writing and distribution of birth-control information and severely punished abortionists and the women who sought them out (Mossuz-Lavau 1991). The effort to stamp out the fledgling French neo-Malthusian (birth-control) movement was carried on with exemplary ferocity even by the left-wing governments of the Popular Front, which quickly learned the virtue of presenting all their innovations, including paid vacations, as pro-family in nature.

Following the defeat of 1940, the collaborationist regime in Vichy simply increased the punishments for these 'crimes' against the unborn and decreed that French women must pay the 'blood tax' of pregnancy and birth as a duty to nation and race (Muel-Dreyfus 1996). Indeed the leaders of the natalist movement were raised to exalted levels in Vichy's New Order, where they were able to implement, without the usual political resistance, measures encouraging large families and births. The movement to maintain the differences between the sexes, which was an important aspect of the desire to return to traditional gender norms in the interwar years, became, under Vichy, a stern ideological imperative.

Following the war the legislative and administrative apparatus created at the very end of the Third Republic and amplified during Vichy to stimulate births was perpetuated with little change. Under a name change, the Haut Comité de la Population continued its work without interruption, and the Catholic and Marxist left-wing parties of the new regime proved themselves adept at aligning themselves with the broad national consensus on 'repopulation' (Mossuz-Lavau 1991; LeBras 1991). Tax premiums were granted to the parents of firstborns and for each subsequent child, and maternity clinics and maternity leaves received generous governmental support, a programme that continues in modified form to the present. By contrast France permitted some forms of abortion only in 1975. As Christine Delphy has argued, despite the liberal abortion law, in practice the state-run clinics that perform abortions in France are so over-crowded that five thousand French women went to the Netherlands in 1992 to get their abortions (Delphy 1996). Contraceptives of most kinds continued to be outlawed until 1967, and, despite the celebrity of the pharmaceutical abortifacient RU-489, the long-persecuted French birth-control movement is still far weaker than movements elsewhere in the West (Corbett 1994).

Meanwhile, the extraordinary postwar economic boom created an unanticipated consumer paradise that took the direction of a huge advertising campaign to appeal to young couples, particularly middle-class couples with kids who lived in cities and who learned to think of government family allowances for each additional birth as a way of financing new household acquisitions (Ross 1995). As Kristin Ross has suggested, the image of a mythic 'ideal couple' was overdeter-mined by a number of factors relating to advertising and consump-tion, procreation and the emergence of a new, 'stable' middle class whose political neutrality was crucial to the end of the 'stalemate society' and the rise of the technocratic state (Ross 1995).

While fertile couples were showered with official largess, 'non-procreative' forms of sexuality were legally repressed as never before. Homosexuals were barred from state service under the Mirguet law of 1960, and, on orders from above, police harassment of gay men in Paris reached heights not previously attained. As if nothing what-ever had changed from the 1890s, savage characterisations of homo-sexuality persisted in the medical literature throughout the 1950s and 1960s (Hocquenghem 1993). Stereotypes about mental instability, effeminacy, laziness and anti-social behaviour circulated in the popular press and were used with little contradiction in political discourse in De Gaulle's new order (Mossuz-Lavau 1991; Hocquenghem 1993; Copley 1989; Badinter 1992).

Perhaps on account of such arrant misinformation, the French public appears to have known little about homosexuality; however, the usual confidence reigned that the traditional respect for privacy in France made discrimination against them unlikely. The summary of a public opinion poll of 1962 sums up this contradictory attitude perfectly:

> Homosexuality is considered an anomaly by the majority of the population and the homosexual as a separate being: but, looking more closely, there is no systematic ostracism. Public opinion seems clearly in agreement with the civil code which tends to consider homosexuality as a private matter, even while morally disapproving of it. This attitude is very different from that which exists in the Anglo-Saxon countries.
>
> (Quoted in Copley 1989: 220)

I would like to conclude by examining some issues related to sexuality in contemporary French society for evidence of continuities with the historical traditions I have considered above. First, the prevalence of self-delusion, not to mention hypocrisy, in sexual matters makes it an open question whether there is some direct relationship between the attitudes people hold about sexuality and their actual behaviour. However, in light of the intense and long-lived combination of affirmation for heterosexual love and disapproval of deviations from it in French society, we might expect to see some effect on very contemporary attitudes and behaviour.

Sex surveys, even the most scrupulously researched, have notable problems; they may, in the questions they ask and the categories they choose, simply be reifying the social myths that circulate in the wider society. For what it is worth, recent sex surveys suggest that French couples have a stronger preference for standard genital penetration and a higher disapproval of masturbation than do Americans, higher rates of sexual satisfaction, and, most remarkably, avowals for frequency of orgasm, and particularly simultaneous orgasm, far higher than Americans claim. The categories are not exactly comparable, but 88.8 per cent of French men and 74.6 per cent of French women claim to have had an orgasm during their last sexual encounter, while 75 per cent of American men and 29 per cent of American women report 'always' to have had an orgasm with their primary partner (Spira and Bajos 1993; Michael and Gagnon 1994).

French marriages end in divorce less often than almost anywhere else in the West. It is true that the marriage rate has fallen drastically in recent years, but surveys seem to indicate that unmarried couples behave pretty much like married ones, and, in any case, children born out of wedlock are at no particular legal or cultural disadvantage. Even more telling is the still very widely held conviction that there is no 'real' marriage in the absence of children. A recent survey indicated that 93.6 per cent of girls and 88.2 per cent of boys expected to have children one day (Corbett 1994; Riffaut 1994).

With some notable exceptions, French intellectuals, including some feminists, are remarkably supportive of the notion that the social and amorous relations of French men and women are unique in western societies. In her recent book on masculinity Elizabeth Badinter has written that 'the solidarity of the sexes has survived everything here, including the most intense periods of question-raising. Virility is less contested on this side of the Atlantic, masculine violence less great, and men have less fear here of women and reciprocally' (Badinter 1992: 18–19; Badinter 1986). Likewise, according to Evelyne Sullerot, 'Men and women in France have always tried to charm and seduce one another, have always loved to talk together, ... even during the years of feminist struggle' (Sullerot 1992: 252). In their recent and hugely popular book of dialogues on men and women Françoise Giroud and Bernard-Henry Lévy follow a similar tack. For Lévy men and women are irreducible categories of being shaped 'in the night of time', and both Giroud and Lévy devote considerable space to the energy each sex expends in devising strategies of seduction (Giroud and Lévy 1993; Ozouf 1995).

Many French writers have focused on the maintenance of sexual difference as the foundation not simply of love and the human species but of a just society as well. Thus the novelist Marguerite Duras has praised 'the fabulous richness of heterosexuality' as compared with the 'incommensurable poverty of homosexuality' (Ince 1996: 159). The psychiatrist and critic Julia Kristeva has also worried about 'the blurring of sexual difference' which she fears will produce two phenomena:

> The first is that we're going to witness the end of a certain kind of desire and sexual pleasure. For, after all, if you level out difference, given that it's difference that's desirable and provokes sexual pleasure, you could see a kind of sexual anesthesia, and this in an incubator society where the question of reproduction will be posed by way of machines and bioscientific methods in order for the species to continue.
>
> (Quoted in Jardine and Menke 1991: 117)

For her part, the feminist writer Luce Irigaray claims that 'What we need for our future civilisation, for human maturity, is a sexed culture'. In the present situation, she has written, women cannot enter the

'between-men cultural world' without relinquishing 'their female identity and relationships with other women', and thus the whole foundation of their social power (Irigaray 1993: 16 and 20; Rosario 1992).

Rehabilitating the ghost of Jean-Jacques Rousseau, the philos-
opher Alain Etchegoyen has gone so far as to predict that 'man and
woman are, in their very difference, the decisive stakes of our era,
especially the years to come. We are very far from having exhausted
the being and consequences of that difference, ... despite the diversion
that consists of denying it, sublimating it into the notion of sexuality.'
Indeed, he apostrophises, 'Let's get back to basics: the difference between
the sexes is genital. All the rest is literature' (Etchegoyen 1997: 34).

It is also revealing that more scientifically serious works continue
to portray the link between human sexuality and reproduction as
'natural' and superior, despite the revolution in behaviour that has
effectively dissociated the two in the twentieth century. The physical
anthropologist Jacques Ruffié portrays reproductive sexuality 'as the
very foundation of society' and coitus as 'indispensable to a couple: it
assures its physical and psychic equilibrium, *especially when it results
in an orgasm in both partners*' (Ruffié 1986: 123 and 181; Charzac-
Brunel 1993). One might easily see a corollary in the claim that,
according to the contemporary sexologist Geneviève Tétart, French
women are distinguished from women elsewhere in preferring
vaginal orgasms. In her experience,

> In France, the most part of our patients ask to be taught how to
> have vaginal orgasms uniquely through coital penetration. I spoke
> of this to an American sexologist who responded in astonishment:
> 'But that is the *magic orgasm*. Tell them that it requires a great
> deal of work and courage to attain. To Americans one teaches
> simultaneous penetration and clitoral stimulation.'
>
> (Tétart, 1997: 158)

George Bataille provided a more poetic account of eroticism in
his now-classic account of eroticism. It was, in his view, fatally
connected to reproduction:

> The consideration I am introducing is linked with life in the most
> intimate way: it refers to sexual activity considered now in the
> light of reproduction. I said that reproduction was opposed to
> eroticism, but while it is true that eroticism is defined by the
> mutual independence of erotic pleasure and reproduction as an

end, the fundamental meaning of reproduction is nonetheless the key to eroticism.

(Bataille 1986: 12–13)

By contrast, even in the most recent literature, homosexual sexual relations, if they do not lead to 'suicidal' impulses (Charzac-Brunel 1993: 67), are still invariably characterised as inferior, as 'monotonous' (Ruffié 1986: 213) or, in the words of France's leading sexologist, Gérard Zwang, an 'extension of infantile and adolescent sexuality', a type of sexual activity that demands 'less erotic effort' from its participants (Zwang 1990, 182–5; Zwang 1997). These uncomplimentary characterisations of the homosexual *vita sexualis* are virtually identical to those employed in French medical discourse since the 1890s, and they appear to serve much the same ideological role in French culture today as before (Nye 1993; Bonnet 1995). It may be, in the end, that the 'tolerance' of private sexuality in which the French take so much pride has always been reserved for a certain kind of sexuality.

A particularly compelling example of this bias was provided by the recent debate in France prior to and during the passage of a law in 1992 on sexual harassment in the workplace. In the early stages of the debate Jacques Séguela, at that time the campaign manager of President François Mitterand, pronounced during a public workshop on the issue, 'Of course I have had the occasion to hump cute chicks on my office carpet. Sexual harassment is the demeanor of all Latin men towards women. In my country we call that courtship. It is the French men's need to seduce at work as well as in the subway. But be careful, in the final analysis, it is the woman who decides' (quoted in Mazur 1996: 38). Owing to a strategy of resistance by socialists and Gaullists alike, the final law confined itself to condemning harassment by individuals in authority; it was mute on the harassment of co-workers and on the existence of a hostile work environment. As Christine Delphy has argued, this legislation narrowly outlaws the use of authority to obtain sex, but is useless as a way of combating harassment whose aim is to humiliate and exclude. 'It is this awareness of gender domination, and the decision to outlaw it', she writes, 'which is at the core of the U.S. legislation and [European Community] recommendation. By contrast, gender domination is recognised by neither the French state nor the wider political class' (Delphy 1996: 152).

This is not particularly surprising in view of the feeble numbers of women who participate in French political life. Before the recent socialist victory in the legislative elections of May 1997, there were only thirty-five women among the 577 deputies in the National Assembly, or about 5.7 per cent, a number which ranked France twenty-sixth in Europe in this category, on a par with Albania, and just ahead of Greece, which brings up the rear. Françoise Giroud, who was the Secretary of State for Women between 1974 and 1976, persists in believing that women can best influence events by means of their vaunted power of seduction, working behind the scenes to get what they want, but the facts seem to suggest otherwise (interview in Porter 1993: 123–4).

Indeed there is evidence that the old fears about depopulation and reproduction still haunt debates about sexuality and the law. These debates are, in turn, indissolubly linked to the current efforts to limit immigration and to the recent political successes of Jean-Marie Le Pen's National Front. As Phillipe de Villiers, a right-wing deputy to the European Parliament recently wrote, 'our identity is in danger: the integration and assimilation of young immigrants is contingent upon the existence of a sufficient number of French [read "race"] children. France's place in the world is threatened: fewer children means less dynamism, a country weakened politically and economically' (quoted in Reggiani 1996: 753). As Andrés Reggiani has remarked about statements like this, 'pronatalism stands close to a vernacular version of eugenics' (1996: 753).

French homosexual activists and civil libertarians in France currently support a measure to allow persons of any sex to engage in a legal 'contract of civil union' which would supplant heterosexual marriage as the legal foundation for stable unions, allowing homosexual couples to enjoy the same benefits and protections as those formally married. The right-wing alliance in power until May 1997 fiercely opposed it, for the reason, in the words of the Minister of Justice, Jacques Toubon, uttered in the autumn of 1995, that 'there is no question of our adopting the contract of civil union. Public order opposes it and it is on the contrary necessary that we favour marriages and births in order for France to remain strong' (Eribon 1996: 12).

Demographers recognise the existence in all historical societies of clear relations between demographic phenomena, patterns of reproduction and structures of sex and gender. In France a profound

demographic trauma that has deep roots in the national consciousness has skewed attitudes towards sexuality, and perhaps sexual
behaviour itself, in ways that make French sexual culture relatively
unique in western Europe. In recent years there has been a notable
defensiveness about the decline of global Francophonia and the
currently weak French presence in the arts. It may well be that the
relatively slow disengagement from the sexual culture of the last
century is another aspect of the self-protective reflexes of a nation
which has badly adjusted to the status of a second-class power.

What is clear is that French men and women seem heavily
invested in a French identity that is committed to a rather
traditional heterosexual 'amour' and its attendant expressions and
techniques which is, potentially at least, reproductively fertile. Many
public figures apparently still feel obliged to contrast this aspect of
Frenchness with the sexuality of other nations. Thus, when François
Mitterand appointed Edith Cresson as France's first woman Prime
Minister in 1991, a British journalist saw fit to publish an interview
he had with her four years previously in which he had observed that
'In Anglo-Saxon countries most men prefer the company of other
men', to which Cresson replied,

> Yes, but the majority of these men are homosexual – perhaps not
> the majority – but in the USA there are already 25 per cent of them,
> and in England and in Germany, it is much the same. You cannot
> imagine it in the history of France. Traditionally, the image of
> Frenchmen has been heterosexual, an image given to them by the
> men of power, by kings, etc. Frenchmen are much more interested
> in women and this is a problem that needs analysis.
>
> (Quoted in Merrick and Ragan 1996: 3; Adler 1993)

Bibliography

Accampo, Elinor, Rachel Fuchs and Mary Lynn Stewart (eds) (1995), *Gender and the Politics of Social Reform in France, 1870–1914*, Baltimore, Johns Hopkins University Press.

Adler, Laure (1993), *Les femmes politiques*, Paris, Seuil, pp. 213–37.

Badinter, Elisabeth (1986), *L'Un et l'autre: les relations entre hommes et femmes*, Paris, Odile Jacob.

— (1992), *X:Y De l'identité masculine*, Paris, Odile Jacob.

Balloul, Patrick (1993), *La Salle de Garde, ou le plaisir des dieux*, Paris, Editions de Loya.

Bardet, Jean-Pierre and Hervé LeBras (eds) (1988), *Histoire de la population française*, vol. 3, Paris, Presses Universitaires de France.

Bataille, Georges (1986), *Eroticism: Death and Sensuality*, San Francisco, City Lights.

Battagliola, Françoise (1995), 'Mariage, concubinage et relations entre les sexes à Paris, 1880–1890', *Genèses*, 18, pp. 68–96.

Berlière, Jean-Marc (1992), *La Police des moeurs sous la IIIe République*, Paris, Editions du Seuil.

Bernheimer, Charles (1989), *Figures of Ill-repute: Representing Prostitution in Nineteenth-century France*, Cambridge (Mass.), Harvard University Press.

Bleys, Rudi C. (1995), *The Geography of Perversion: Male-to-male Sexual Behaviour Outside the West and the Ethnographic Imagination*, New York, New York University Press.

Bonnet, Marie-Jo (1995), *Les Relations amoureux entre les femmes*, Paris, Odile Jacob.

Brenot, Philippe (1994), *La Sexologie*, Paris, Presses Universitaires de France.

Carol, Anne (1995), *Histoire de l'eugénisme en France: les médecins et la procréation, XIXe–XXe siècle*, Paris, Seuil.

Charzac-Brunel, Marguerite (1993), 'Le Déni de la différence des sexes et les effets pervers dans le couple', in Xavier Lacroix (ed.), *Homme et femme: l'insaissable différence*, Paris, Cerf.

Cole, Joshua H. (1996), '"There are Only Good Mothers": The Ideological Work of Women's Fertility in France Before World War One', *French Historical Studies*, 19, 3, pp. 639–72.

Copley, Anthony (1989), *Sexual Moralities in France, 1780–1980: New Ideas on the Family, Divorce and Homosexuality*, London, Routledge.

Corbett, James (1994), *Through French Windows: An Introduction to France in the Nineties*, Ann Arbor, University of Michigan Press.

Corbin, Alain (1990), *Women for Hire: Prostitution and Sexuality in France after 1850*, Cambridge (Mass.), Harvard University Press.

Daston, Lorraine and Katharine Park (1985), 'Hermaphrodites in Renaissance France', *Critical Matrix*, 1, 5, pp. 1–18.

Davidson, Arnold (1987), 'How to do the History of Psychoanalysis: A Reading of Freud's *Three Essays on the Theory of Sexuality*', *Critical Inquiry*, 14, pp. 252–77.

Dean, Carolyn J. (1992), *The Self and Its Pleasures: Bataille, Lacan, and the History of the Decentered Subject*, Ithaca, Cornell University Press.

Delphy, Christine (1996), 'The European Union and the Future of Feminism', in R. Amy Elman (ed.), *Sexual Politics and the European Union: The New Feminist Challenge*, Providence (R.I.) and Oxford, Berghahn Books, pp. 147–58.

Dottin-Orsini, Mireille (1993), *Cette femme qu'ils disent fatale: textes et images de la misogynie fin-de-siècle*, Paris, Grasset.

Eribon, Didier (1995), 'Le Nouveau combat des gays et lesbiennes', *Le Nouvel Observateur*, 13–19 June, 12.

Etchegoyen, Alain (1997), *Éloge de la fémininité*, Paris, Arléa.

Foucault, Michel (1980a), *The History of Sexuality: vol. 1: An Introduction*, New York, Random.

— (1980b), 'The Politics of Health in the Eighteenth Century', in Colin Gordon (ed.), *Power/Knowledge: Selected Interviews and Other Writings, 1972–1977*, New York, Pantheon, pp. 166–82.

Fraisse, Geneviève (1989), *Muse de la raison: la démocratie exclusive et la différence des sexes*, Paris, Alinea.

Fuchs, Rachel (1992), *Poor and Pregnant in Paris: Strategies for Survival in the Nineteenth Century*, New Brunswick (N.J.), Rutgers University Press.

Gauthier, Marie-Véronique (1992), *Chanson, sociabilité et grivoiserie au XIXe siècle*, Paris, Aubier.

Giroud, Françoise and Bernard-Henri Lévy (1993), *Les Hommes et les femmes*, Paris, Orban.

Guerrand, Roger-Henri and Francis Ronsin (1993), *Le Sexe apprivoisé: Jeanne Humbert et la lutte pour le contrôle des naissances*, Paris, Edition la Découverte.

Hanna, Martha (1996), 'Natalism, Homosexuality and the Controversy over *Corydon*', in Jeffrey Merrick and Bryant T. Ragan Jr (eds), *Homosexuality in Modern France*, New York, Oxford University Press, pp. 202–24.

Harsin, Jill (1985), *Policing Prostitution in Nineteenth-century Paris*, Princeton, Princeton University Press.

Hekma, Gert (1994), '"A Female Soul in a Male Body": Sexual Inversion as Gender Inversion in Nineteenth-century Sexology', in Gilbert Herdt (ed.), *Third Sex, Third Gender: Beyond Sexual Dimorphism in Culture and History*, New York, Zone, pp. 213–40.

Herdt, Gilbert (1994), 'Third Sexes and Third Genders', in Gilbert Herdt (ed.), *Third Sex, Third Gender: Beyond Sexual Dimorphism in Culture and History*, New York, Zone, pp. 21–84.

Hesnard, Angelo (1933), *Traité de sexologie normale et pathologique*, Paris, Payot.

Hocquenghem, Guy (1993), *Homosexual Desire*, Durham (N.C.), Duke University Press.

Hunt, Lynn A. (ed.) (1993), *The Invention of Pornography: Obscenity and the Invention of Modernity*, New York, Zone.

Huss, Marie-Monique (1990), 'Pronatalism in the Inter-war Period in France', *Journal of Contemporary History*, 25, pp. 39–68.

Ince, Kate (1996), '*L'Amour la Mort*: The Eroticism of Marguerite Duras', in Alex Huges and Kate Ince (eds), *French Erotic Fiction: Women's Desiring Writing, 1880–1990*, Oxford, Berg, pp. 147–74.

Irigaray, Luce (1993), *je, tu, nous: Toward a Culture of Difference*, New York, Routledge.

Jardine, Alice A. and Anne M. Menke (eds) (1991), *Shifting Scenes: Interviews on Women, Writing, and Politics in Post-68 France*, New York, Columbia University Press.

Knibiehler, Yvonne (1987), *Les Pères aussi ont une histoire*, Paris, Hachette.

Koos, Cheryl A. (1996), 'Gender, Anti-individualism, and Nationalism: The Alliance Nationale and the Pronatalist Backlash against the *Femme Moderne*, 1933–1940', *French Historical Studies*, 19, 3, pp. 699–725.

Lamont, Michèle (1992), *Money, Morals, and Manners: The Culture of the French and American Upper-middle Class*, Chicago, University of Chicago Press.

LeBras, Hervé (1991), *Marianne et les lapins: l'obsession démographique*, Paris, Olivier Orban.

Lipton, Eunice (1987), *Looking into Degas: Uneasy Images of Women and Modern Life*, Berkeley, University of California Press.

Louis, Marie-Victoire (1994), *Le Droit de cuissage: France, 1860–1930*, Paris, Les Editions de L'Atelier.

McLaren, Angus (1990), *A History of Contraception from Antiquity to the Present Day*, Oxford, Blackwell.

Matlock, Jann (1994), *Scenes of Seduction: Prostitution, Hysteria, and Reading Difference in Nineteenth-century France*, New York, Columbia University Press.

Mazur, Amy G. (1996), 'The Interplay: The Formation of Sexual Harassment Legislation in France and EU Policy Initiatives', in R. Amy Elman (ed.), *Sexual Politics and the European Union: The New Feminist Challenge*, Providence (R.I.) and Oxford, Berghahn Books, pp. 35–50.

Merrick, Jeffrey and Bryant T. Ragan, Jr (1996), 'Introduction', in Jeffrey Merrick and Bryant T. Ragan Jr (eds), *Homosexuality in Modern France*, New York, Oxford University Press.

Michael, Robert T., John H. Gagnon *et al.* (1994), *Sex in America: A Definitive Survey*, Boston, Little, Brown.

Mossuz-Lavau, Janine (1991), *Les Lois de l'amour: les politiques de la sexualité en France (1950–1990)*, Paris, Payot.

Muel-Dreyfus, Francine (1996), *Vichy et l'éternel féminin*, Paris, Seuil.

Nye, Robert A. (1984), *Crime, Madness and Politics in Modern France: The Medical Concept of National Decline*, Princeton, Princeton University Press.

— (1993), *Masculinity and Male Codes of Honor in Modern France*, New York, Oxford University Press.

— (1996), 'Michel Foucault's Sexuality and the History of Homosexuality in France', in Jeffrey Merrick and Bryant T. Ragan Jr (eds), *Homosexuality in Modern France*, New York, Oxford University Press, pp. 225–41.

Offen, Karen (1984), 'Depopulation, Nationalism, and Feminism in Fin-de-siècle France', *American Historical Review*, 89, pp. 648–76.

Ory, Pascal (ed.) (1997), *La Censure en France à l'ère démocratique (1848–)*, Paris, Editions Complexe.

Ozouf, Mona (1995), *Les Mots des femmes: essai sur la singularité française*, Paris, Fayard.

Pedersen, Jean Elizabeth (1996), 'Regulating Abortion and Birth Control: Gender, Medicine, and Republican Politics in France, 1870–1920', *French Historical Studies* 19, 3, pp. 673–98.

Peniston, William A. (1996), 'Love and Death in Gay Paris: Homosexuality and Criminality in the 1870s', in Jeffrey Merrick and Bryant T. Ragan Jr (eds), *Homosexuality in Modern France*, New York, Oxford University Press, pp. 128–45.

Perrot, Philippe (1981), *Les Dessus et les dessous de la bourgeoisie: une histoire du vêtement au XIXe siècle*, Paris, Fayard.

Phillips, Roderick (1988), *Putting Asunder: A History of Divorce in Western Society*, Cambridge, Cambridge University Press.

Pick, Daniel (1989), *Faces of Degeneration: A European Disorder*, Cambridge, Cambridge University Press.

Porter, Melinda C. (1993), *Through Parisian Eyes*, New York, Da Capo Press.

Raffalovich, Marc-André (1896), *Uranisme et unisexualité: étude sur les différentes manifestations de l'instinct sexuel*, Paris, Masson.

Reggiani, Andrés Horacio (1996), 'Procreating France: The Politics of Demography, 1919–1945', *French Historical Studies*, 19, 3, pp. 725–54.

Riffaut, Hélène (1994), *Les Valeurs des Français*, Paris, Presses Universitaires de France.

Roberts, Mary Louise (1994), *Civilization without Sexes: Reconstructing Gender in Postwar France, 1917–27*, Chicago, University of Chicago Press.

Rosario, Vernon A. (1992), 'Sexual Liberalism and Compulsory Heterosexuality', *Contemporary French Civilization*, 16, 2, pp. 262–79.

— (1996), 'Pointy Penises, Fashion Crimes, and Hysterical Mollies: The Pederasts' Inversions', in Jeffrey Merrick and Bryant T. Ragan Jr (eds), *Homosexuality in Modern France*, New York, Oxford University Press, pp. 146–76.

— (1997), *The Erotic Imagination: French Histories of Perversity*, New York, Oxford University Press.

Ross, Kristin (1995), *Fast Cars, Clean Bodies: Decolonization and the Reordering of French Culture*, Cambridge (Mass.), MIT Press.

Ruffié, Jacques (1986), *Le Sexe et le mort*, Paris, Odile Jacob.

Sautman, Francesca Canadé (1996), 'Invisible Women: Lesbian Working-class Culture in France, 1880–1930', in Jeffrey Merrick and Bryant T. Ragan Jr (eds), *Homosexuality in Modern France*, New York, Oxford University Press, pp. 177–201.

Schneider, William (1990), *Quality and Quantity: The Quest for Biological Regeneration in Twentieth-century France*, Cambridge, Cambridge University Press.

Sibalis, Michael David (1996), 'The Regulation of Male Homosexuality in Revolutionary and Napoleonic France', in Jeffrey Merrick and Bryant T. Ragan Jr (eds), *Homosexuality in Modern France*, New York, Oxford University Press, pp. 80–101.

Singer, Irving (1987), *The Nature of Love: The Modern World*, 3 vols, Chicago, University of Chicago Press.

Spira, Alfred and Nathalie Bajos (1993), *Les Comportements sexuels en France*, Paris, La Documentation Française.

Stora-Lamarre, Annie (1990), *L'Enfer de la IIIᵉ République: censeurs et pornographes*, Paris, Imago.

Sullerot, Evelyne (1992), *Quels pères? Quels fils?*, Paris, Fayard.

Tétart, Geneviève (1997), 'Le Clitoris, le vagin? Pourquoi pas les deux …', *Panoramiques*, 28.

Thompson, Victoria (1996), 'Creating Boundaries: Homosexuality and the Changing Social Order in France', in Jeffrey Merrick and Bryant T. Ragan Jr (eds), *Homosexuality in Modern France*, New York, Oxford University Press, pp. 102–27.

Tomlinson, Richard (1985), 'The "Disappearance of France", 1896–1940: French Politics and the Birth Rate', *The Historical Journal*, 28, 2, pp. 5–15.

Zwang, Gérard (1990), *Pathologie sexuelle: les troubles de la fonction érotique et du comportement sexuel de l'adulte*, Paris, Maloine.

— (1997), 'Où en est la sexologie?', *Panoramiques*, 28, pp. 5–31.

5

Italy: sexuality, morality and public authority

Bruno P. F. Wanrooij

While even today one should be cautious in expressing general judgements about sexuality, women and the family in Italy, this is even more true for the first decades of the nineteenth century, when the various states existing on Italian territory were characterised by widely different social and economic conditions, cultural traditions and legal systems. Women in the Lombard provinces under Austrian rule and in the Grand Duchy of Tuscany, for instance, were allowed to administer and dispose of their property. Elsewhere they needed the authorisation of their husband or a male member of the family. According to the civil codes of some Italian states the legal minority of women lasted for all their life and, in the case of matrimony, responsibility over them was transmitted from the father to the husband.

It would be difficult to overestimate the differences existing not only between the various states but also between rural areas and cities and between the social classes. The whole of Italy shared however, the unifying influence of Catholic religion, and many states left the regulation of the private life of individual citizens almost entirely to the church. When legislation was introduced during the second half of the eighteenth century, it often challenged Catholic doctrine only in as far as it added new impediments to matrimony, as has been shown by Spinelli (1950–1). The legal code which was adopted in Modena in 1771, for example, punished marriages between persons belonging to different social classes. In Naples the civil code made lack of paternal consent an impediment to the matrimony of minors. Legislation was particularly strict in the province of Trent under Habsburg rule where from 1816 until 1918 it was necessary to obtain a special licence in order to marry. This licence was withheld by state functionaries if the spouses depended upon charity.

Although, in theory, the consent of the partners was the sole condition for a valid marriage, the family and the local community exercised a strong influence, and in doing so often enjoyed the support of public authorities. At least until the end of the eighteenth century, in the families of the aristocracy and rich bourgeoisie, the father decided whether his sons and daughters should marry, whom they should marry and when they should marry. The opinions of young people themselves were taken into consideration, but were not decisive. According to Di Simplicio (1994) freedom of choice was uncommon even for young people from the lower middle class. Generally, the arrangements made by parents made it difficult for young people to adopt a different solution, and marriages contracted against the will of the family were rare.

In the case of the sharecroppers' families of central Italy the landlord also wielded some power. As married women abandoned their original family to join that of their husbands, a landlord who needed the workforce would try to delay the date of marriage. The landlord's right to intervene in decisions regarding the intimate life of families was removed from the sharecroppers' contracts only in 1919–20. In practice it continued to exist even later.

The most important single institution governing the family was without any doubt the Catholic church. The Papal State provides an interesting example of the functioning of Catholic doctrine regarding sexuality because here both spiritual power and temporal power were in the hands of the clergy. As pointed out by Pelaja (1994 and 1996), the Catholic juridical tradition of granting exemptions from existing rules allowed those residing in the states governed by Rome to enjoy a measure of flexibility elsewhere unknown. As a result, the severity of the legislation regarding sexuality was mitigated by a close examination of personal cases. Premarital sexual intercourse could be excused if it was a prelude to marriage, and in this case could even become a valid argument for dispensation from impediments or exemption from payment for the marriage licence. According to Catholic doctrine, the *Sponsalia*, or betrothal, did not legitimise premarital sexual intercourse, but among the poor different attitudes were rather common, and even moralists showed some tolerance for the *delectatio in tactibus* between engaged young people.

The status of premarital sex was ambivalent in most penal codes. A law adopted in Tuscany in 1754 depenalised sexual relations before matrimony, but continued to consider seduction – sexual relations obtained after a false promise of marriage – a criminal offence. Even though the promise of marriage followed by sexual intercourse did not formally oblige the seducer to marry his partner, women would often accept sexual relations after such a promise, hoping that social pressure would be strong enough to convince their partners if these were unwilling to keep their promise.

The efforts of the Catholic church to control the intimate life of the faithful, which had been much intensified after the Council of Trent, transformed non-procreative and non-conjugal sexuality into the quintessence of sin. The negative attitude towards sexuality had its roots in a strong misogynistic prejudice, but perhaps the attempt to discipline sexual life should also be viewed in the context of a society in which sexual violence was widespread.

The obligation of the faithful to confess their sins initiated a slow process of interiorisation of the moral norms which had been reformulated by the Council of Trent. As Pino Lucà Trombetta (1991) has explained, frequent confessions allowed the clergy to acquire a degree of control over the intimate life of the faithful which had been unknown in the past.

The interiorisation of the moral standards defined by the Council of Trent is one explanation for the decrease in the number of requests for separation and of trials for the desertion of a spouse. The lack of alternatives, determined by the 'confessional' character of the Italian regional states of the eighteenth century, may well be another reason for the resignation with which women especially accepted their fate. A combination of legal persecution, social pressure and interiorisation of religious norms also explains the decreasing frequency of illegal couples whose union had not been sanctified by matrimony.

All this contrasts with Italy's reputation for libertinism which emerges from most eighteenth-century travelogues written by upper-class foreigners on their grand tour. This image was based, above all, on the role played by the *cicisbeo* in high society. The *cicisbeo*, who had as his main duty to assist aristocratic ladies in their social life, was chosen by common agreement of husband and wife, and became so fashionable that it was almost impossible for a lady not to have one. Most foreign observers were convinced that the *cicisbeo* – or gallant – was an official lover, but evidence for this is scarce. More likely, the *cicisbeo* provided compensation for the lack of affection and sentiment which characterised the relationship between spouses in arranged marriages. The *cicisbeo* thus marks a moment of crisis in the history of aristocratic marriages.

During the second half of the century the psychological distance between husband and wife became less profound and a development started which led to the creation of marriage based on the ideal of intimate companionship. The age difference between husband and wife, which in the past had contributed to reinforcing hierarchical relations between spouses, was no longer accepted without discussion. According to Barbagli (1984), the relations between parents and children also became more affectionate. In the cities of the north, in Liguria and in Tuscany this development was accompanied by a decline in the birth rate.

During the second half of the nineteenth century all over Europe state authorities became more interested in the family. Healthy citizens and demographic growth were considered a necessary condition for colonial expansion. As George Mosse (1985) has shown, the intertwining of nationalism and respectability coincided with the rise of the nation state. The unchallenged dominance of the male head of the family over his wife and children was defended on the grounds that the subordination of the family to its head was analogous to – and also a direct cause of – the subordination of the subjects to their sovereign. Because the family was considered to be the primary unit of society, it was assumed that obedience and continence within the family by analogy would translate into obedience to public authorities and stability of government.

Also, in Italy politicians were convinced that it was necessary to have more control over the private life of citizens if the new state was to become strong and powerful. Attention to the advancement of the moral conditions of the population was determined by changes in the relationship between the state and the Catholic church. After the unification of Italy, the conflict with the Holy See and, more generally, the process of secularisation, forced the state to intervene in a more direct way. While trying to take over the role of the church, the state hardly ever changed judgements about what was morally acceptable and what was not, and often limited itself to defending moral values elaborated by the church.

Shortly after unification, which was completed in 1871 when Rome was declared capital of the kingdom, the political class showed its desire to keep up moral standards by staging a campaign against pornography. While urging the prefects to apply existing legislation with more severity, Minister of the Interior Giovanni Lanza explained the reasons for his concern:

> All those who are honest and moral know how much these obscene images and licentious books harm young people, and they are aware of the fact that these forms of licence corrupt young people, make them vicious, and give them habits which are harmful not only for their moral well-being, but also for their physical and intellectual development. This ... cannot be tolerated by people of free and noble principles. The corruption of mores leads to the decadence of the Nation.
>
> (Carelli 1891: 529–30)

As Gibson (1986) has pointed out, the introduction in 1860 of regulated prostitution can also be seen as a public demonstration of the desire to defend the moral standards of the Italian population. The system elaborated by venereologist Casimiro Sperino followed the example set by France and Belgium: prostitution was concentrated in licensed brothels, and prostitutes were obliged to register and to pass a fortnightly medical check. Discrimination was based not only on sex but also on social class: the only clients who were obliged to undergo a medical check were ordinary soldiers.

Protests against regulated prostitution led in 1875 – after a visit to Italy by the British feminist Josephine Butler – to the foundation of the Italian section of the British, Continental and General Federation for the Abolition of Government Regulations of Prostitution. The abolitionists saw poverty as the main cause of prostitution, but this view was opposed by scientists like Cesare Lombroso who denied the importance of economic conditions and claimed that all prostitutes shared a form of moral insanity which predisposed them to prostitution. This idea of biological destiny made it possible to ignore male responsibility, and undermined the position of the abolitionists.

Anna Maria Mozzoni, one of the founders of the abolitionist movement, had already denounced the effects of regulated prostitution on gender relations in Italy in 1870. She pointed out how young men, by associating with prostitutes, lost all respect for women. The tolerant attitude towards young men who visited brothels was also inspired by the idea that it was necessary to provide them with an outlet for their sexual instincts. The famous physiologist Paolo

Mantegazza made it clear that, if the choice was between masturbation and visits to prostitutes, the latter solution was preferable. The fear of the consequences of masturbation which had been described in the most gloomy terms by Tissot and his Italian imitators prevailed over the condemnation of prostitution at least until the beginning of the twentieth century, when new voices could be heard which underlined the danger of venereal diseases. Only at that point did the moral condemnation of masturbation become less rigid, and some authors admitted that 'onanism', albeit 'against nature and revolting', represented less of a social danger than prostitution.

In spite of attempts by public authorities to improve the moral standards of the population, Catholics continued to criticise the new state and suggested that only religious education would be able to stop decline, notwithstanding the opinion of those who believed that morality could thrive 'without the threat of divine punishment'.

While Catholics and lay observers disagreed about the causes of moral decline, they often shared the same negative view of contemporary society. Their impressions were based on numerous sociological and anthropological studies regarding the living conditions of the lower classes published during the last decades of the nineteenth century.

Conservatives had always positively contrasted the strict moral norms of rural areas with the moral decay of the cities, but reading the volumes published by the Parliamentary Committee of Investigation on Agriculture they discovered to their dismay a rather different image of the countryside. The conditions of the poor peasants in the south of Italy, in particular, were described in extremely negative terms:

> Fathers sell their sons and daughters for whom they feel no love. Husbands are only interested in the property of their spouses and care about nothing else. Procuring, incest, uxoricides ... prostitution, and bastardy have all reached dreadful proportions, and, what's worse, are not even hidden ... If rape is rare, the explanation is the ease with which women give themselves up at the first request which makes a higher frequency impossible.
>
> (Damiani 1884: 35)

The authors also worried about changes in the structure of the family. In fact, although the patriarchal, multiple-family household was still frequent among sharecroppers in Tuscany, Emilia Romagna and other regions, there were many complaints about its decline. According to Emilio Morpurgo, who wrote about the Veneto area, the transform-ation of the traditional family was a result of the combined effects of poverty and population growth. Other observers attributed the crisis more moralistically to the desire for luxury of young women, and to their unwillingness to accept the authority of their mothers-in-law. Often the authors expressed the fear that the tendency of young people to elude the control of the male head of the household would lead to a more general revolt against all authority.

Studies of the living conditions of the urban lower classes revealed similar problems. According to an investigation among Roman workers published in 1897, on average six persons slept in the same room: father, mother, sons and daughters and often also subtenants. Social scientists underlined that in these circumstances children could hardly be expected to preserve their innocence.

The idea of youthful innocence itself was at the centre of a heated discussion. The first books on sex education, analysed by Rifelli and Ziglio (1991) and Bonetta (1990), often put a strong accent on the moral aspects and preferred not to give any concrete information, fearing that this might stir untimely the sexual instincts of young people.

This attitude began to change during the first decade of the twentieth century, when pathologist Pio Foà started to tour Italy to give lectures about sexual life. Pio Foà was also the driving force behind the publication in Italy of a series of books on sex education by Sylvanus Stall, Emma Drake and Mary Wood Allen, which had been an international bestseller.

The problems related to juvenile prostitution convinced some observers to ask for the introduction of new measures to protect young people. The Italian government participated in the 1902 Paris Conference against white slavery, but did not employ much energy in concrete actions. This was perhaps in part due to the fact that some authors were convinced that young girls in the south of Italy became prostitutes because of their precocious sexuality. During a discussion about the reform of the Penal Code, Senator Maggiorani had warned in 1875 that a law which would make sex with girls under the age of twelve a statutory offence risked putting men at the mercy of young prostitutes who would try to extort money by threatening them with denunciation. In 1909 the Court of Cassation declared that sexual intercourse with a consenting minor was not a crime and should not be considered 'corruption'. The verdict was interpreted in a positive manner by writers who favoured a more liberal attitude with regard to sexuality, but in reality only confirmed existing stereotypes about the sexuality of young girls from the lower classes, and served to exclude any idea of male responsibility.

The fear of sexual disorder and the worry about a breakdown of the traditional family led in 1894 to the foundation of a League against Pornography, which in 1899 widened its scope and became the League for Public Decency. Most members of the League were young men from the urban middle classes. While stressing the importance of high moral standards for the internal cohesion of the nation, the middle classes transformed chastity into a patriotic duty and based their own demands for social and political leadership on the claim of moral superiority. They explained the immorality of the lower classes by poverty and attributed the tendency for debauchery of the upper class to excessive wealth. Sexual continence, on the contrary, distinguished the bourgeoisie and wealthy merchants from the licentious and frivolous nobility, while at the lower end of the social ladder it marked off the virtuous lower middle class from the proletariat.

The actions of the League for Public Decency were directed mainly against obscene art and literature, pornography and immoral theatre. Links were established with the Bureau International contre la Littérature Immorale, and members of the League were present at the anti-pornography conferences of Colonia (1904), Bordeaux (1905) and Paris (1910). Much less energy was dedicated to the attempt to introduce legislation in favour of paternity tests. Generally, the social purity movement was characterised by a conservative political stance and its members often preferred to ask for the intervention of the magistracy and of police forces instead of appealing to a public opinion which anyway did not seem to be very responsive. In their dealings with the lower classes the members of the League displayed a mixture of paternalism and contempt: while trying to obtain the support of the workers, they ignored economic problems and denounced the influence of the socialist movement which, according to their opinion, ruined families and corrupted the young.

The poor did not always appreciate attempts at moralisation. When, in 1904, Giovanni Lorenzoni, on behalf of the progressive Humanitarian Society of Milan, asked for separate dormitories for male and female rice-weeders, both men and women protested.

Young seasonal workers evidently were happy to be able to escape from control by their parents, and wanted to have a good time without bothering too much about morality.

The League also censured, without much success, the changes in courtship behaviour and gender roles which occurred in the big cities of northern Italy during the 1890s. Although it became more common in this period to see young women from the middle classes and higher classes walking in the streets without a chaperon, the extent of the diffusion of new models of behaviour should not be exaggerated: as late as 1912 the German sociologist Robert Michels noted the prudery which in Italy surrounded all physical expressions of love (Michels 1912: 171–2).

Changes in gender roles were hampered by legal rulings. The penal code which had been adopted in 1889 underlined the inferior position of women within marriage and gave strong legal support to male authority. The Code included clear distinctions between husband and wife as far as their sexual rights were concerned. While adultery was considered a crime for women, who risked a term of prison from three to thirty months, the extramarital affairs of their husbands were tolerated, and men could be prosecuted only in cases of public concubinage.

In the attempt to outline the limits of male and female behaviour moralists received the welcome support of medical science. As Roberto Ardigò put it, 'positivism saved morality thanks to science' (Ardigò 1878: 11–13). While trying to reveal the physical and biological roots of male and female behaviour, scientists switched with ease from description to prescriptions as to how 'real' men and 'real' women should behave, and thus gave a rational base to pre-scriptive rules. The scientific view reflected social stereotypes about gender roles according to which a woman's role should be confined to motherhood and marriage. The moral categories of virtue and vice were replaced by the concepts of normality and abnormality, health and disease, but often the scientists in doing this simply gave new prestige to traditional moral judgements.

All these aspects emerge clearly from discussions about female sexuality. Most authors agreed that women were sexually passive and attributed this fact both to their biology and to the influence of society. The 'biological destiny' of women was often used to oppose equal rights. According to Enrico Ferri, the psycho-sexual energy needed for maternity was compensated by limited sensibility. In order to preserve this precarious balance he suggested that it was unwise for women to get involved too much in social or political activities (Ferri 1908: 160–3). Those who claimed that the apparent lack of sexual passion of women was only a tribute to social conventions were a minority, but even they shared the view that the life of women, much more than that of men, was determined by their biology.

Another thing which sparked off a debate among scientists was homosexuality. The legislation of the eighteenth century had provided severe punishment for homosexual acts, in line with the moral condemnation pronounced by the Catholic church. Followers of the Enlightenment like Cesare Beccaria had criticised the excessive severity of the laws, and had asked for a clear distinction between religious norms and state legislation. On the basis of similar principles, after the French Revolution most Italian states maintained the provisions of the Napoleonic Code, which had been extended to Italy in 1804, and did not reintroduce laws against homosexual acts. Noteworthy exceptions were the Kingdom of Sardinia, where 'indecent assaults against nature' could be punished with up to ten years of hard labour, and the Lombard provinces under Austrian rule. After Italian unification the repressive legislation of the Kingdom of Savoy was applied to the rest of Italy excluding the territory of the ancient kingdom of Naples. Only in 1889, with the introduction of the new penal code, were regional differences in the treatment of homosexual acts eliminated and homosexuality depenalised. The new situation, however, did not exclude other forms of legal persecution, based on accusations regarding indecent acts, corruption of minors or pornography.

Scientists like Lombroso legitimated the social persecution of homosexuals by pointing to the similarity between criminality and homosexuality, as both were considered expressions of a primitive stage of human development. The physical appearance of male and female homosexuals, which allegedly revealed traces of the original hermaphroditism, was supposed to be sufficient proof for this theory. Other scientists preferred to underline the influence of social and environmental circumstances and claimed that 'pseudo-homosexuality' could be a result of excessive prudishness, poverty or isolation. The feminist movement was accused of favouring the diffusion of lesbianism because it had inspired a hatred against men. Only very few scientists in Italy shared the more positive idea of homosexuality proposed by Richard von Krafft-Ebing and others, whose works had been translated into Italian.

The literature of the early twentieth century shows increasing difficulties in defining gender identity. As early as 1912 some authors who worried about changes in gender roles asked for war, convinced that violence would create new opportunities to reaffirm the gender identity of men. Similar ideas were widespread: one of the young members of the League for Public Decency, Egilberto Martire, accused pacifism of sapping the strength and vitality of the nation, because it expressed a general lack of vigour. Intellectuals adhering to the futurist movement viewed war as an opportunity to promote the modernisation of Italian society and to cancel many obsolete traditions. The idea that the war could be a vehicle of change convinced progressives – among them Benito Mussolini – to break away in 1915 from the socialist movement and to give their support to intervention.

War created great problems for the Neo-Malthusian League, which had been founded in 1913 by Luigi Berta and Secondo Giorni. Within a few years the League had succeeded in creating strong links with the socialist party. It had founded its own periodical *L'Educazione Sessuale*, it had published numerous books with information about birth control, and it had created a network for the sale of condoms. During the war, however, the League was forced to suspend its activities for technical reasons, but also because of the widespread opinion that the power of Germany and the strength of its army were the result of population growth. If the number of citizens was decisive for a nation's force to resist military attack, then perhaps birth control was anti-patriotic.

Against the expectations of many, war failed to re-establish traditional gender identities. For one thing, the need to keep up the production of arms and munitions made it necessary to employ more women in paid labour. While they became more active in production, women moved out of the private sphere which tradition had reserved for them. The futurists were among the first to sense the changes which were taking place in the position and in the self-image of women who had undergone a transformation from 'vain dolls' to 'human beings who are conscious of their present and future role' (Rosà 1917: 1). The war did not have the regenerating effect on men which some observers had hoped for. On the contrary, the cruelty of modern warfare often disturbed their psychological equilibrium.

When the soldiers returned from the battlefields, they had to face a new challenge. Some of them accepted the emancipation of women, but interpreted this in such a way as to create a conflict between sexual rights and political and social-economic demands. According to this view, women's struggle for socio-economic and political rights was an impediment to the conquest of sexual rights and ignored the more profound desires of female nature.

The effects of the war on gender relations and sexual morality were contradictory and often short-lived, but for a brief period it seemed that the war had cancelled traditional customs and had introduced a new lifestyle. Italy enjoyed its 'roaring twenties'. Young women were allowed to move about more freely in the cities and to meet people of their own age at parties where they listened to jazz music and danced the charleston. Among the urban middle classes the traditional courtship pattern with its official betrothal and strict control by parents and society gradually lost its influence and 'flirting' became more common.

The most convinced upholders of tradition feared that this sort of modernisation would lead to the dissolution of gender identity and longed for a return to the values and customs of a patriarchal and rural society. The so-called modern girl was accused of following the American example of birth control and sexual freedom. Changes in fashion contributed to the idea that the differences between the sexes were gradually disappearing. Women had their hair bobbed and wore short, tight dresses; men – wrote a society columnist in 1922 – looked like cocottes. The main result of the changes in gender roles therefore seemed to be the creation of a so-called 'third sex' of masculine women and feminine men.

The reaction to these changes in some cases reflects a 'male homophobic panic'. Although certainly not a conservative, the futurist poet Marinetti shared the dislike of blurring gender identities, because he feared that this might lead to the disappearance of 'male' values such as aggressiveness, force and courage. For the same reason he condemned homosexuals as enemies of progress and revolution.

The concrete results of the postwar period were limited: some improvements were introduced in the legal position of women, but women failed to obtain the vote. Owing to Catholic mobilisation, the proposal for the introduction of divorce which had been forwarded in Parliament in 1921 was not approved. The fate of the proposal to introduce sex education in secondary schools was no better.

Notwithstanding their initial and rather instrumental backing of some demands of the women's movement, the Fascists were fierce opponents of any change in the relationship between men and women, and tried to re-establish the 'natural' order in order to gain male support. For this reason they violently opposed the new role of women and tried to force them to return to the household. The Fascist way of life received the enthusiastic support of young men who wanted to express the 'male' values of activism, courage and force through violent actions against political opponents. Thus, while combating the working-class movement, these young men, often with a middle-class background, also wanted to re-establish their dominion over women.

Soon after the March on Rome (1922), the Fascist government organised an anti-pornography campaign. Repression was justified on the grounds that it was necessary to save the energy spent in the search for sexual pleasure in order to reconstruct the nation. The heavy accent on public virtues certainly did not cancel private 'vices', but it did create a situation in which hypocrisy was considered normal and necessary.

The members of the League for Public Decency tried to influence political authorities by suggesting the introduction of extremely severe measures against immorality. They failed, however, to obtain full support: when Dino Segre in 1923 was accused of pornography after the publication of *La cintura di castità* (*The Chastity Belt*) a number of important Fascist leaders – among whom was the head of the organisation of Fascist intellectuals, Pietro Gorgolini – stood up in his defence.

While censorship and repression were used against popular publications which diffused ideas in favour of sexual liberation or gave information about birth control, there were also more subtle ways of proceeding. The Società Italiana per lo Studio delle Questioni Sessuali had been founded in 1921 by Aldo Mieli, with the aim 'of disseminating serious and well-pondered information about sexual matters, and to instruct the masses in order to provide them with some norms and ideas about hygiene, education and morality'. Until 1928 its periodical – the *Rassegna di Studi Sessuali* – continued to publish articles about controversial issues such as the paternity test, premarital medical examination and eugenics, notwithstanding ever increasing difficulties. Permission for publication was granted as long as the discussion about sexuality and sexual morality remained limited to specialists. After the departure of Mieli, and particularly after the nomination, in 1931, of Corrado Gini as the new director, the *Rassegna* became an instrument of Fascist population policy.

Despite the general atmosphere of conformity, even during the 1930s some unorthodox books continued to be published. Edoardo Tinto published between 1932 and 1934 a *Dizionario di sessuologia* which tried to elaborate a new sexual morality, based no longer on religious faith but on science. Among other books which contributed during the 1930s to diffusing a non-orthodox view of sexual pleasure were Theo van de Velde's manual for a perfect marriage, Marie Stopes's *Married Love* and Bronislaw Malinowski's study of sexual life among the 'savages'.

Perhaps the best-known aspect of Fascist population policy is the 'battle' in favour of demographic growth which Mussolini announced in 1927 in the so-called Ascension Day speech. All possible measures were used to convince couples to have more children: subsidies and tax reductions for large families, jobs and better career chances for prolific fathers, higher taxation for bachelors, etc. The Opera Nazionale Maternità e Infanzia (Mother and Child Welfare Association), which had been founded in 1925, co-ordinated the activities of private charitable institutions which offered sanitary education and medical care. The Fascist penal code of 1930 made propaganda in favour of birth control a crime, but it did not affect the production of condoms, which were deemed necessary to protect against venereal diseases men who had contacts with prostitutes.

Fascist population policy was a failure: notwithstanding the efforts of the Catholic church and of the government, the birth rate continued to decline during the 1920s and 1930s. Some historians have seen this decline as a result of a semi-conscious refusal by women to obey the orders of the political leaders. Luisa Passerini (1984) defines birth control in this sense as a kind of practical critique of women's oppression. It seems more likely that the decision to have children was linked with short-term economic crises and with long-term general trends like urbanisation. As shown by Gribaudi (1987), the decision to limit the number of children was often part of a rational strategy aiming at improving the living standard of the family. The desire to facilitate upward social mobility was therefore probably the main reason why individuals decided to postpone or put off marriage, to delay the date of birth of children or to limit their number.

According to the communist leader Ruggero Grieco (1936), higher moral standards could result only from improvement of the living conditions of the working class. Without this improvement moralistic discourses were nothing but rhetoric. Most Fascists, however, condemned as pure selfishness the fact that women preferred the immediate advantages of comfortable living to the more profound joys of motherhood. Giovanni Franceschini (1941), author of a sex manual and influential member of the movement in favour of public decency, went as far as to declare that poverty was a necessary condition for population growth; higher living standards would only make women more egoistical and lead to an increase of nervous diseases.

In the absence of more concrete measures to improve economic conditions, the Fascist leaders tried to reinforce the position of the male as head of the family. They proved, however, unable to stop changes in gender relations: notwithstanding legislation and social practices which were decisively masculinist, many men felt unsure about their predominance and denounced the economic independence of women as well as their emotional autonomy.

As a result of the refusal of women to comply with the Fascist idea of womanhood, complaints about the masculinisation of women abounded. Ferdinando De Napoli, a medical doctor, warned against the risk of the creation of a 'third sex', neither man nor woman. Rather unconventionally, he emphasised that sex was as important for women as it was for men, or even more so. Women depended on men not only for psychological and economic support, but also to satisfy their own physical needs: chastity – warned De Napoli – could lead to homosexuality (De Napoli 1934: 347–66).

The question of whether men would be able to recover their supremacy was the subject of discussion. Not even their virility could be taken for granted: in 1936 the Court of Appeal of Naples condemned a man for having refused to have sexual intercourse with his wife. The same years saw a growing number of publications dealing with male impotence and lack of vigour. Educators suggested military training and sports as the appropriate means to strengthen the willpower of young men. Boy scouting provided an education based on the ideals of strength and purity. At the same time this ideal of 'muscular Christianity' served the bellicose purposes of the Fascist regime.

Although the Catholic church often acted as a loyal ally of the Fascists and certainly was not in favour of feminism, it nevertheless strongly opposed the Fascist double morality which allowed men to ignore the moral rules to which women were subjected. The biographies of young men who were both chaste and virile, good sportsmen and part of modern life were held up as an example for Catholic youth. These new saints helped to redesign the image of the Catholic male.

While Fascism had left many old problems unsolved, the end of the Second World War added new ones: a new lifestyle was introduced by the American troops stationed in Italy and made popular by American movies showing independent women and angry young men. Secularisation once more seemed to threaten social stability, and the proposal to introduce divorce legislation raised fears about the disintegration of family life. All this convinced Monsignor Montini – the future pope Paul VI – that the family had become 'the great invalid of the postwar period'.

Like their predecessors, the Christian Democrats who formed the government after the Second World War demonstrated their adherence to traditional morality by staging a campaign against pornography. On the occasion of the IX National Congress for Morality Prime Minister Alcide De Gasperi solemnly announced the creation of special police forces and invited 'honest citizens' to participate in the battle for moralisation.

The 1950s in Italy were characterised by the dominant position of the Catholic church and by conservative public opinion. However, it would be a mistake not to recognise the attempts made to eliminate some of the more obvious examples of a double standard of morality. Bianca Bianchi, for example, convinced Parliament to change the legal position of children born out of wedlock. The indication *N.N.*, which marked them as illegitimate, was removed from their identity cards; paternity tests were allowed more often, and natural fathers obtained the right to recognise their children, even if, at the moment of conception, they had been officially married to another woman.

It took more time to do away with the regulation of prostitution, because many people continued to see prostitution as a necessary outlet for the sexual instincts of unmarried young men. According to public opinion surveys, quite a few women shared this opinion. When Lina Merlin in 1948 advanced her proposal to abolish the closed house system, she therefore met with much opposition. Even among those who adhered to her proposal, not all shared Merlin's matter-of-fact approach and her aversion to 'Salvation Army mentality'. According to members of the Christian Democrat Party, the struggle against regulated prostitution should be part of a more general strategy aiming at re-establishing male authority in the family. They wanted men to become more aware of their moral responsibilities, and refrain not only from visits to brothels, but also, more generally, from pre- and extramarital sex and from the use of contraceptives. The division among the supporters of abolitionism, the secret desire of many members of Parliament to ignore the problem, and the opposition of parts of public opinion caused a major delay, and only in 1958 did Lina Merlin manage to get her proposal for the abolition of regulated prostitution through Parliament.

While Catholics could accept the moderate attempts for sexual reform of the 1950s, they feared the introduction of new lifestyles and of different values by American movies and popular culture. Marriage counselling was introduced with the declared purpose of re-enforcing male authority and thereby saving the traditional family. With these aims in mind, Don Paolo Liggeri created in Milan, in 1948, the first Catholic marriage counselling agency. The diffusion of similar agencies all over Italy marks a particular phase in the history of the family when people were convinced that 'scientists can explain why a marriage is a failure'.

Don Paolo Liggeri's position regarding sexual morality can be described as one of 'enlightened asceticism'. He underlined the positive value of sexuality within marriage, but was convinced, at the same time, that continence gave young, unmarried people an opportunity to strengthen their willpower. It should be recognised that the Catholic movements active in marriage counselling and sex education often expressed innovative ideas about the role of sexuality within marriage and about gender relations. More traditional moralists certainly did not share their positive opinion about sex education. Nor did they appreciate the attempt to counter the influence of popular sex manuals by publishing manuals more in line with Catholic doctrine regarding sexual morality.

While positive opinions about sexual pleasure were not a novelty for theologians, the openness with which Catholic priests addressed the problems of sexual life was new, and a source of scandal. In his autobiography Don Paolo Liggeri recalls how his attempts to give information about sexual life often created problems. L'Osservatore Romano, the official newspaper of the Vatican, condemned 'excessive realism' in the description of the pleasures of the senses. It was suggested that the importance which Catholic authors attributed to sexuality might create the impression that sexual harmony was a value *per se*.

Catholic educators and marriage counsellors were convinced that sexual harmony could reinforce the sense of unity of the couple and thereby help to prevent the failure of marriages. This opinion was shared by the majority of Italian public opinion. In a survey of 1951, 68 per cent of the women interviewed declared that satisfactory sexual relations were essential for the success of marriage. In the attempt to save marriages Catholic counsellors started to propagate the idea that more sexual harmony was necessary. They explained that relations between the spouses were perfect when 'husband and wife reach complete satisfaction, after having experienced simultaneously the paroxysm of pleasure: *orgasm*'. To reach this result, all expressions of physical love were legitimate as long as they contributed to strengthen the unity of the married couple and did not lead to exaggerated sensualism aroused by 'whims and absurd technicalities'.

Catholic discourse in favour of sexual harmony as a precondition for the success of marriages had unforeseen, and certainly undesired, results, and was used by young men to ask their girlfriends for the so-called *prova d'amore* (love test). A young girl who was interviewed by Gabriella Parca told her how the request of the so-called 'love test' could well become a form of blackmail (Parca 1959: 17–18).

If we want to believe the results of numerous inquiries carried out during the 1960s and 1970s, many women had a negative opinion of their own sexual life, in particular women living in the south of Italy and in provincial towns where traditional male attitudes often ignored all forms of affection. Only very few of the interviews done by Gabriella Parca (1959), Lieta Harrison (1966 and 1972), Fausta Cecchini (1977) and others speak of a satisfactory sexual life, and most women seemed to consider sexual relations almost entirely as part of female duties.

Catholic marriage counsellors agreed with the negative opinion of many women regarding male behaviour in sexual relations, and tried to convince husbands to pay more attention to their wives' reactions, to show more affection and tenderness, to be more patient, and to dedicate more time to foreplay. More generally, men were asked to abandon their traditionalist attitudes: they were invited to show more interest in the education of their children and to take their responsibilities as fathers more seriously.

The idea that a happy sexual life was a precondition for a happy marriage was new, but had its roots in the more traditional ideas about conjugal duties. In a book about the crisis of matrimony Mario Elia stressed the duty of spouses 'to put their body at the disposal of their partner' (Elia 1962: 318–19). A passive attitude was not considered sufficient to fulfil conjugal duties.

Notwithstanding the dominant position of the Catholic church in Italian society during the 1950s, some unorthodox voices could be heard. In 1956 the Italian Association for Demographic Education (AIED) was founded with the aim of defending the idea and the practice of voluntary and conscious limitation of the number of children, and to combat existing legislation against birth control. In its activities the AIED tried to make it clear that birth control was not simply a personal problem but had important social repercussions. Perhaps also for this reason lay forces, socialists and communists joined the campaign in favour of birth control, which found growing support among the general public. In 1952, 55 per cent of Italians agreed with the necessity of limiting the number of children. Even though, under these circumstances, very few magistrates were willing to prosecute people for propaganda in favour of birth control, in 1965 the Constitutional Court still declared that detailed information about contraceptives should remain illegal because it offended public morality. The Court did not condemn more theoretical pleas in favour of birth control. Only in 1971 was legislation which forbade 'propaganda in favour of birth control' declared anti-constitutional.

Catholic theologians never formally approved complete separation between sexuality and procreation, but under certain circumstances they were willing to tolerate sexual acts which had no immediate links with procreation. The condemnation of forms of procreation which were not the result of conception during a natural sexual act left no room for discussion. Already in 1897 the Sant'Ufficio had answered 'non licet' to the question 'an adhiberi possit artificialis mulieris faecundatio'. The condemnation of artificial insemination was repeated in the 1930 encyclical against birth control, *Casti connubii*, and then, once more, in September 1949, on the occasion of the IV International Congress of Catholic medical doctors.

In 1959 the decision of the Court of Cassation to condemn a woman who had accepted artificial insemination with sperm from a donor created a heated debate. The prestigious Jesuit periodical *Civiltà Cattolica* published an article by Salvatore Lener in which this form of insemination was rated the worst form of adultery. Two Christian Democratic members of Parliament, Gonella and Manco, proposed punishing by law not only women who permitted similar practices to be carried out on themselves but also the donor, the consenting husband and whoever else was involved.

The movement in favour of sexual liberation of the 1960s was often characterised by strong male prejudices and by an even stronger anti-homosexual bias. In the 1950s, fear of social disorder had once more suggested a link with the presumed increase in the number of homosexuals. According to psychiatrist Mario Vinci (1954), 'sexual inversion' had become much more significant and in some Italian regions the number of homosexuals had reached up to 1 per cent of the total population. The results of an inquiry regarding the clients of brothels were even more worrying: cases of impotency, 'latent homosexuality' and masochism were so frequent that conclusions about the emasculation of the Italian male seemed justified.

Only a few isolated voices tried to lift the curtain of silence which surrounded the issue of homosexuality. The short-lived monthly magazine *Sesso e Libertà* published a number of articles in 1952 and 1953 by male and female homosexuals in defence of homosexuality. Books like Ettore Mariotti's *La neofilia* (1952) and Giorgio Punzo's *Lettere erotologiche* (1956) were even more important for the history of homosexuality because they were not limited to an apology, but also underlined the positive aspects of homosexuality. Similar opinions were received very coldly by medical science in Italy, which during the late 1950s and early 1960s rediscovered the problem of homosexuality. It was the common opinion among medical doctors that at least in a number of cases it was possible to cure homo-sexuals: discussion concerned the choice of the best method. According to a physician from Milan, Gino Olivari (1952), manly sports such as boxing, sexual relations with prostitutes and an active, 'male', way of life could help his patients to overcome their tenden-cies. Other experts suggested using intensive electro-shock therapy. The Italian specialists in sexology – a booming science in the early 1960s – tried to prevent homosexuality being considered as 'normal':

> if normal human sexuality is characterised by the fact that the anatomical, physiological, instinctive, rational and social aspects of men and women complete each other, then it is clear that a

homosexual has to be considered abnormal. The question whether homosexual tendencies are more or less frequent is not at all relevant ...

Under no circumstances can homosexuality be considered a simple variation of the normal human behaviour, and therefore homosexuality rightly is an object of study of medical science.

(Santori 1963)

One understands why one of the first public appearances of the gay movement FUORI (Fronte Unitario Omosessuale Rivoluzionario Italiano) was at a congress of sexology in April 1972.

Given the attitudes of public opinion and medical science, it is not surprising that in the 1960s members of Parliament tried to introduce legislation against homosexuality. Similar attempts had failed under Fascism because Minister Alfredo Rocco was convinced that a special article which would make homosexual acts between consenting adults a criminal offence would create the wrong impression that homosexuality was a serious problem in Italy. Moreover, he trusted that police measures would be sufficient to punish homosexuals who dared to 'come out'. In the 1960s the situation changed: fearing that young people could become homosexuals as a result of 'propaganda', the social democrat Bruno Romano proposed to punish not only persons who committed 'homosexual offences' but also the authors of books and movies in favour of homosexuality, and whoever contributed to defending this crime. Romano's failure to convince Parliament to approve similar proposals was probably the result of an attitude of repressive tolerance, and certainly did not express a desire to promote gay liberation. In case of need other laws could be applied: in 1968 the Court of Appeal of Rome condemned Aldo Braibanti to a prison term of nine years for the moral subjugation of his younger friend. Almost ten years later a Catholic group protested against 'rampant sexual perversion' when members of the gay movement participated in the activities organised by the students of a secondary school in Ciampino.

Notwithstanding opposition, during the late 1960s and 1970s a radical change in the legal framework of sexuality and the family took place. In 1968 the Constitutional Court declared that the distinction between men and women with regard to adultery was contrary to the Constitution. In 1970 Parliament approved a proposal for the introduction of divorce which was confirmed by referendum a few years later. Finally, in 1975 a new family law was adopted, based on the recognition of equal rights for men and women and on a democratic idea of family relations.

The radical changes of the 1970s, when traditional morality was questioned openly and no longer respected, forced Catholic organisations to take up a position of defence. Catholic educators and moralists who wanted to oppose the diffusion of more liberal lifestyles once more asked for the repressive action of the state. Whereas in the past they had tried to participate in the ongoing process of modernisation, they now contributed to the reaction against modern society.

The effects of secularisation should not be exaggerated: still today in Italy the Catholic church plays an important role and is decisive in the orientation of public opinion on issues such as artificial insemination, the rights of homosexuals and euthanasia. On the other hand, it is also necessary to recognise the fact that dissident voices have easy access to mass media, and that new lifestyles and mentalities are gaining ground in Italy, creating the conditions for the recognition of alternative sexualities and changing sexual and gender identities.

Bibliography

Aldrich, R. (1993), *The Seduction of the Mediterranean: Writing, Art and Homosexual Fantasy*, London and New York, Routledge.

Ardigò, R. (1878), *La morale dei positivisti*, in *Opere filosofiche*, Padua, Draghi, 1893.

Babini, V. P., F. Minuz and A. Tagliavini (1986), *La donna nelle scienze dell'uomo: Immagini del femminile nella cultura scientifica italiana di fine secolo*, Milan, Franco Angeli.

Barbagli, M. (1984), *Sotto lo stesso tetto: Mutamenti della famiglia in Italia dal XV al XX secolo*, Bologna, Il Mulino.

Barbagli, M. and D. I. Kertzer (1992), *Storia della famiglia italiana 1750–1950*, Bologna, Il Mulino.

Bonetta, G. (1990), *Corpo e nazione: L'educazione ginnastica, igienica e sessuale nell'Italia liberale*, Milan, Angeli.

Buttafuoco, A. (1985), *Le Mariuccine: storia di un'istituzione laica: l'Asilo Mariuccia*, Milan, Angeli.

Canosa, R. (1981), *Sesso e stato: Devianza sessuale e interventi istituzionali nell'ottocento italiano*, Milan, Mazzotta.

Carelli, L. (1891), 'L'art. 339 e le pubblicazioni ed esposizioni oscene', *La Scuola Positiva*, 1, 11–12.

Cavaglion, A. (1982), *Otto Weininger in Italia*, Rome, Carucci.

Cecchini, F. (1977), *Sesso amaro: Trentamila donne rispondono su maternità sessualità aborto*, Rome, Editori Riuniti.

Damiani, A. (1884), 'Relazione sulla I circoscrizione (prov. di Caltanisetta, Catania, Girgenti, Messina, Palermo, Siracusa e Trapani)', *Atti della giunta per l'inchiesta agraria e sulle condizioni della classe agraria*, Rome, Forzani, 13.

De Giorgio, M. (1992), *Le italiane dall'Unità a oggi: Modelli culturali e comportamenti sociali*, Rome and Bari, Laterza.

De Grazia, V. (1992), *How Fascism Ruled Women: Italy, 1922–1945*, Berkeley, California University Press.

De Napoli, F. (1934), *Da Malthus a Mussolini: La guerra che noi preferiamo*, Bologna, Cappelli.

Di Simplicio, O. (1994), *Peccato penitenza perdono: Siena 1575–1800. La formazione della coscienza nell'Italia moderna*, Milan, Angeli.

Elia, M. (1962), *Matrimonio in crisi*, Rome, Arti e Scienze.

Ferrante, L., M. Palazzi and G. Pomata (1988), *Ragnatela di rapporti: Patronage e reti di relazione nella storia delle donne*, Turin, Rosenberg & Sellier.

Ferri, E. (1908), in *La Ginecologia Moderna*, 1, 2–3.

Franceschini, G. (1941), *Vita sessuale: Fisiologia ed etica*, Milan, Hoepli.

Gibson, M. (1986), *Prostitution and the State in Italy: 1860–1915*, New Brunswick (N.J.) and London, Rutgers University Press.

Greco, G. (1985), *Peccato, crimine e malattia tra Ottocento e Novecento*, Bari, Dedalo.

— (1987), *Lo scienziato e la prostituta: Due secoli di studi sulla prostituzione*, Bari, Dedalo.

Gribaudi, M. (1987), *Mondo operaio e mito operaio: Spazi e percorsi sociali a Torino nel primo Novecento*, Turin, Einaudi.

Grieco, R. (1936), 'Per la salvezza delle nuove generazioni', *Lo Stato Operaio*, 10, 10, 670–3.

Groppi, A. (1994), *I conservatori della virtù: Donne recluse nella Roma dei Papi*, Rome and Bari, Laterza.

Harrison, L. (1966), *L'iniziazione: Come le adolescenti italiane diventano donne*, Milan, Rizzoli.

— (1972), *La donna sposata: Mille mogli accusano*, Milan, Feltrinelli.

Horn, D. G. (1994), *Social Bodies: Science, Reproduction, and Italian Modernity*, Princeton, Princeton University Press.

Kertzer, D. I. (1993), *Sacrificed for Honor: Italian Infant Abandonment and the Politics of Reproductive Control*, Boston, Beacon.

Kertzer, D. I. and R. P. Saller (1992), *The Family in Italy from Antiquity to the Present*, New Haven and London, Yale University Press.

Livi Bacci, M. (1977), *A History of Italian Fertility during the last two Centuries*, Princeton, Princeton University Press.

Lucà Trombetta, P. (1991), *La confessione della lussuria: Definizione e controllo del piacere nel cattolicesimo*, Genoa, Costa & Nolan.

Macrelli, R. (1981), *L'indegna schiavitù: Anna Maria Mozzoni e la lotta contro la prostituzione di Stato*, Rome, Editori Riuniti.

Mariotti, E. (1952), *La neofilia: Contributo agli studi di psicopatologia sessuale*, Rome, Editori Mediterranea.

Michels, R. (1912), *La morale sessuale*, Turin, Bocca [1944].

Mosse, G. L. (1985), *Nationalism and Sexuality: Respectability and Abnormal*

Sexuality in Modern Europe, New York, Fertig.

Olivari, G. (1952), *Omosessualità*, Milan, private publication.

Parca, G. (1959), *Le italiane si confessano*, Florence, Parenti.

Pasi, A. and P. Sorcinelli (1995), *Amori e trasgressioni: Rapporti di coppia tra '800 e '900*, Bari, Dedalo.

Passerini, L. (1984), *Torino operaia e fascismo: Una storia orale*, Rome and Bari, Laterza.

Pelaja, M. (1994), *Matrimonio e sessualità a Rome nell'ottocento*, Rome and Bari, Laterza.

— (1996), 'Marriage by Exception: Marriage Dispositions and Ecclesiastical Policies in Nineteenth-century Rome', *Journal of Modern Italian Studies*, 1, 2, 223–44.

Piccone Stella, S. (1993), *La prima generazione: Ragazze e ragazzi nel miracolo economico italiano*, Milan, Angeli.

Punzo, G. (1956), *Lettere erotologiche: Trilogia erotologica minore*, Naples, C. Martello.

Rifelli, G. and P. Moro (1989), *Sessuologia clinica*, 1, *Sessuologia generale*, Bologna, CLUEB.

Rifelli, G. and C. Ziglio (1991), *Per una storia dell'educazione sessuale 1870–1920*, Florence, La Nuova Italia.

Rosà, R. (1917), 'Le donne del posdomani', *L'Italia Futurista*, 2, 181.

Santori, G. (1963), 'Introduzione', *Aspetti patogenetici dell'omosessualità*, Turin, Minerva Medica, 7–16.

Società italiana di demografia storica (1990), *Popolazione, società e ambiente: Temi di demografia storica italiana (secc. XVII–XIX)*, Bologna, CLUEB.

Spackman, B. (1996), *Fascist Virilities: Rhetoric, Ideology and Social Fantasy in Italy*, Minneapolis, Minnesota University Press.

Spinelli, L. (1950–1), 'Le legislazioni matrimoniali degli stati italiani preunitari con riferimento al sistema concordatario', *Studi urbinati di scienze giuridiche ed economiche*, 19, 3, 183–232.

Valmaggi, L. (1927), *I cicisbei: Contributo alla storia del costume italiano nel secolo XVIII*, Turin, Chiantore.

Vinci, M. (1954), 'Contributo alla genesi dell'omosessualità', *Annali di Neuropsichiatria e Psicoanalisi*, 1, 3, 469–80.

Wanrooij, B. (1990), *Storia del pudore: La questione sessuale in Italia 1860–1940*, Venice, Marsilio.

6

Sexual cultures in Germany and Austria, 1700–2000

Franz X. Eder

Austrian and German historiography has had a contradictory tradition concerning sexuality. German-speaking cultural historians and historically orientated ethnographers rated high in the European history of manners at the end of the nineteenth century. By investigating 'exotic' variants of sex-life, Austrian and German founders of the sexual sciences touched on historical terrain. Although their uncritical and positivistic use of sources no longer satisfies modern standards, studies like Eduard Fuchs's *Illustrierte Sittengeschichte* (1909–16) determined the historical view of sexuality in German-speaking countries up to the 1970s, when new approaches to the social and political history of sexuality came from gay and lesbian movements rather than from established academic historiography. Though European and American historians were already working with 'sexual' sources from German-speaking areas, sexuality did not become a topic of academic analysis till the 1980s. During the last two decades professional historians have published many regional studies, but an overview, or comparative approaches, are still missing.

This chapter provides an initial synthesis of the history of sexuality in German-speaking countries. Socio-economic and gender-specific differences provide a focus for the history of peasant, middle-class and proletarian sexuality and for the politicisation and medicalisation of sexual desires from the eighteenth to the early twentieth century. Following the constructivist turn of paradigmatic discussion about sexuality and its meaning in history, the term *sexual desire* will be preferred and it will be employed according to Isabel V. Hull's definition:

> Sexual desire and its possible modes of expression were fashioned within the contours of one's particular life condition. These

conditions were material, mental, physical, social, and accidental, and they differed by Stand [estate], wealth, gender, age, and so on ... Desire is not a 'force' that must be constrained, but something that actually comes into being within a set of circumstances. It is an act of will, but it is never free.

(Hull 1996: 47)

Gemieth und Lieb – sexual desire in peasant society

During the eighteenth and nineteenth centuries marriage was the dominant reference system for sexual desire among peasants and legitimated sexual expression. All sexual acts outside the marital context were seen as illicit, though certain manifestations were not perceived as 'sexual', since they had no connection with marriage. Most historical studies on peasant sexuality in German-speaking areas – as well as the sources used – reflect this focus. There are investigations of premarital sexual life and courtship, breach of promise (failure of wedding wishes and illegitimacy), sexual disagreements within marriage, and adultery (including prostitution). We do not know much about the everyday and 'unproblematic' sexual life of peasants – most sources reflect the deviant sexual margins.

Premarital sexual life mostly began with selecting a marriage candidate, not primarily on the basis of love (in the modern sense) but for socio-economic reasons. Estate, property, inheritance, ability to work, reputation of the individual and of their parental estate were central criteria. According to Reinhard Sieder 'it would be a mistake to separate the sexuality of peasants from its "socioeconomic" determination and to interpret it "for its own sake"' (Sieder 1987: 59). But emotional factors also played an important role: *Gemieth und Lieb* (soul/feelings and love) were a response to positively coded traits and attitudes of the potential partner and contributed to the emergence of sexual desire. Last but not least one must not underestimate the effect of bodily attraction and physical communication: in peasant body language – nearer to the early modern than modern bodily model – everything sticking out from the body, and all 'open' parts, were interesting and attractive. The intense interrelation between intimate awareness of the body and positive emotions in former centuries must not be disregarded. On the contrary, these were important for the development and stability of love connections.

In peasant societies sexual desire and lust were experienced towards potential partners whose bodies, characters and properties represented the fulfilment of one's own social destiny. The endogamous marriage system additionally contributed to the stability of the village society. Values such as respectability, health, robustness, modesty and other emotio-material norms of the peasant existence therefore formed arguments for marriage as well as motivating sexual actions in all social groups – even the lower rural classes. Affective and social as well as economic factors were invested – in Bourdieu's sense – as symbolic and material capital in the sexual and reproductive system of the village in a gender-specific way. Men's symbolic capital of honour permitted deviations from sexual expression within marriage: though the active and experienced male 'seducer' was not widely accepted in peasant culture, his behaviour was attributed to virility. For female honour and modesty women had to defend their 'capital', which could fundamentally influence their future. Loss of honour led to the margins of the social domain regulated by family and community.

Typically, in cases of fornication the promiscuous woman was punished differently. According to Ulrike Gleixner women were defined 'as defensive, repelling and sexually passive and therefore had to state their consent; however men were defined as active and wanting, their acts expressed and explained their will' (Gleixner 1994: 114). The attitude towards pregnant, so-called 'weakened' or 'fallen' women whose partners had broken marriage promises, reveals this asymmetry: women were the deceived persons, yet expected to take care of the reciprocity of achievement and return. They ran all the risks in premarital relationships.

Family, peer group and community regulated gender-specific behaviour, through social mechanisms of courtship and licit sexual connection, and the prevention and penalisation of deviant sexual behaviour. The best-known courtship custom was the *Kiltgang* (also *Gasslgehen, Nachtfreien, Fensterln,* etc.) widely practised in northern Europe. Adolescent male peer groups made nocturnal visits to the windows of unmarried women but also collective or individual visits to their sleeping chambers. Depending on age, sexual approaches might be verbal or even physical. But most men followed the strict rules of the peer group and were observed by its members. *Coitus interruptus* or even full coitus signalled the final phase of individual courtship, no longer directly supervised by others. After promise of marriage, coitus was practised in bed rather than, for example, outside in the meadow, symbolising intention to marry. When we can trust and generalise from Tyrolian court records, premarital coitus also functioned to test female fertility.

Rural premarital sexual culture was aimed at long-term relationships. Short-range contacts and frequent partner changes were not usual, and were attributed to carelessness towards the socio-sexual system. In spite of the tolerance of premarital conception, virginity was considered a virtue to be defended not only by a woman herself but also by the community. Male peer groups had to keep outsiders from night-visiting in their own village and expose dishonourable sexual behaviour within the community by charivari-like customs uncovering and protesting against socio-sexual deviance.

Besides the peer group the *domus* (*house*) – in the persons of the *Hausvater* (father/head of household) and the *Hausmutter* (mother of household) – regulated the sexual behaviour of its members. Until the disintegration of the old patriarchal system during modernisation and industrialisation, these two authorities controlled their children's courtship via strategy and ritual until engagement and Christian wedding. They also had to supervise servants, who were not permitted marriage or sexual activities. After the Reformation their task was under permanent strain between church and state forbidding premarital sexual activities, and social practice permitting intercourse after engagement. Patriarchal authority over servants clashed with changing demands of the peasant economy from the first half of the nineteenth century. Both phenomena are visible in the development of illegitimacy and its contemporary interpretation. During the nineteenth century Austrian and German regions had the highest illegitimacy rates in Europe, peaking between the 1810s and the 1870–80s, with a climax in the 1850s and 1860s. Edward Shorter (1971) saw this as evidence for a 'first sexual revolution' in the second half of the eighteenth and the first half of the nineteenth century, caused by a radical change in mentality, due to industrialisation and the wish for self-fulfilment and emancipation among large sections of the population. According to Shorter this mental modernisation was driven by capitalism, forcing profit-orientated thinking and individuality, and the extension of elementary education. Therefore increasing illegitimacy could be seen as the expression of a new self-realising subject, more and more liberated from old social and moral rules through a free(r) sexual life.

The critics of this hypothesis stress socio-economic and legal factors, given that illegitimacy had existed in rural areas for centuries. Legitimate and illegitimate fertility even followed similar seasonal patterns, high during wintertime and low during the intensive working phase in summer. In interrogation protocols one finds mostly the following pattern: premarital conceptions and illegitimate births resulted from long-term relationships and took place after a marriage promise, not only among the rural lower classes and servants but also among non-inheriting siblings. Illegitimacy was not primarily a class-specific phenomenon, but one of access to the family inheritance. At the end of the eighteenth century this started to change and there were increasing rates in regions with the *Anerbenrecht* form of inheritance, which did not force peasants to split their estates. Illegitimacy was also high during the first phase of the agrarian revolution in regions of large estates with a high demand for workers, recruited from unmarried servants, siblings of heirs to estates and their illegitimate children. Demand for labour led to increasing mobility and eroded the patriarchal dependency of servants. The agrarian revolution was an important factor in the increase of the rural proletariat, a group with much concubinage and high illegitimacy rates. All poor and unpropertied social groups were subject to the tightening up of political marriage restrictions (*Ehekonsens*) from the 1820s, enforced in Germany until 1868–70 and in most of the Austro-Hungarian Empire until 1868.

The polarisation of rural society into well-to-do peasants and poor lower classes (frequently living in concubinage) seems to have altered the orientation of peasant culture towards Christian matrimony. Erosion of the power of the head of the household apparently widened the scope of rural workers' practices. In extreme cases peasants were forced to accept servants having lovers, completely contrary to traditional law and order. In Württemberg Neckarhausen (from the 1830s) female servants remained single and had their illegitimate children fostered, having decided to live without husbands while they could earn their highest wages. Premarital conceptions and additional legitimation of non-marital children were so widespread in Carinthia that the term *Carinthian wedding* was devised: non-marital pregnancies were not considered shameful if there was intention and the chance to marry. But in most rural regions high illegitimacy rates were due to fluctuations in the labour market and rural exodus leading to less stable affairs between servants. Records of infanticide reveal that an illegitimate child was still an existential threat for the 'abandoned woman'.

Within the village, illegitimacy, like sexual deviance in general, was assessed according to a variety of factors. Family and household, neighbours, peer groups and, ultimately, the whole community participated in the production and regulation of sexual desire. This was true also in cases of sexual violence against females. Rape within and outside the family was regulated in the first instance by family and village. Where offences within marriage came to court, men of all social classes stressed their marital rights and the female duty of marital coitus. Outside marriage female victims had to prove that they had not provoked the man, had defended their honour, did not experience pleasurable sensations and, especially, were not promiscuous. This gender-specific definition of sexual desire became an important perspective in the middle-class vision of a new society during the eighteenth century.

The power of sexual drives and the weakness of respectable man – the middle classes

In German historiography middle-class sexuality has had a distinct emphasis, with literary and scientific discourses primarily the focus of analysis. Few serious investigations use other sources, such as autobiographical writings or court records, which might present a more differentiated picture of the socio-sexual practices and sexual acts and desires of the middle classes. Therefore this section concentrates on the two most important middle-class discourses on sexuality in the German-speaking countries during the eighteenth and nineteenth centuries: the scientific discourses on masturbation and on female desire. These provide insight into the styles of thinking and imagination of their producers – middle-class men (mostly in academic professions). The discursive construction of sexuality also became a driving force in the self-interpretation of the middle-class subject from the final decades of the eighteenth century, contributing to social practice and the emergence of middle-class identity.

Medicine, psychiatry and pedagogy supplied central impulses for the development of discourses on sexuality. From the late eighteenth century these located the 'natural place' of gender difference in the genitals, the nervous system and the brain. Medical, psychological and pedagogic scientists based their new moral and social system on these postulated 'facts of nature'. But they also focused on the (self-)construction of sexual desire. In their view the new middle-class body was the most personal property of the individuum, differentiated from the artificial body of the nobility. It was to be used appropriately to its 'nature'; not beyond a certain degree and in support of life energies: 'natural behaviour', 'health', 'efficiency' were recurrent demands, aiming at productive use of sexual desire; both to shape individual destiny and to construct middle-class society. Middle-class virtues such as vitality, energy and activity were metaphorically united in the sexual drive and materially in the genitals.

However, men and women were tied to sexuality in a different way. Female being and (gender) identity were bound to the genitals and their effects on the nervous system and the brain. Meanwhile male scientists questioned female sexual desire: in their imagination (and writings) active female desire, so-called female *Wollust* (lust) mutated to passive *Liebestrieb*, desire for love, during the eighteenth century. Under the old view *Wollust* occupied only part of female existence – also true for the male – but *desire for love* could influence the entire female being. This was coded in relation to the male *Wollust* – to be cultivated and satisfied but also pacified by the first. Along with reproduction, this new sexual task formed the main contribution of women to the further development of civilisation and the realisation of the civil society. This passive form of sexuality denied women any possibility of achieving the most important qualities of middle-class men – working actively and rationally for individuation and participation in middle-class society. The sexual wishes and fears of the (male) creators of sexual knowledge defined this new ideal. During the first half of the nineteenth century a new academic (sub)discipline, 'gynaecology', defined women as determined by the pathological processes of their genital organs (e.g. during puberty and menstruation), postulating direct connections with the brain and nervous system and thereby legitimising physicians to operate on the supposed physiological causes of nervous disease.

During the last two decades of the eighteenth century the discourse on masturbation focused directly on the male body. Boys and men were the targets of physicians and also philanthropists, the first professional pedagogues in the German-speaking areas. Still influenced by the old humoral theory, scientists believed that the unnatural loss of semen, the most important human fluid, would lead not only to bodily ruin but to persisting and incurable mental damage. The basic conditions of middle-class society were questioned and polarised in the metaphoric code of masturbation discourse: reason versus (sexual) desire, moderation versus excess, promotion of life versus the fight against death. They feared that the destruction of the *ancien régime* would suspend existing sexual morality, leaving sexual desire unregulated, leading to inevitable social and political chaos.

During the second half of the nineteenth century, discourses on sexuality were also initiated via assumed connections between the genitals and the brain/nervous system and the theory of evolution, especially ideas of degeneration. Two hypotheses linked the two fields: ontogenesis was believed to copy phylogenesis, while scientists designated the (occidental) male as the climax of phylogenetic development. However, women – as well as lower-class people and Jews – were located near so-called *primitives*, allegedly closer to nature and dominated by atavistic drives, their apparently pathological genital–brain complex embodying wrong developments during the process of civilisation.

At the end of the nineteenth century a broad grouping of theorists as well as practical men saw female sexuality as an important element of the woman question. Did intellectual work negatively affect reproductive capacity? Were females predestined to mental motherhood? These and similar questions dominated debates about the natural social roles of men and women during the *fin de siècle*. The ideology of a special female sexuality was a perfect instrument for, by a discourse of substitution, discussing and canalising the crisis of male middle-class identity. As Christina von Braun has emphasised, the sex-identity of the male was located *in* the female and *embodied* by her. In many cases these discourses were wishful thinking by isolated scientists. But such scientific constructions of sexuality could be found in practical and popular works, household manuals, popular medical writings and encyclopaedias. Following the reading revolution of the late eighteenth century, these texts were employed as advisers by middle-class men and women.

Fiction was also influential in constructing sexual knowledge. The literary concept of reasonable love was transformed into romantic love during the eighteenth and nineteenth centuries, with sexualisation of the love ideal as one outcome. At the end of the eighteenth century the old social order was gradually questioned through sexualised motifs. A characteristic trope for the dissolution of boundaries between nobility and middle classes was 'infanticide': a nobleman seduces a middle-class girl without intending marriage; after the birth of an illegitimate child, the woman – who still loves the nobleman – kills the baby in an attack of madness. In a second fashionable motif, 'incest', authors problematised new emotional and sexual intimacy within the family. And last but not least, from the late eighteenth century literary discourse also centred on the conditions for middle-class marriage, querying whether friendship or erotic love formed the proper basis for lifelong partnership. Finally, in Romanticism the ideal of the love match overcame rational argument. Niklas Luhmann has emphasised that gender bias was maintained: in the love code of the nineteenth century, 'the male loves love, the female loves the man' (Luhmann 1982; 172).

The actual relationship between middle-class love and sexual desire remains controversial. Autobiographical writings prove that the ideal had wide resonance. With increasing domestic privacy new intimate and more reflective forms of sexual practice emerged. But the love match did not have the importance ascribed in fiction: money, social status and prestige dominated partner selection. During the nineteenth century among the middle classes love, intimacy and sexual desire were emotions which had material causes and were constructed through communication and body contacts during marriage. Because of wide age differences between spouses – ten years and more was usual – conflicts persisted between the very different views, ideals and experiences of love and sexuality of men and women.

On the way to respectability – sexual desire among the working classes

For a long time the history of proletarian sexuality was determined by the bourgeois ideology of contemporary observers, and even some socialist theorists painted a rather one-sided picture of working-class sexual desire and experience. According to this, male and female workers no longer repressed their sexual drives, as a result of changing working and housing conditions, particularly overcrowding (leading to precocious sexual knowledge), collaboration of the sexes at work (permanently stimulating sexual acts), lack of social surveillance (preventing sanctions against deviant behaviour) and religious and cultural deracination (preventing internalisation of moral norms). To bourgeois authors it was also clear that the materialistic and atheistic ideology spread by the labour movement contributed to this moral decline. The consequences of unrestricted proletarian sexuality seemed especially visible in big cities: high illegitimacy rates, numerous abortions, increasing urban prostitution, widespread venereal diseases and – after the turn of the century – dramatically decreasing birth rates. To combat the apparently excessive sexual lives of the working classes various measures were proposed: some advocated the Malthusian way of total sexual abstinence (assisted by a general anti-marriage policy for the lower classes) and others neo-Malthusian regulation of the sexual drive (with strong efforts towards domesticisation of the working classes).

The new history of sexuality emphasises that contemporary authors were greatly influenced by their own bourgeois morality. This interpretative revision has been based on sources – contemporary sexual surveys and reports, memoirs and autobiographies, oral history interviews of workers, more detailed demographic analysis exploring the general conditions for the emergence and shaping of sexual desires in the proletarian environment – which reveal a rather different picture. The sexual as well as family lives of workers now appear more heterogeneous: class membership was not the only important factor constituting proletarian sex-life – education, religious affiliation, social origin, urban or rural background, material conditions and the prospects for setting up a family were also important.

The variants of proletarian sexual life may be located between the following poles: first-generation unskilled and semi-skilled workers, mostly Catholics living in a rural environment or of peasant background; and second- and third-generation skilled workers, educated at least to primary level, organised in the labour movement, and Protestant or less influenced by the church. The sexuality of the first pole remained closer to peasant constructions; that of the second approached bourgeois ideology. Workers did not just adopt or imitate bourgeois sexual practices: in spite of differences within the working classes there was a specifically proletarian construction of sexual desires during the nineteenth and twentieth centuries.

In contrast to contemporary bourgeois images, proletarian sexual life was not free, unrestricted or unsuppressed, as evidenced in perceptions of the sexual in everyday family life. Though most lived in crowded circumstances, children never – or only secretly – watched their parents' sexual activities and, when they did so, the experience never became a topic of family conversation. If several people slept in one bed – experienced by children as positive emotional and physical contact – there was mostly strict separation of sexes. The silence around sexual matters caused children to associate their observations, and also their own sexual experiences such as masturbation or menstruation, with uncertainty, shame and fear. In spite of all strategies to conceal sex, workers and their children nevertheless had attitudes to the body which differed from the middle classes'. Until the 1860s and 1870s, nakedness, for example during bathing or even in the factory, seemed to cause no moral outrage. Only after the end of the nineteenth century did there arise a more prudish relationship with the body and a lower threshold of shame.

Around the mid nineteenth century autobiographers mentioned 'sexual victimisation stemming directly from the particular vulnerability of poor children and adolescents both in the home and in the workplace' (Maynes 1992: 406). Because of the many non-related household members – above all in the sub-proletarian environment – sexual matters were not concealed to the same extent. But this did not provide any positive sex education for co-resident children and adolescents, and the negative reactions arising from ignorance and silence might cause lifelong rejection of sexual matters. Adolescents gained their earliest sexual knowledge and sometimes their first experiences among friends and in the workplace. According to autobiographies, the factory was a very important place for constructing working-class desire; sex was a major topic but approached only indirectly via risqué remarks, crude jokes and ambiguous talks on intimate affairs between adults and the married – curiously watched by the young and unmarried. This 'sex education' in the workplace led to the internalisation of certain sexual norms for men and women and supported the construction of both positive and negative sexual objects. The qualities rendering a person desirable or repulsive could be learnt, and how to distinguish potential candidates for sexual relations and marriage from dissipated, unfaithful and corrupted individuals. Especially for females, workplace gossip determined who belonged among the moral workers and who were classified as 'fallen' women or potential prostitutes.

But sexual gossip in the workplace was not necessarily an affirmative sex education. In most autobiographies analysed, the first sexual experiences at the factory were determined by insecurity – similarly experiences with non-related lodgers and persons who came only to sleep in the workers' household. Carola Lipp stressed that many male adolescents experienced (and sometimes only dreamt about) their first sexual 'adventures' as seduction by an older 'lascivious' woman. Because of the common household constellation within the workers' family, these young men moved 'between powerless feelings towards women experienced as strong and identification with paternal aggressiveness. The tension between these two poles partly explains male showing-off of strength, and the pressure and even aggression, occasionally involved in sexual acts in the workers' environment' (Lipp 1990: 229).

Young women often experienced their first sexual acts as traumatic; harassment and abuse were significant aspects of their experience. The socio-sexual power relations between the sexes were manifested in the sexual conditions and relationships in the factory. Young women were often confronted with unwanted sexual advances and sexual blackmail from foremen or white-collar workers taking advantage of their position. This might explain why the respectable working classes supposed that sexual excess and exploitation were characteristics of the bourgeoisie and therefore dissociated themselves from sex or thought they should not be exposed to such immorality.

Most workers' first sexual contacts took place within a relatively stable relationship or engagement – but quite early, at the age of sixteen or seventeen. In the urban working-class environment traditional peasant forms of choosing a sexual and marriage partner were replaced by regulation by family, neighbourhood and workmates, who supported certain relationships and demonstrated acceptance or condemned misalliances through gossip and other sanctions. But these forms of regulation were continuously losing effectiveness within anonymous working and living conditions. The number of delayed legitimations – indicating social pressures on parents of illegitimate children – clearly declined. Female workers got into complicated sexual bargains, granting sexual favours in exchange for the limited material security of future marriage. Acceding too fast to a sexual offer threatened a woman's reputation; on the other hand, continued denial reduced her chances on the marriage market.

Many couples experienced before marriage that sexual contacts led to illegitimate children. Political marriage restrictions prevented from marrying people without property and lacking adequate savings or income (in some regions factory work was not accepted as sufficient). Some couples postponed marriage because they could not afford to start a household. Some fathers did not keep their promise of marriage. The highest rate of illegitimacy in the working classes was reached in the mid nineteenth century and declined slightly during its final decades, a trend which accelerated during the first decades of the twentieth century, first among skilled workers, then among the unskilled.

Sometimes interpreted as the last relics of a specifically peasant sexual culture, these phenomena were based on totally different socio-sexual logic, common to urban and rural lower classes, among whom delaying the consummation of sexual desire seemed necessary only if marriage was imminent – a highly uncertain prospect for younger workers with low wages and insecure employment. After the decision to marry or to 'get together' there were no moral incentives to postpone consummation. In a social background where affection and love – not to mention sexual matters – were seldom spoken of, sexual experiences were central to emotional communication, the creation of physical closeness and the construction of a feeling of 'being together'. 'We shall marry if we expect a baby' was the (sometimes unspoken) agreement of working-class couples – but then the date of marriage was postponed from birth to birth.

From most accounts, patriarchy in working-class families resulted in very different forms of male and female sexual desire. Male workers were described as insisting on their 'marital rights', as occasionally violent and as not very co-operative over family planning. Male workers' self-image as the supporter of the family – which did not correspond to the actuality of substantial female contributions to household income – favoured their own emotional and sexual needs. Because of long working hours, sexual life was reduced to weekend evenings at the time when husbands returned from bars. Oral history interviews with Berlin workers during the Weimar Republic show that violence was an 'almost ritual, habitual, banal, omnipresent part of life which also determined its rhythm' (Brücker 1995: 349).

For female workers violence was one reason why most saw sex increasingly as a burden and threat, while the chance of further pregnancies, dangerous births and an additional person to feed apparently had a negative effect on sexual desire. While in peasant households increasing numbers of children also meant more available labourers and future security for aged peasants, in the workers' family, especially after the prohibition of child labour, a large number of children meant resources were no longer sufficient and the family was exposed to the 'poverty trap'. Fear of conception, refusal of the husband's undesired advances and above all contraceptive measures form vital elements in all autobiographical writings by female workers. However, in many cases, male workers interpreted their wives' attitude as undermining their own marital rights and made this an occasion for violence and also as legitimating contact with prostitutes.

The working classes still had a very high rate of abortion during the first decades of the twentieth century. Terminations were carried out by the women concerned, female neighbours or professional abortionists and more or less formed part of the everyday experience of most women. Apart from traditional herbal abortifacients, instruments and chemicals were employed; none the less abortion was still extremely dangerous, with possible sequelae of infection and internal injury. Interruption of pregnancies in the working-class milieu was primarily practised by older married female workers.

Prevention of pregnancy was thus of central concern to female workers. In a 1914 survey 65–75 per cent of workers mentioned practising some kind of birth control, most frequently the rather risky practice of *coitus interruptus*, which required male co-operation. Douching, employed by many women, was very unreliable. Because of cost, condoms were not widely used until the 1920s. Pessaries and diaphragms were complicated to use and involved an expensive visit to the doctor. Sexual abstinence and non-coital sex seem also to have been practised but have hardly been investigated. For urban, educated groups of workers it may be true, as James Woycke declared in a more general form, that:

> During the 1920s, the third stage of diffusion saw the mass acceptance of modern [mechanical and chemical] contraception by people in all classes of society. The impact of war, revolution, and inflation intensified socio-economic pressures to control fertility; more extensive and overt marketing and advertising increased awareness and availability of contraceptives.
>
> (Woycke 1988: 169)

Changing attitudes towards family limitation, especially increased prevalence of the view that everybody can take charge of his or her own life course as well as of the 'fate' of their children, and the decline of fatalistic and religious beliefs, were a significant precondition for increased demand for new and cheaper contraceptives. In memoirs and autobiographies workers expressed gender-specific arguments concerning the question of contraception. Women wanted to limit the number of children from fears of additional work and the negative implications for their own health; men because of the burden on household finances. Many factors caused this alteration in working-class mentality, including secularisation by the urban way of life, ideologisation by social democratic and communist parties and improvement of the elementary school system (increase in literacy), as well as the increasing movement towards bourgeois family ideals. In Max Marcuse's interviews with three hundred couples in 1917 many workers thought that a large number of children was synonymous with unmodern behaviour. For workers at the beginning of the twentieth century it was the case that 'a minimum of intimacy and individuality ... is both the condition and the consequence of a smaller number of children' (Rosenbaum 1992: 194). In general the bourgeois domesticisation of the working classes was pushed ahead by success in forming families, extensive family planning and regulating sexual desire.

Economic and social misery was also the reason why female workers became prostitutes. Among lower-income groups the boundary between a transitional form of prostitution – regarded by women as a legitimate deal with their own body during periods of economic uncertainty – and a professional one was difficult to determine. This may explain why promiscuous or prostitutional behaviour was registered and strictly sanctioned, particularly by female workers. But a distinction has to be drawn between social strata within the working classes: respectable workers accused poorer workers of immoral behaviour and even having prostitutes as wives, and declared themselves free from such 'dirty vices'. Meanwhile the contemporary bourgeoisie suspected all female workers of being potential 'whores'. Along with the debate on combating venereal diseases the 'question of prostitution' became the starting point for increasing politicisation and medicalisation of sexual desire during the second half of the nineteenth and the first half of the twentieth century.

The politicisation and medicalisation of prostitution

From the mid nineteenth century political, scientific and church observers agreed that the supposed increase in the number of prostitutes in large cities was responsible for the seemingly rapid spread of venereal diseases. However, recent historical studies demonstrate that their statistics have to be handled with the utmost caution: the landscape of prostitution in Germany and Austria in the nineteenth and early twentieth centuries was dominated by individual street prostitutes rather than the brothel system of former centuries. The law did not permit prostitution as such, but transferred powers of regulation to the local police, the vice squad, acting on local directions. Prostitutes' customers – we know little about their social profile – were not prosecuted. Criminalisation led to a very incomplete rate of registering prostitutes and thus to unrepresentative statistics. Therefore, published figures on prostitution – for example in Vienna thirty to fifty thousand prostitutes – were based on estimates and tell us more about the moral indignation of the producers.

Similarly, people disagreed about definitions. The maximal version of the Viennese police in 1861 included not only professional prostitutes but also 'occasional whores' – women who provided 'indecent satisfaction' not as a business but from 'greed'. The police also wanted to observe private mistresses and kept women, and for them 'prostitution' became a metaphor for all non-marital sexual activities of women. Given such unreliable data, it is not legitimate to speak of a (rapid) increase of prostitution from the mid nineteenth century. Even the increased number of registered prostitutes cannot bear this interpretation, because of differing rates of registration.

The social origins of prostitutes was a long-standing controversy. According to contemporary opinion – revived by some historians – a large number had worked as urban domestic servants, the rest as waitresses, actresses and the like. Recent studies have shown that prostitutes were recruited primarily from the lower classes and socially declining groups of the middle classes, whose professional classification varied over the years. Both the assumption that domestic servants especially tended to practise prostitution, and the contemporary myth that no 'fallen' woman could return to normal existence, turned out to be wrong. 'For a considerable proportion of females even before the turn of the century prostitution was a phase especially in periods of unemployment and they did not continue the business' (Jušek 1993: 78).

The expansion of street prostitution – forced by strict police persecution of any form of procuration – had the effect that, in a sense, prostitutes became a part of the supply of goods in cities, their bodies regarded as having exchange value in the general marketplace. Though prostitution was concentrated in certain areas, it became

153

more publicly visible. To the respectable bourgeoisie this symbolised definite moral decline. However, around 1900 prostitution was not merely discussed as a moral problem but interpreted as a sign of the adverse development of modern urban society – isolation, allegedly spreading 'nervosity' and the supposed disruption of family life through sexual excess and venereal diseases. In consequence large prohibited areas were erected which prostitutes were not allowed to enter. Police measures were strengthened to include investigations and observations, and also coercive inspection of registered prostitutes and even many other women suspected by the police of being prostitutes.

Vice squad infringements against 'respectable women' and also the first investigations and reports about the miserable living conditions of prostitutes led to vehement criticism of police methods. Representatives of the bourgeois and proletarian women's movement in particular, members of morality societies and abolitionists, agitated against existing regulation. Some of them turned against the unequal treatment of males and females under the law and also against coercive inspections (imposed only on women); others demanded general moral renewal or total abolition of all regulation. Regardless of the faction to which critics belonged, their common aim was to address at public protest meetings and in newspaper articles the 'double standard' of bourgeois society.

Yet they disagreed strongly about the causes of prostitution. One opinion was that catastrophic social and economic conditions mainly forced women into prostitution; others believed that the 'born whore' – the female equivalent of so-called 'born criminals' – was condemned to her business by 'moral insanity'. Public debate about prostitution made it possible also to address the sexual desires of men: even those who thought that men had a stronger sexual drive demanded that male sexual behaviour should be restricted to marital intercourse. The *syphilisation* of the prostitute and the stigmatisation of her behaviour as congenital disease, as well as the criminalisation of her 'occupation', were expected to cause men to reject this kind of sexual activity. However, one of the most serious consequences of the politicisation and medicalisation of prostitution at the turn of the century was the fact that the 'prostitute developed from an amateur to a "professional", who no longer regarded her activities as a survival strategy in difficult economic periods, but as an occupation' (Ulrichs 1994: 147).

Because of the inefficiency of registration and control over clandestine prostitutes, the surveillance system was increasingly attacked. After 1900 a swing of opinion among all factions involved can be noticed, for instance at the 1903 and 1905 congresses of the German Society for the Fight Against Venereal Diseases (Deutsche Gesellschaft zur Bekämpfung der Geschlechtskrankheiten). Within the German Empire Prussia in 1907 ended the surveillance of prostitution – on condition that prostitutes underwent periodical medical inspections. This first attempt at decriminalisation failed because of resistance by the vice squad, which in practice continued to act according to the penal law. During the First World War there was even further tightening up of regulation by the military administration, which regarded the health of soldiers as supreme. Brothels were permitted in the areas behind the war zone, but means to protect both prostitutes and clients had to be provided. The Law for the Fight against Venereal Diseases (1927) finally abolished coercive measures in Germany and established that prostitutes could move around freely (except in the neighbourhood of churches and schools). Public health offices continued to ask for health certificates and, in the case of venereal infections, ordered medical treatment and supervision. The police could take action only if a prostitute offended against decency or invited to sexual offence in a 'molesting manner'.

The revival of regulation and the return of the brothels during National Socialism cannot be interpreted as an expression of Nazi moral condemnation of extramarital sexual desires. On the contrary prostitution was totally subordinated to Nazi health policy. They saw a ready-made solution against venereal diseases in replacing street prostitution with a system of brothels. During the Second World War the Wehrmacht ran about five hundred brothels in the occupied territories, in which prostitutes' health was checked and soldiers had to use freely distributed condoms; they also had to disinfect after intercourse in special rooms. There were sixty similar brothels for coerced workers (*Zwangsarbeiter*) until 1943. From 1942 brothels were installed in concentration camps, in which women inmates were forced to work.

According to Nazi ideology all prostitutes belonged to the category of 'mentally and morally inferior' persons, and thus became victims of coercive eugenic sterilisations from the beginning of the Nazi regime. They shared this fate with a group which from the late nineteenth century increasingly became central in medical, political and public discourse – the homosexuals.

The 'homosexual' between penalisation, psychiatry and emancipation

Around 1800 in German-speaking countries there were three distinct discourses on same-sex (erotic) desire: 'The moral theology of love, the cultural history of male eros, and an enlightened vision of Sokratic love' (Hekma 1989: 439). Because of the anthropological turn of the Enlightenment, the first increasingly lost its importance; the second changed during Romanticism into an ascetic, anti-erotic image of male friendship; the last, however, led to the first apologias for erotic male love during the nineteenth century. These apologias made public a form of sexual desire referred to as the 'unmentionable sin' until the eighteenth century. During the first half of the nineteenth century same-sex desire was still discussed along the lines of the classical *Male Love of the Greeks* – the title of Heinrich Hössli's decisive work published in 1836–8. With Karl Heinrich Ulrichs's writings about the *Mysteries of Male–Male Love* (1864–79) the debate gained a new quality: thenceforward autobiographical records and philosophical, medical and anthropological reflections aimed at social emancipation of the *Urninge*.

A major task of this emancipation discourse was reform of the penal law. After the abolition of capital punishment for sodomy and same-sex offences (Austria, 1787/1803, Prussia, 1794), some countries continued liberalising their codes, while, in German territories in which the Code Pénal was implemented, simple and consensual same-sex acts were no longer punished. In Austrian penal law, however (established 1803, tightened up 1852), same-sex sexual offences in general were punished with several years' prison; in the Prussian *Allgemeines Landrecht* (1794) only sexual offences between men. The 1851 revision of the Prussian penal law defined same-sex acts as only a minor offence, nevertheless imposing prison from six months to four years. In 1871 the Prussian, not the more liberal Bavarian, version, became article 175 in the penal law of the German Empire.

This situation explains why research on *Homosexualität* – a term introduced by Austro-Hungarian author Karl Maria Kertbeny in 1869 – in Germany and Austria was dominated by sexual-pathological investigations and the views of sexual science. Before the 1860s 'old' forensic medicine and physiologically orientated physicians were consulted concerning same-sex offences. From the 1870s 'new' sexual pathologists increasingly took their place. Psychiatrists, mainly, developed a comprehensive system of *psychopathia sexualis* initially for legal and clinical use, eventually for the wider public interested in medical and psychological questions. Within this system contrary sexual feeling was most prominent. Mutual influences between the empirical discourse of emancipation, psychiatric casuistry and scientific theory-building can be observed: in many cases patients identified themselves in the medical categorisations and explanation of *psychopathia sexualis*, and their self-reports strongly influenced the psychiatric construction of knowledge.

Both sides focused on the nature and causes of homosexuality. Following contemporary degeneration theories, some thought that homosexuality was a pathological and degenerate aberration in evolution; others defined it as one of manifold natural variations or 'intermediate stages' of human sexual life. According to the latter view, homosexual acts should be judged not by legal but by moral norms. Most participants in the discussion saw the homosexual's personality as highly determined by the sexual, with no facet of physical or psychic life uninfluenced by the sexual peculiarity – homosexuals were supposed to be the marionettes of their sexual desires. Psychiatrists and sexual scientists declared themselves to be specialists in exploring the genuine homosexual self as well as treating 'contrary sexual feelings'.

Same-sex desires between women did not become an object of study until the 1890s, when female homosexuals were included in systems designed for men. If the male homosexual lacked manliness, his female counterpart – the so-called 'man-woman' – had too much. With the psychologisation and psychiatrisation of the homosexual, not only was anal penetration – believed to mimic heterosexual coitus – interpreted as a sexual offence but also acts which only resembled penetration. The specific psychic constitution of the male and female homosexual became of more interest than actual acts.

The publications of scientists, statements of persons concerned and of various institutions fighting against the laws discriminating against homosexuals had little effect on policy-making. Politicians were primarily interested in whether the state could legitimately interfere in moral matters. Even the repeatedly submitted petitions of Magnus Hirschfeld's Scientific-Humanitarian Committee (Wissenschaftlich-humanitäres Komitee, WhK) and his attempts to bring the discussion on to a more rational scientific level did not alter the situation. Even the WhK survey (1903/4) which asked about the sexual orientation of some thousands of Berlin students and metal workers attracted public attention but did not effect a legal reform (6.0 per cent of the students answered that they were partly and 1.5 per cent that they were exclusively gay; among the metal workers the percentages were 4.3 and 1.1). The Krupp, Bülow, Eulenburg and Moltke scandals were the reason why article 175 became a topic in everyday fights between political parties. Left-wing parties in particular denounced existing judicial practice as class justice and spoke of homosexual bonding and moral decline at the highest levels of government.

After the First World War freedom of opinion, press and assembly led to a boom in homosexual organisations and publications and films on the topic. It was a time of flourishing gay and lesbian subcultures, with bars and music halls in the bigger cities. For the most important sex reform institution of the interwar period, the Berlin Institute for Sexual Science (founded in 1919), the fight for the liberation of homosexuals was one of its essential tasks. In the 1920s social democratic and communistic parties even spoke (more or less) for the abolition of punishment for consensual same-sex acts. Nevertheless article 175 remained unreformed during the interwar period. Members of the left parties did not restrain themselves from using the reproach of homosexuality: the Röhm affair especially contributed to the stereotype of the homosexual Nazi – a myth also propagated by anti-Fascist exiles.

Nazi sexual and health policies were designed against same-sex desire. According to Nazi biological racism, homosexuals threatened the growth of the *Volk*, quantitatively by wasting procreative potential, and qualitatively through their alleged 'hereditary inferiority'. But Nazi homophobia was based also on the difficult demarcation between homosocial and homoerotic relationships within their own organisations. Homosexuality was seen as a contagious social disease, which could spread easily via Nazi male bonds, especially within the *Wehrmacht*, and thereby destroy 'pure' male friendships. After 1935 the penal law imposed sentences of up to ten years both on sexual acts resembling intercourse and on all other forms of male–male sexual contacts. Sexual acts between females were not covered, as Nazi ideology defined women as completely dependent on men in sexual matters, and lesbian relationships were considered an insignificant social issue which would not endanger the *Volksgemeinschaft*.

Unlike the Holocaust, persecution of homosexuals was neither planned nor carried out systematically: although courts sentenced some fifty thousand persons for 'offences against nature' (*Unzucht wider die Natur*) before 1945 and the Central Office for the Fight Against Homosexuality and Abortion (Reichszentrale zur Bekämpfung der Homosexualität und Abtreibung, founded in 1936 by secret order of Heinrich Himmler) and Gestapo recorded about ninety thousand persons, '"only" between 5,000 and 15,000 of these persons were deported to the concentration camps' (Oosterhuis 1994: 389). From the outbreak of war capital punishment was introduced for 'exceptionally hard cases' of homosexuality. It is impossible to estimate the number of persons suspected to be homosexuals or sentenced under article 175 forced to undergo medical 'treatment', i.e. castration or sterilisation, coercive measures which could be imposed for various homosexual crimes after 1933. In subsequent years, so-called 'voluntary' sterilisation was introduced as a precondition for release from 'preventive custody' and as a chance to escape deportation to a concentration camp. The National Socialists continued a process – at least as regards political and scientific discussion of various measures – going back to the late nineteenth century.

Birth control and the struggle for modernity

At the turn of the century demographers discovered that even in central Europe, not only in nations such as France, regarded as decadent and degenerate, had the fertility rate declined. Thenceforward the reproductive behaviour of the population became a long-term political issue in Austria and Germany. Population statistics seemed to confirm the worst fears about nations dying out: until the turn of the century the crude birth ratio (the number of live births per thousand inhabitants) was between 30 and 40, then declined rapidly to 10–20. Apart from other regional differences, Protestant areas started earlier and took off faster than Catholic ones. In the case of Germany there was a close relationship between urban and rural fertility rates. Workers had the highest fertility, the amorphous group of independents experienced intermediate levels, and officials and salaried employees had fewest children. The difference between the last group and the first two however, at least in absolute terms, was less for more recent cohorts because of differences in cohort-to-cohort fertility reduction. Within the first three decades of the twentieth century – less than two generations – the number of marital births had fallen by half.

Thus, for many politicians and scientists the 'question of procreation' became the most important question in modern 'civilised nations', and the fight against the declining birth rate seemed imperative for the maintenance of the state, the economy and military strength. But this demographic perspective and fear that the nation might be eliminated was only one aspect. In German-language areas the debate began when the fertility decline was not perceived as very threatening: in contrast to France, where the birth rate declined much earlier and the demographic transition was discussed intensively following the 1856 census, in Germany even around 1900 it was seen as a consequence of demographic normalisation, given the extremely high fertility rates (about 37–9 births per thousand females) up to the 1880s.

More important than worries about the future demographic development of the nation state were fears of the radical upheavals of modernity and of social, economic and cultural chaos. Critics of modernity have rightly recognised the change in sexual behaviour as a factor in cultural and social upheaval. The national 'procreation question' made possible discussion of another delicate side of modernisation, just about being solved by a major part of the population: the separation of sexual desire from reproduction. The critics of individual birth control within churches, political parties and morality associations wanted to maintain and revive the old system, deploying not only moral arguments but increasingly theories from the (natural) sciences. These included eugenics and race hygiene, influenced not yet by images of degeneration but by the idea of increasing 'procreation quality' to reduce social misery, diseases and crime. The arguments of the opponents of conscious birth control – who still dominated the discourse before the First World War – reveal that this was not only a fight over social hegemony but also a gender conflict. Active female sexual desire aimed at pleasure not procreation was seen as a degeneration of the sexual drive and described as leading to the destruction of marriage, the family and posterity.

In comparison to the large number of opponents of birth control, only a few German eugenicists and racial hygienists recommended neo-Malthusianism (continence and the use of contraceptives) and eugenic measures (castration and sterilisation of people who would not improve 'population quality'). Early eugenic thinking focused on improving the quality of life in industrial society. For most socialist theorists regulation of procreation was important: the future socialist 'power man' would be created by both social progress and biological improvement based on scientific research. Only a few (mostly female) social democratic politicians spoke for practical use of contraceptives and so-called 'preventive intercourse'. In the 'birth strike debate' within the German Social Democratic Party (1913) the vast majority of male party members spoke against these interests of women, believing that female birth denial would undermine the class struggle and that the use of contraceptives was indecent, unaesthetic and an expression of sexual denial.

During the First World War everybody who supported birth control was regarded as a national enemy. Contraception was thought to jeopardise the demographic and military strength of the nation, and most political parties accepted the idea that the state should intervene to favour natality. The wartime 'abortion panic' contributed to this attitude: medical surveys showed that for the women concerned abortion meant nothing morally reprehensible and criminal and that there was a discrepancy between strict abortion laws – the Austrian (article 144) and German (article 218) penal code threatened up to five years' prison – and abortion practice.

Even after the war conflicts about abortion continued. For conservatives, it signalled the catastrophic moral state of society in general and of the working classes in particular. With their exceptionally low birth rates and large number of abortions the working classes were regarded as sexually anarchic. The left, however, saw regulation of abortion as unjust social legislation, which ignored the crimes of the rich. While the first demanded increased penalties, the latter supported an indication model for abortions. Even leading figures on the left spoke against individual freedom of choice, and wanted to make the decision for abortion dependent on social and eugenic factors and agreement by the public health officers. Although left parties did not really support the idea of sex reform in general, they led a broad social movement against the abortion paragraphs. In Germany their campaigns led to the most liberal abortion law in western Europe, with simple abortion only a minor offence with low sentences. The Supreme Court of the Reich exempted abortions on medical indications from punishment in 1917.

The political struggle against abortion laws, and reports on the social and physical consequences of existing abortion practices, meant that contraceptives became increasingly accepted in the 1920s as the best means of rational family planning. Under the sexual offence laws advertisement and distribution of 'preventive means' – but not their manufacture – were still prohibited. Nevertheless contraceptives of every kind could be obtained as 'hygiene products' by mail-order and in chemists' shops. In bigger cities Sexual Information Centres and organisations of informed lay persons distributed contraceptives and even established contacts with doctors who performed abortions. From the mid-1920s physicians increasingly supported the use of contraceptives, which widened their authority and competence in the matter of sexual regulation. The medical profession also urgently warned against the most commonly practised method of contraception – *coitus interruptus* – and advised new chemical and mechanical means. In general the interwar period can be seen as having a more positive attitude towards sexual reforms – an attitude supported by psychoanalysts such as Sigmund Freud and popular writers on sex such as August Forel. Nevertheless the public debate on the 'procreation business' was still experienced by a large part of the population as 'causing a public nuisance'. Numerous sex scandals concerning literature, theatre and film also provide evidence of this common negative attitude.

New methods of birth control helped to spread more self-determined and less fearful sexual practices for females – and also for males. However, increasing medicalisation and politicisation of birth control led to further regulation, with state intervention in sexual matters seen as legitimate and even necessary. Physicians advanced to the position of sex specialists, to be consulted not only on individual problems but in political questions. Finally the discussion on population and health policy stressed the qualitative and not the quantitative improvement of the *Volkskörper*, the 'body' of the people. The discourses of the interwar period prepared the ground for Nazi ideology in many respects, but can also be differentiated by means of their plurality: the spectrum of opinion included Social Darwinists, who insisted on the social privileges of the fittest and demanded racial hygiene, as well as eugenists, who wanted to achieve better 'procreative hygiene' primarily through public welfare and preventive medicine.

Most advocates of all these 'schools', however, believed it necessary to prevent the most 'inferior' members of society from procreating. After the Great Depression of the late 1920s this opinion was strengthened by the belief that eugenic sterilisation could reduce welfare and health spending. The question of whether it should be carried out only with the consent of the person concerned or against his or her will was decided on the latter side: yet the laws were not changed and sterilisation was permitted only for medical reasons. Nevertheless – as in many other countries – even before the Nazis thousands of eugenically motivated sterilisations took place in Germany. As with many other questions of 'procreation' gender bias was obvious: a high percentage of the persons sterilised were 'inferior' women, thought to be a great danger to hereditary 'purity', and who, as unmarried mothers, would also be a burden on the state.

On the basis of the Law for the Prevention of Offspring with Hereditary Diseases (1933) about four hundred thousand eugenic sterilisations were carried out on 'inferior' persons, half of them female, under Nazi rule. These were ordered by law, carried out under compulsion and took place within a systematic inquiry apparatus. Anti-natalist interventions included prohibition of 'racially mixed marriages' and 'extramarital racial mixing' – according to the Law for the Protection of the German Blood and the German Honour (1935) – and of marriage of so-called 'people with hereditary diseases' – according to the Law for the Protection of the Hereditary Health of the German People (1935). Apart from the racial element, all diseases, deviations and anomalies included in Nazi policy had been discussed in psychiatry and eugenics during previous decades.

> Together with this 'antinatalist' measure, 'pronatalist' enactments like the wartime imposition of the death penalty for abortion, were part of a dual strategy for the state control of fertility. 'Compulsory motherhood' for 'valuable' Germans and 'compulsory sterilisation' for the 'unfit' were two faces of the Nazi 'body politics' which systematically deprived individuals of reproductive rights and freedoms.
>
> (Quine 1996: 92)

A range of pronatalist interventions by the Nazis included the 'matrimony loan' system, the 'Mother Cross' decoration and severe prosecution of individual abortions (coercive abortions on anti-natalist grounds were nevertheless practised). In principle sexual desire was seen as a positive force when connected with the hope of 'hereditary healthy' and 'racially pure' offspring. Christian moral objections were no longer important to the Nazis: this, among other things, resulted in illegitimate children no longer being stigmatised by law from 1940. In general, public health offices and officers became concerned with all sexual matters: their anamnesis, tests and inspections included questions on pregnancies, venereal diseases, impotence and sexual life in general. In thus doing, they made the sexual desires and feelings of nearly every person – not just the objects of forensic medicine – a topic of public communication.

In rural areas particularly these inspections, as well as information about (coercive) sterilisations, seem to have contributed to a more reflective attitude towards sex-life and, as Gisela Bock stressed, even to 'sexual enlightenment': those who had not known until then could read up in the leaflets of the Hereditary Health Courts that sterilisation ended the ability to procreate but did not reduce sexual pleasure, and that therefore lust and procreation were not necessarily linked. None the less, the Nazis were extremely conservative concerning individual birth control: the sale of contraceptives was strictly forbidden, and sexual activities other than for reproductive purposes were portrayed as being injurious to the body of the *Volk*.

The question of whether their pro-natalist and anti-natalist policies can be seen as the cause of the increase in fertility during the 1930s, or whether this was an effect of economic recovery after the years of depression, is still debated. There is, however, no doubt about the Nazis' attitude towards the 'sexual' characteristics of the genders: in Nazi ideology females were mainly defined as totally under the influence of the sexual: either active, demonic and engulfing vamps or pure, desexualised and conceiving mothers. The image of the male included the eugenically and racially 'pure' heterosexual 'power man', but incorporated male friendships and 'sterile' male bonds cleansed of sexual connotations.

What about sex? – commercialisation and 'liberalisation' after 1945

In the 1950s and 1960s a conservative sexual ideology was re-established, anchoring sexual life in marriage once more and defining sexual matters as personal and private. At the end of the 1960s the students' rebellion, women's liberation and the gay and lesbian emancipation movement initiated a period characterised by so-called 'sexual liberalisation'. During a single decade the idea of sexuality as well as major aspects of sexual behaviour, particularly of younger people, changed radically and led to almost entire destruction of the traditional model of marriage. Since then it has been of no importance whether sexual activities happen inside or outside of marriage, and questions of sexual experience and orgastic satisfaction were the focus of interest. During the 1980s and 1990s the construction of sexual desire has increasingly become a paradox: On the one hand the media commercialised sex and suggested that nothing was more important in life than sexual stimuli and satisfaction. On the other hand the results of empirical sex research showed that on average sexuality was and is still remote from the manifold practices presented in sex-talk shows on television. During recent years especially young people experienced a decline in sexual lust and a spread of erotic insensibility. Without going into details of the different developments in the German-speaking countries, this section deals with changes in the sexual lives of youth and young adults. Changes since the 1960s have been most far-reaching within these groups and have therefore been investigated in detail. (An extensive chapter on the general development of sexuality in the second half of the twentieth century can be found in my forthcoming study on the history of sexuality from 1700 to the present.)

In the period of reconstruction between 1945 and the 1960s an attitude of general renunciation and a very strict sexual morality orientated towards marriage and the family predominated. Public discourse of the 1950s and 1960s promoted virginity until marriage and especially rejected masturbation. Officials proceeded against *Schmutz- und Schundliteratur* (literature of mud and trash) and delegated sex education to parents alone. In 1949 the first representative survey of German sexual life revealed, however, that, in contrast to this discourse, the first changes in sexual practice could be observed. But until the mid-1960s young people, especially young women, continued to 'restrict their premarital coitus activities to their later marriage partner. Their "permissiveness in the case of love" was in reality "permissiveness in the case of love and the prospect of marriage"' (Schmidt 1993: 16).

The first shock for conservative sexual morality came from the new youth culture at the end of the 1950s. Rock 'n' roll *à la* 'Elvis the pelvis' and new youth journals like *Bravo* made sexuality a hot topic of public discussion. But the majority of Germans and Austrians once again turned against both female sexual expressiveness and the feminisation of men, 'reminiscent of Nazi hostility toward jazz and swing specifically and of Nazi attacks on Jews, blacks, homosexuals, and Sinti and Roma more generally … Taken together, these voices shaped … discourse in which a rejection of (female) sexual expressiveness was linked to definitions of black culture and working–class culture as sexual and therefore unacceptable' (Poiger 1996: 591). Nevertheless one has to stress that already ten years before the 'sexual revolution' young females especially repudiated the clean and un-erotic female type in their new fashion and dancing styles. They also questioned the self-restrained and controlling man, who represented the anti-type of the rock 'n' roller and the so-called *Halbstarke* (hood).

From the 1960s the rebellious rock 'n' roller was countered by the marketing of a soft, desexualised youth type, the 'teenager' (using the English word). Even though teenagers used words like 'sexy' and 'petting', they represented the retreat of the sexual into the private, anti-political life within marriage. While West German and Austrian youth culture and politics aimed at disciplined privati-sation of the sexual, East German officials tended to the contrary: after the building of the Berlin Wall in August 1961, the new youth culture was connected with anti-Americanism and with the capitalistic orientation of West Germany and therefore the officials in the East persecuted and disapproved of it more strongly than in the West.

During the late 1960s the 'dirty' secret that the postwar generation made out of sexuality – and also of their political past – was the reason why young people withdrew from the parental culture. For them sexual experiences and liberation became a political act as well as a question of identity. Their search for a new way of life was strongly influenced by increasing sexualisation of the public by the media: there was for example the discussion of the 'pill', available on the market from 1961 and offering for the first time not only a safe and relatively cheap contraceptive but also a means to render women independent of the co-operation of their sex partners. In the German Democratic Republic the pill was provided free of charge and abortion was also legalised. By the end of the 1960s, the 'sex-wave' began to roll over the German-speaking countries: by popularising the results of contemporary sex research, new movies and books on sex education – most famous were Oswalt Kolle's productions in West Germany and Siegfried Schnabl's in the GDR – were published. The first soft porno movies, the so-called 'schoolgirl reports' and 'housewife reports' were shown in cinemas, and Beate Uhse founded sex shops in German cities.

The social group which made intensive experiments with the new 'sex' was students, female students in particular. Until the 1960s these young adults had their first coitus four years later than, for example, young workers. From the late 1960s students clearly advanced their sexual activity: in 1966 only around twenty per cent of female and thirty per cent of male students had had coitus; in 1981 around sixty per cent of females and eighty per cent of males had already had this experience. At the same time their coitus activity began to increase dramatically. Attitudes to many sexual questions also changed: for example, virginity was no longer seen as a positive prerequisite for marriage, and the sexual double standard was rejected as a relic of the conservative morality of parents. Relationships between students became more and more limited in duration and based only on love and partnership.

During the 1970s legislation on *Unzucht* (vice) and abortion was also liberalised. But even today, for example, in Austria there is unequal legal treatment of homosexual men (according to age etc.), a fact which demonstrates that, in spite of a greater public acceptance, some groups of the population were and are excluded from full equality and from total sexual liberalisation. In the course of time the changes which first influenced the life of students have become the general pattern of sexual behaviour, and can also be detected in demographic changes. Since the 1960s the number of marriages and births has considerably declined and the number of divorces has increased – altogether the model of the nuclear family has increasingly lost importance as the dominant way of life.

From the 1970s to the present the changes in the sexual life of young people have not been so dramatic. Today the sexuality of Austrian and German youth is still 'permissive, tolerant about sexual matters, orientated towards partner and love as well as egalitarian with regard to moral ideas about boys and girls' (Schmidt 1993: 34). But during the last years sex researchers have found that premarital and non-marital monogamous partnerships are increasing. The number of coital partners has diminished slightly and especially boys (also girls) rarely describe their sexual desires as urgent. While in the 1970s the search for sexual experience led to a retreat from parents, today the sexuality of young people is more often integrated into their parents' family lives. Boys and young men mainly see their sexuality as more connected with love and relationship. At the same time both sexes have demystified sexuality: to 'have sex' is no more an outstanding sensation but on a par with other experiences and events. This increasingly rational sexual life has consequently led to more use of contraceptives, especially condoms. Females also take more sexual initiative, they express their wishes directly and get them met.

The increase in fidelity and the romanticisation of joint sexual relationships were falsely seen as reactions to the threat of AIDS. This hypothesis misses the main causes of this development: the present form of social construction of the sexual desire is a response to sexual norms orientated towards consumption and the myth of sexual liberalisation. But it also embodies the wish for intimacy and safety in a society which has abolished the old sexual morality and replaced it with a new morality of negotiation and consensus. It is a demand for authenticity in a world of second-hand events, where people are confronted with too many goods for satisfaction and have less potential for desire. It is the response to over-sexualisation which has resulted in its opposite − at the moment we can hardly be affected by erotic and sexual stimulation. It is also an attempt not only to pacify sexuality within (almost) equal relations between the sexes but also to maintain and support sexual excitement as a central factor in the construction of sexual desires. And last but not least it is the effort to see homosexual as well as heterosexual desires of men and women not as an all-embracing nucleus but only as one − nevertheless very important − aspect of modern male and female identity.

Note

An extended version of the section on the sexual desire of peasants was published as Eder 1997a. Thanks to Markus Cerman and Lesley Hall for their assistance in translating this article.

Bibliography

Beck, Rainer (1983), 'Illegitimität und voreheliche Sexualität auf dem Land: Unterfinning 1661–1770', in Richard van Dülmen (ed.), *Kultur der einfachen Leute: Bayerisches Volksleben vom 16. bis zum 19. Jahrhundert*, Munich, Fischer, pp. 112–50.

Becker, Peter (1990), *Leben und Lieben in einem kalten Land: Sexualität im Spannungsfeld von Ökonomie und Demographie. Das Beispiel St Lamprecht 1600–1850*, Frankfurt am Main, Campus.

Bei, Neda *et al.* (eds) (1986), *Das lila Wien um 1900: zur Ästhetik der Homosexualitäten*, Vienna, Edition Spuren.

Bergmann, Anna (1992), *Die verhütete Sexualität: die Anfänge der modernen Geburtenkontrolle*, Hamburg, Rasch & Röhring.

Blazek, Helmut (1996), *Rosa Zeiten für rosa Liebe: zur Geschichte der Homosexualität*, Frankfurt am Main, Fischer.

Bleibtreu-Ehrenberg, Gisela (1978), *Tabu Homosexualität: die Geschichte eines Vorurteils*, Frankfurt am Main, Fischer.

Bock, Gisela (1986), *Zwangssterilisation im Nationalsozialismus: Studien zur Rassen- und Frauenpolitik*, Opladen, Westdeutscher Verlag.

Breit, Stefan (1991), *Leichtfertigkeit und ländliche Gesellschaft: voreheliche Sexualität in der frühen Neuzeit*, Munich, Oldenbourg.

Brücker, Eva (1995), 'Und ich bin heil da 'rausgekommen: Gewalt und Sexualität in einer Berliner Arbeiternachbarschaft 1916/17 und 1958', in Thomas Lindenberger and Alf Lüdtke (eds), *Physische Gewalt: Studien zur Geshichte der Neuzeit*, Frankfurt, Suhrkamp, pp. 337–65.

Czarnowski, Gabriele (1991), *Das kontrollierte Paar: Ehe- und Sexualpolitik im Nationalsozialismus*, Weinheim, Deutscher Studien Verlag.

Derks, Paul (1990), *Die Schande der heiligen Päderastie: Homosexualität und Öffentlichkeit in der deutschen Literatur, 1750–1850*, Berlin, Rosa Winkel.

Dienel, Christiane (1995), *Kinderzahl und Staatsräson: Empfängnisverhütung und Bevölkerungspolitik in Deutschland und Frankreich bis 1918*, Münster, Westfälisches Dampfboot.

Eder, Franz X. (1994), 'Die Historisierung des sexuellen Subjekts: Sexualitätsgeschichte zwischen Essentialismus und sozialem Konstruktivismus', *Österreichische Zeitschrift für Geschichtswissenschaften*, 5, 3, pp. 311–27.

— (1996), 'Durchtränktsein mit Geschlechtlichkeit: zur Konstruktion der bürgerlichen Geschlechterdifferenz im wissenschaftlichen Diskurs über die Sexualität (18.–19. Jahrhundert)', in Margret Friedrich and Peter Urbanitsch (eds), *Von Bürgern und ihren Frauen: Bürgertum in der Habsburgermonarchie 5*, Vienna, Cologne and Weimar, Böhlau, pp. 25–47.

— (1997a), 'Sex-appeal versus "Gemieth und Lieb": zur Entstehung der sexuellen Begierde in der bäuerlichen Kultur des 17.–19. Jahrhunderts', in Institut für Wirtschafts- und Sozialgeschichte, Universität Vienna (ed.), *Wiener Wege der Sozialgeschichte: Themen – Perspektiven – Vermittlungen*, Vienna, Cologne and Weimar, Böhlau, pp. 277–98.

— (1997b), 'Von "Sodomiten" und "Konträrsexualen": die Konstruktion des "homosexuellen" Subjekts im deutschsprachigen Wissenschaftsdiskurs des 18. und 19. Jahrhunderts', in Barbara Hey *et al.* (eds), *Que(e)rdenken: weibliche/männliche Homosexualität und Wissenschaft*, Innsbruck, Studienverlag, pp. 15–39.

Finck, Petra and Marliese Eckhof (1987), *Euer Körper gehört uns! Ärzte, Bevölkerungspolitik und Sexualmoral bis 1933*, Hamburg, Ergebnisse.

Freunde eines Schwulen Museums in Berlin e. V. (eds) (1990), *Die Geschichte des Paragraphen 175: Strafrecht gegen Homosexuelle*, Ausstellungskatalog, Frankfurt am Main, Rosa Winkel.

Gleixner, Ulrike (1994), *Das Mensch und der Kerl: die Konstruktion von Geschlecht in Unzuchtsverfahren der Frühen Neuzeit (1700–1760)*, Frankfurt am Main and New York, Campus.

Grau, Günter (ed.) (1992), *Homosexualität in der NS-Zeit: Dokumente einer Diskriminierung und Verfolgung*, Frankfurt am Main, Fischer.

Grossmann, Atina (1995), *Reforming Sex: The German Movement for Birth Control and Abortion Reform 1920–1950*, New York, Oxford University Press.

Grumbach, Detlev (ed.) (1995), *Die Linke und das Laster: schwule Emanzipation und die Linke*, Hamburg, MännerschwarmSkript.

Hacker, Hanna (1987), *Frauen und Freundinnen: Studien zur 'weiblichen Homosexualiät' am Beispiel Österreich 1870–1938*, Weinheim and Basel, Beltz.

Hagemann, Karen (1991), *Eine Frauensache: Alltagsleben und Geburtenpolitik, 1919–1933*, Pfaffenweiler, Centaurus.

Hekma, Gert (1989), 'Sodomites, Platonic Lovers, Contrary Lovers: The Backgrounds of the Modern Homosexual', in Gerard Kent and Gert Hekma (eds), *The Pursuit of Sodomy: Male Homosexuality in Renaissance and Enlightenment Europe*, New York, Harrington Park, pp. 433–55.

Herzer, Manfred (1992), *Magnus Hirschfeld: Leben und Werk eines jüdischen, schwulen und sozialistischen Sexologen*, Frankfurt am Main and New York, Campus.

Hull, Isabel V. (1996), *Sexuality, State, and Civil Society in Germany 1700–1815*, Ithaca and London, Cornell University Press.

Jellonnek, Burkhard (1990), *Homosexuelle unter dem Hakenkreuz: die Verfolgung von Homosexuellen im Dritten Reich*, Paderborn, Schöningh.

Jušek, Karin J. (1993), *Auf der Suche nach der Verlorenen: die Prostitutionsdebatten im Wien der Jahrhundertwende*, Habilitation, University of Groningen.

Jütte, Robert (ed.) (1993), *Geschichte der Abtreibung: von der Antike bis zur Gegenwart*, Munich, Beck.

Kienitz, Sabine (1995), *Sexualität, Macht und Moral: Prostitution und Geschlechterbeziehungen Anfang des 19. Jahrhunderts in Würtemberg. Ein Beitrag zur Mentalitätsgeschichte*, Berlin, Akademie.

Knodel, John E. (1974), *The Decline of Fertility in Germany, 1871–1939*, Princeton, Princeton University Press.

— (1988), *Demographic Behavior in the Past: A Study of Fourteen German Village Populations in the Eighteenth and Nineteenth Century*, Cambridge, Cambridge University Press.

Krafft, Sybille (1996), *Zucht und Unzucht: Prostitution und Sittenpolizei im München der Jahrhundertwende*, Munich, Hugendubel.

Kuzniar, Alice A. (ed.) (1996), *Outing Goethe and His Age*, Stanford, Stanford University Press.

Lautmann, Rüdiger (ed.) (1993), *Homosexualität – Handbuch der Theorie- und Forschungsgeschichte*, Frankfurt am Main and New York, Campus.

Lautmann, Rüdiger and Angela Taeger (eds) (1992), *Männerliebe im alten Deutschland: sozialgeschichtliche Abhandlungen*, Berlin, Rosa Winkel.

Lipp, Carola (1990), 'Die Innenseite der Arbeiterkultur: Sexualität im Arbeitermilieu des 19. und frühen 20. Jahrhunderts', in Richard van Dülmen (ed.), *Arbeit, Frömmigkeit, Eigensinn*, Frankfurt am Main, Fischer, pp. 214–59.

Luhmann, Niklas (1982), *Liebe als Passion: zur Codierung von Intimität*, Frankfurt am Main, Suhrkamp.

Maynes, Mary Jo (1992), 'Adolescent Sexuality and Social Identity in French and German Lower-class Autobiography', *Journal of Family History*, 17, 4, pp. 397–418.

Medick, Hans (1980), 'Spinnstuben auf dem Dorf: jugendliche Sexualkultur und Feierabendbräuche in der ländlichen Gesellschaft der frühen Neuzeit', in

Gerhard Huck (ed.), *Sozialgeschichte der Freizeit: Untersuchungen zum Wandel der Alltagskultur in Deutschland*, Wuppertal, Hammer, pp. 19–49.

Mitterauer, Michael (1983), *Ledige Mütter: zur Geschichte illegitimer Geburten in Europa*, Munich, Beck.

Mosse, George L. (1987), *Nationalismus und Sexualität: bürgerliche Moral und sexuelle Normen*, Munich and Vienna, Hanser.

Müller, Klaus (1991), *Aber in meinem Herzen sprach eine Stimme so laut: homosexuelle Autobiographien und medizinische Pathographien im 19. Jahrhundert*, Berlin, Rosa Winkel.

Oosterhuis, Harry (1994), 'Reinheit und Verfolgung: Männerbünde, Homosexualität und Politik in Deutschland (1900–1945)', *Österreichische Zeitschrift für Geschichtswissenschaften*, 5, 3, pp. 388–409.

Pallaver, Günther (1987), *Das Ende der schamlosen Zeit: die Verdrängung der Sexualität in der frühen Neuzeit am Beispiel Tirols*, Vienna, Gesellschaftskritik.

Paul, Christa (1994), *Zwangsprostitution: staatlich errichtete Bordelle im Nationalsozialismus*, Berlin, Hentrich.

Plant, Richard (1991), *Rosa Winkel: der Krieg der Nazis gegen die Homosexuellen*, Frankfurt am Main and New York, Campus.

Poiger, Uta G. (1996), 'Rock 'n' Roll, Female Sexuality, and the Cold War Battle over German Identities', *Journal of Modern History*, 68, pp. 577–616.

Quine, Maria Sophia (1996), *Population Politics in Twentieth-century Europe: Fascist Dictatorship and Liberal Democracies*, London and New York, Routledge.

Rohlje, Uwe (1991), *Autoerotik und Gesundheit: Untersuchungen zur gesellschaftlichen Entstehung und Funktion der Masturbationsbekämpfung im 18. Jahrhundert*, Münster and New York, Waxmann.

Roper, Lyndal (1994), *Oedipus and the Devil: Witchcraft, Sexuality and Religion in Early Modern Europe*, London and New York, Routledge.

Rosenbaum, Heidi (1992), *Proletarische Familien: Arbeiterfamilien und Arbeiterväter im frühen 20. Jahrhundert zwischen traditioneller, sozialdemokratischer und kleinbürgerlicher Orientierung*, Frankfurt am Main, Suhrkamp.

Schmid, Pia and Christina Weber (1986), 'Von der "wohlgeordneten Liebe" und der "so eigenen Wollust des Geschlechtes": zur Diskussion weiblichen Begehrens zwischen 1730 und 1830', in Jutta Dalhoff *et al.* (eds), *Frauenmacht in der Geschichte: Beiträge des Historikerinnentreffens 1985 zur Frauengeschichtsforschung*, Düsseldorf, Schwan, pp. 150–65.

Schmidt, Gunter (1988), *Das grosse Der Die Das: über das Sexuelle*, Reinbek bei Hamburg, Rowohlt.

— (ed.) (1993), *Jugendsexualität: sozialer Wandel, Gruppenunterschiede, Konfliktfelder*, Stuttgart, Ferdinand Enke.

Schoppmann, Claudia (1991), *Nationalsozialistische Sexualpolitik und weibliche Homosexualität*, Pfaffenweiler, Centaurus.

— (1993), *Zeit der Maskierung: Lebensgeschichten lesbischer Frauen im 'Dritten Reich'*, Berlin, Orlanda.

Schulte, Regina (1979), *Sperrbezirke: Tugendhaftigkeit und Prostitution in der bürgerlichen Welt*, Frankfurt am Main, Syndikat.

Shorter, Edward (1971), 'Illegitimacy, Sexual Revolution and Social Change in Modern Europe', *Journal of Interdisciplinary History*, 2, pp. 237–72.

Sieder, Reinhard (1987), *Sozialgeschichte der Familie*, Frankfurt am Main, Suhrkamp.

FRANZ X. EDER

— (1994), 'Die Ordnung des Hauses und die Liebe der Jungen: zur Sexualkultur Lediger in bäuerlichen Gesellschaften um 1800', in Oto Luthar (ed.), *Pot na grmado: der Weg auf den Scheiterhaufen: The Road to Pile*, Ljubljana, Historical Seminar Ljubljana, pp. 297–327.

Soden, Kristine von (1988), *Die Sexualberatungsstellen der Weimarer Republik 1919–1933*, Berlin, Hentrich.

Spree, Reinhard (1984), 'Geburtenrückgang in Deutschland vor 1939: Verlauf und schichtspezifische Ausprägung', *Demographische Informationen*, pp. 49–68.

Staupe, Gisela and Lisa Vieth (eds) (1996), *Die Pille: von der Lust und von der Liebe*, Berlin, Rowohlt.

Tenfelde, Klaus (1992), 'Arbeiterfamilie und Geschlechterbeziehungen im Deutschen Kaiserreich', *Geschichte und Gesellschaft*, 18, 2, pp. 179–203.

Theweleit, Klaus (1977), *Männerphantasien*, 2 vols, Frankfurt am Main, Deutscher Taschenbuch Verlag.

Ulrichs, Karl Heinrich (1994), *Forschungen über das Räthsel der mannmännlichen Liebe*, ed. Hubert Kennedy, 4 vols, Berlin, Rosa Winkel.

Usborne, Cornelie (1994), *Frauenkörper – Volkskörper: Geburtenkontrolle und Bevölkerungspolitik in der Weimarer Republik*, Münster, Westfälisches Dampfboot.

Weingart, Peter et al. (1988), *Rasse, Blut und Gene: Geschichte der Eugenik und Rassenhygiene in Deutschland*, Frankfurt am Main, Suhrkamp.

Wernz, Corinna (1993), *Sexualität als Krankheit: der medizinische Diskurs zur Sexualität um 1800*, Stuttgart, Enke.

Westphal, Hannelore (1988), *Die Liebe auf dem Dorf: vom Wandel der Sexualmoral und der Prostitution auf dem Lande*, Braunschweig, Holtzmeyer.

Woycke, James (1988), *Birth Control in Germany, 1871–1933*, London and New York, Routledge.

7

Spain: the political and social context of sex reform in the late nineteenth and early twentieth centuries

Richard M. Cleminson & Efigenio Amezúa

Recent work has suggested that 'sexual cultures' should be considered in the context in which they are produced and that these circumstances are highly specific (Weeks and Holland 1996). While a clearer picture of the sexual cultures of Spain is beginning to emerge, there are a large number of gaps in the historiography of sexuality in this country. Even though there has been an increasing number of studies on gender and women's experience since 1700 (Buxán 1997; Simón Palmer 1974–9; Kirkpatrick 1990), a limited number of texts on homosexuality (Mirabet i Mullol 1985) and others centred on the history of sexual morality (Vázquez Gârcía and Moreno Mengíbar 1997), there are few monographic studies on sexology and sexual theory in Spain (Amezúa 1991; Sánchez Granjel 1974), and certainly no full-length texts on the creation of sexuality, identities and the sexual question in modern times. Nevertheless, as with other countries' sexual cultures, stereotypes and myths abound, including the aphrodisiac qualities of 'Spanish fly', the masculine pride and coqueterie of *donjuanism*, the fieriness of 'Latin' blood and the more recent daring sexual play of the Pedro Almodóvar film industry (Smith 1992).

This chapter aims to provide an overview of sexual cultures in Spain, to allow comparison and contrast between different countries in Europe and to provide some ideas for possible further research. While Amezúa has in the past concentrated upon the intellectual and theoretical debates in Spain in the late nineteenth and early twentieth centuries regarding sexology, and Cleminson on the socio-cultural aspect of some movements' negotiation of sexuality, this chapter attempts to twin the theoretical with the social dimension in which debates and activities around sexuality were played out. Here we concentrate on the late nineteenth and early twentieth centuries and make no attempt to document earlier or later periods, which should be the subjects of further work.

This chapter aims to provide a background for the understanding and situating of debates and practices within the context of place and time. The situating of sexuality within a specific historic framework is crucial to an understanding of its workings. Sexuality here is understood to constitute a field of individual and social relations and is seen as a dynamic, multifaceted site for the unfolding of social relations between men and women, children, ideological groupings and material conditions. Emphasis is placed on what we understand to be the peculiarities of Spain and those aspects which the country held in common with the rest of Europe. Within this framework it is also necessary to understand that 'Spain' itself is formed of a large number of different material and social conditions which vary significantly from region to region.

This study on Spain is organised into a number of sections which cover the social and political background of the country in the late nineteenth and early twentieth centuries; the first modern conceptualisation and manifestation of the sexual question in the form of popular guide books and pamphlets on sexuality; the growth of scientific and sexological material; social and political movements around sexuality; and the 'progressive' sex reform movements of the 1930s. Some final remarks are made on the subject of the triumph of General Francisco Franco after the Civil War of 1936–9. Throughout, the authors will attempt to comment on the emergence of sexuality as an issue of importance in the conflict between a traditional society and a more modern one as well as paying attention to some specific developments around rural/urban differences, marriage, gender roles, the role of science and sexology and the importance of the Catholic church.

The historico-social dimension: Spain in the nineteenth and twentieth centuries

Because the workings of sexuality cannot be understood outside the context in which they were negotiated and produced, the social and political conditions which characterise Spain during our period of study are discussed here. While Spain has traditionally been viewed as different from the rest of Europe, there are many parallels which can be drawn. Nevertheless, the road to 'modernity' in the European sense has been a tortuous one for the country because of the continued existence of an array of structural peculiarities mainly eliminated or at least attenuated in northern and other western European countries of the time.

Spain from the days of the 'unification' under the Catholic monarchy of Ferdinand and Isabella (1492) to the beginning of the twentieth century was largely a country where a variety of traditional feudal or semi-feudal forms existed. The monarchy and the Catholic church, both backed by an army which regularly intervened in politics by means of the *pronunciamiento* or *coup d'état* and which saw itself as the saviour of the nation, were extremely powerful central-ising institutions within a generally weak, even though centralist state. The influence of the monarchy and church began to wane only during the liberal projects of the nineteenth century, which, under the impetus of the French Revolution of 1789 and the Enlightenment, attempted to introduce what was understood as a European-type democracy into the country. This strengthened the legislative and organising power of the state, its legitimacy in social and political affairs, the rise of professional groups and the construction of a *national* state, not one made up of quasi-independent cantons (Barton 1993). The liberal regimes of the nineteenth century attempted to curb the traditional power blocs of Spanish society. The disentail-ments of church property in a series of mid-century reforms were one example of this conviction to structurally alter social and economic relations. Despite these attempts, the country was still torn by internal strife, dysfunctional democracy, corruption, secessional wars (the Carlist wars), military coups, workers' revolts: the face not of one Spain but of many Spains, fragmented according to wealth, politics, class and many other differences.

A window of opportunity for a different system of political organisation was represented by the brief Republic of 1873–4, which nevertheless collapsed as a result of traditionalist opposition and revolu-tionary workers' revolts. Subsequent to the demise of the Republic and the restoration of the monarchy a period of rotation of political power between conservatives and liberals, the *turno pacífico*, was inaugurated (Carr 1983). The peaceful process of power-swapping was characterised by electoral fixes and widespread political corruption. In addition to political corruption, the defeat of the Spanish forces particularly in Cuba meant that the so-called 'Disaster' of 1898 stripped Spain of most of the last remnants of empire, occasioning general decline, economic hardship and spiritual doldrums.

The tremendous strain that the loss of the empire placed, in different ways, on all sectors of society led to an institutionalised political process termed *regeneracionismo* which was designed, through a 'revolution from above', to regenerate Spain, to purify politics and to encourage public participation in Spanish life (Ben-Ami 1978: 1–2; Balfour 1995, 1997). While this project ultimately failed, it paved the way for the opening of a modernisation process which would see its more mature fruits only in the Second Republic of 1931–6. Before the onset of the Republic, however, Spain was once again plunged into dictatorship at the hands of General Miguel Primo de Rivera (1923–30). Crucially, though, and of importance for our study here, is that Primo's regime brought about a process of modernisation of infrastructures, as well as later opposition from university professors and students over democracy and the role of knowledge and culture in society. But conflict and renewal were not present merely in the privileged quarters of the intelligentsia; rather, they were widespread and fundamental: 'Pornographic literature together with the Tango, the Charleston, and the cinema, which in the early years of the Dictatorship were reaching the most backward and remote villages, were already accentuating there the struggle between "old" and "new"' (Ben-Ami 1978: 35; on 'erotismo blando' see Trigo 1907; Fortuny 1929).

In this broader ambience new sciences such as sexology could begin to flourish. This development, however, was uneven and problematic. The conflicts between fusty morality and emerging sexology were especially apparent in the thwarted attempt by sex reformers to hold a conference on eugenics in 1928. This event encapsulated many aspects of sexual hygiene and sexual morality, but was outlawed after Catholic opposition (Alvarez Peláez 1985; Pérez Sanz and Bru Ripoll 1987). In addition to this act of legal repression, and despite the opening up of ideas on sexual 'delinquency' and 'deviancy', penalties for persistent homosexual acts between both sexes were established. There had previously been penalties only for members of the armed forces.

This period contrasts in many ways with the Second Republic, which represented for many the historic opportunity to push the country into modernity. A period when culture, education, new ideas and changing social mores were prominent issues, the Second Republic saw the clearest advances in terms of the opening up of sexological material and its dissemination and popularisation.

The sexual culture of the times

Spain during most of the period analysed here was still largely a traditional, agrarian society in which the Catholic church wielded great influence in all social affairs, from voting patterns to issues of sexuality. Access to education was limited to a (male) elite; in 1870 approximately sixty per cent of the population was illiterate (Brenan 1990: 50), in comparison to France with its seventy per cent literacy rate (Alvarez Junco 1995: 47). The situation was even worse for girls, often kept at home to perform domestic chores rather than attending what limited schooling there was available. Tradition was strong, especially in rural areas, as can be seen in the rules which guided courtship and marriage, with strong gender differences established for males and females and resulting clear gendered spheres of employment and profile in communities. This long process, known as the *noviazgo*, had to follow certain rigid formulae guided by public opinion, modesty and decency.[1] Tradition was also strong in respect of widowhood, as women, especially in small communities, were not expected to remarry or even so much as look at another man. Strict gender roles, bolstered by early nineteenth-century discussions of biological differences between the sexes, were by the end of the century current coinage in most circles (Martínez 1990).

In Spain the Catholic church failed to modernise and adopted a firmly counter-reformation stance. Along with other influences, Catholicism constructed the destiny of women as reproducer of children. Womanhood became a sin, the mother became the realisation of the central role that the female of the species should fulfil (Alvarez Peláez 1990: 184). Women's experience embodied the Catholic aspirations of home and hearth (Lannon 1987). Women in the church itself played no part in ecclesiastical decision-making and were told by male priests to obey their husbands: men were deemed to be in positions of authority and social responsibility, while women were for domesticity, motherhood or sexual renunciation. Sex was denigrated and women were represented as embodying the 'eternal feminine' where virginity was idealised in angelic dimensions (Ruiz Amado 1926). This was so much the case that by 1930, according to

177

the law professor Jiménez de Asúa, who would become President of the Republic in exile, Catholicism was to be blamed for 'the dryness of the Spanish soul, the intolerance, the horror of nudity and hygiene, the consideration of sexual intercourse as a sin ... all the sad characteristics of the Spaniard' (Ben-Ami 1978: 34), a harsh judgement indeed.

As a result of Catholic influence, abortion and birth control were seen as religious matters, or questions of religious morality. Unsafe, unregulated abortion and infanticide (especially of baby girls) were common practices (Alvarez Peláez 1990). It was only in the Republic that birth control was decriminalised. Nevertheless, as has been pointed out, it is extremely difficult to map women's (and men's) knowledge and use of birth-control methods. The historian Alvarez Peláez (1990) has suggested two main avenues: by studying personal and family communications, and by looking at professional information on the area. Nevertheless, usage is difficult to determine and information is scarce since most sectors were silent on the issue of birth control or were negative (Nash 1991). Even in leading medical journals such as *El Siglo Médico* few details were available. Radical sex reform movements or more institutionalised ones such as the eugenics movement or the Spanish League for Sex Reform (see below) were the principal outlets for material of this variety.

If there had been a more developed feminist movement in Spain, it might have been able to pioneer some of these issues. However, radical or militant feminism failed to develop as a large movement and any prominent women's organisation was generally middle-class and educated (Capmany 1970). It was only during the First World War that feminism grew as women took up jobs in the factories. Despite this, feminist organisations remained rather conservative. For example, the second objective of the National Association of Spanish Women (Asociación Nacional de Mujeres Españolas, ANME), established in 1918, read as follows: '[The Association should] seek that every Spanish mother, in perfect harmony with the [female] school teacher, inculcate in the child, from its earliest age, the love of the motherland, which is unique and indivisible' (González Calbet 1988). According to another historian, feminism was viewed by those who opposed it as another heresy in the line of the French Revolution. There was an intense reaction in Spain against the notion of feminism, which was presented by its opponents as aiming to destroy the family, society and Spain itself: 'There is no doubt that the enormous importance of the Church as a social institution and its influence in political, economic and educational affairs, was an important factor in the delay in the development of Spanish feminism' (Scanlon 1976: 6–7). The linkages between nationalism, the female sphere defined as family and reproduction, and the submissive role that the church prescribed for women are to be seen clearly in these examples.

Despite certain attempts by more humanitarian legislators to ease the working hours of women in factories in the industrial heartland of Catalonia and some laws on maternity benefits – often unimplemented as a result of a lack of factory inspectors (Balcells 1974: 23) – most feminist demands until the late 1920s and 1930s reflected middle-class concerns and were directed towards suffrage for women or less radical demands. This emphasis arose from the constituency on which much of the feminist movement drew. The Catalan Institute of Culture and Popular Library for women, for example, was used mainly by middle-class women (Capmany 1966: 71–4), and few women apart from the intellectually and socially privileged listened to the Spanish endocrinologist Gregorio Marañón, whose research and views on sexuality were prominent in his own milieu and in wider society (Aranguren 1972: 19). Despite this middle-class bias there is a history of women's activism in social struggles in working-class areas, discussed below (Kaplan 1992).

Other areas of sexual cultures, including homosexuality, are particularly in need of deeper analysis. Probably as a result of a poorly developed homosexual subculture, there has been little published on the period discussed here. Study of a developing demi-monde of cabarets, prostitution and transvestism in the 1920s would reveal interesting insights into these areas. There was a growing culture of the cabaret style *cuplé* in the early twentieth century and links between transvestism, the erotic novel and more visible homo-sexuality were made by the erotic writer Alvaro Retana (see his erotic novel of 1919, *Las locas de postín*, on homosexuality and transvestism amongst the aristocratic class) (Pérez Sanz and Bru Ripoll 1989: 40–1). Homosexual imagery also emerged in artistic circles, particularly in the work of the poet and playwright Federico García Lorca (Smith 1998).

In order to understand more fully what contributed to the sexual culture of the period, we now consider early sex advice literature, twentieth-century sexology and one working-class counter-cultural movement in the shape of anarchism.

Prelude to scientific sexology: popular sex advice literature

The relationship between popular sex advice manuals and booklets, scientific sexology, and sexual mores and behaviours is not an unproblematic one. There is no straightforward relationship between their production and changes or consistencies in sexual behaviour and there is no obvious correlation; we cannot easily determine the effects of either popular manuals or institutionalised sexology on different audiences. Despite these difficulties, sexology, along with a number of other factors, such as the rise of professional groups, the arrival of ideas from abroad, the building of the nation state, political and religious demands, new forms of literature and the novel, and the changing face of masculinity and femininity can be analysed to build up a picture. We cannot analyse all these factors here so we concentrate on popular sexual advice literature as a prelude to 'scientific' sexology and as an important aspect of the sexual cultures of the time. In what follows we consider a number of writers and doctors who took the sexual question to heart and produced guides or short pamphlets on a variety of subjects.

The doctor Pedro Felipe Monlau i Roca is our first figure. Travellers or foreigners who came to the city and court of Madrid would use as a vade-mecum a guidebook written by Dr Pedro Felipe Monlau, entitled *Madrid en la mano* (1850, *Madrid at your Fingertips*), but married couples would use another guide written by this doctor and humanist. This was his *Higiene del matrimonio o Libro de los casados* (1853, *Marriage Hygiene or the Book of Newly Weds*). The success of this book built on Monlau's *Higiene privada* (1846). Monlau was probably the first to provide a systematic, in-depth version of an early marriage and health guide for couples, similar to those that proliferated in Britain and other countries in the mid nineteenth century (Hall 1991). In his 1853 book, before moving on to less 'politicised' comment, there is a four-page attack on socialism, Saint-Simonism and communism for their affront to the family, and relief that divorce is not on the agenda in Roman Catholic countries. According to the preface:

> various useful notions are brought together which are generally unknown. Important advice on the maintenance of the individual's health, considered in the state of matrimony, useful rules on domestic harmony, the education and upbringing of the family, and common errors and concerns are combated. I believe, therefore, that the objective of this book is pertinent, and that its

reading can be but beneficial to married persons or those about to be married, for whom it has been written. I believe I have hit the mark with this guide – all that remains now is for the intelligent public to share my feeling.

(Monlau 1853: v)

Indeed, the enquiring public did share his feeling and a total of thirteen editions were published. We could even talk of a real 'best-seller'. *Marriage Hygiene* became a bedside table book, hidden away but used to view all that which was morbid as well as relevant to the conjugal hearth.

Monlau can be considered the most significant figure, or even the designer, of this genre in Spain. It has been maintained that nine-teenth-century sexual literature was dominated by psychiatrists (alienists) and asylum doctors, which is to some extent true, but little interest has been shown in works which are outside this reper-toire. It is interesting, for example, to note the importance of the general practitioner who was present at the birth, upbringing, death, fortunes and misfortunes of the family, and the role of the erotic novelists referred to above who often justified their work as alleviating sexual ignorance (Trigo 1908; García Lara 1986).

Another author claims special attention for the large quantity of his publications: Amancio Peratoner. He wrote twenty-four differ-ent publications and was considered frivolous by some, by others an enlightened bearer of sexual knowledge, and by others an author of 'camouflaged pornography'.[2] His publications appeared in many editions from the 1860s to the 1890s and were on subjects such as venereal disease, ways of avoiding pregnancy, ideas on homo-sexuality and polemics on onanism, all inviting the reader to find out more about the particular subject (Peratoner 1874, 1876).

Later than Peratoner were Dr Suárez Casañ's *Conocimientos de la vida privada* (*The Facts of Private Life*). The first of this series on sex education appeared in 1889, published by Maucci, comprising twenty small hundred-page booklets with black and white photographs inside a colour cover. They sold for the price of 0. 25 céntimos each, quite cheap for the time. Subjects included were: pregnancy, the secrets of the marriage bed, venereal diseases, impotence, lesbian love, pederasty and the solitary vices. A second series was begun after this successful first one. Suárez Casañ (1903: 8) himself commented that the success of the first series encouraged him to continue publishing scientific ideas from all countries and instructions on intimate and family life: 'Will we fulfil our noble undertaking? It will fall to the supreme, infallible and unquestionable judgement of the public to say yea or nay.'

The case of Dr Fernando Mateos Koch illustrates another important area in the creation of a 'sexual culture': that of the nascent sex clinic (Foucault 1973; Alvarez-Uría 1983; Alvarez-Uría and Varela 1994). He wrote candidly: 'Our desire, the aim of our work, is none other than to indicate the conditions in which man and woman should come together in order to exercise the sexual relation satisfactorily' (1891: 4). Koch's work appeared, according to our research, from 1891 to 1903 and in nearly every one of his publications the address of the clinic is given (Puerta del Sol-Arenal, 1, 1°, Madrid). Criticism of his works was contested by Koch (1891: 3) in the following terms: 'Nothing is further from our desire than that which has been represented as our subject area: pornography. [What we are looking at] is true physiology, hygiene and pathology of the reproductive functions.' The process whereby sex research and writing about sex were professing to be a serious 'scientific' realm rather than immoral or lewd pornography is evident here. This may imply that the age was neither one of utter repression of the sexual question nor an unproblematic onward march towards clarity and detached analysis. The role of sexologists in the ordering of the state is an interesting subject, and one author, Fernando Alvarez-Uría (1983), has argued that centralisation, the growth of the power of the medical and psychiatric profession, and the creation of the modern state can all be linked (Rose 1985).

While some of these theoretical issues are still to be pursued, this survey has viewed what was in many ways a popular orientation towards the sexual question of the times, representing a thirst for knowledge, the rise of the small sex clinic and advice centre, and cheap but well-produced sexological material which all helped to establish the legitimacy of sex literature to the detriment of a traditional and largely Catholic monopoly on the subject. We now turn to official or scientific sexology.

The rise of scientific, institutionalised sexology

The rise of European sexology in the nineteenth century has been well documented elsewhere. One can detect a move away from concepts of vice and madness towards the growing concept of sexuality as an important factor in the make-up and functioning of human beings as well as the 'professionalisation' of the sexual question. Krafft-Ebing's 1886 *Psychopathia Sexualis* is a landmark in this process; with this volume the idea of sexuality gains currency, even though other sexologists such as Havelock Ellis, Magnus Hirschfeld and Ivan Bloch would disagree with the pathological tone of the book (Robinson 1977). In Spain we note a 'second golden age' (the Golden Age of Literature was the sixteenth century) or a 'silver age' in the scientific and intellectual life of Spain (Mainer 1981; Tuñón de Lara 1970). Within this cultural renaissance, growing contemporaneously with the perceived moral and physical decline of the country after the loss of empire and the ensuing crisis, we will highlight certain ideas, events and journals. The voices of specialists, either from the medical profession or from biologists, endocrinologists and psychologists, were more easily heard in the early twentieth century as this 'silver age' took up momentum. Among the many figures who were important in the deepening of intellectual concerns on a wide variety of subjects, including sexology, was the Nobel prize winner Santiago Ramón y Cajal. Many of those who were active in the sphere of sexology had some connection to his endeavours.

Ramón y Cajal's presidency of the newly created Council for the Expansion of Scientific Studies and Research (Junta de Ampliación de Estudios e Investigaciones Científicas) was important in this sense. Over the thirty years of the Council's existence (1907–38), nearly two thousand young researchers trained in the universities of Europe came back to Spain, bringing 'new knowledge' into the country. With this historic phenomenon without precedent, the principal foci of sexological innovation were introduced into Spain. This may explain why Spanish was the first language to enjoy a complete translation of the full works of Ellis (1913) and Freud (two versions from 1922–1935) as well as other single volumes written by Bloch (1924) and Forel (1925), for example.

This foreign input was complemented by that of indigenous writers such as César Juarros, Gregorio Marañón, Luis Jiménez de Asúa, Jaime Torrubiano and Hildegart Rodríguez who published extensively in the 1920s and 1930s: a veritable 'discursive explosion' on sexuality. While all these writers approached the sexual question differently, it is important to note that all coincided on some central points. Within the general ambience of new ideas, the importance of sexuality within influential intellectual and scientific milieux was established, including medicine, pedagogy, psychology, law and culture in general. It was a question, as Juarros (1930: 4) stated, of removing sexuality from a position of 'ignoble lowliness' to elevate it to one which was firmly located within a modernising, purportedly scientific framework. We now consider some of the consequences of this endeavour.

A part of creating an intellectual culture where discussions on sexuality were possible was the series of conferences given by the scientist Gregorio Marañón in the home of the Madrid intelligentsia, the Ateneo, in 1915. His first address was on 'Sex, sexual life and internal secretions', during which he affirmed that 'The sexual life is not something trivial or superficial, but rather the root of human biography' (1915: 86). Marañón lamented that so little emphasis had been accorded to sexuality: 'sexuality has been considered the source of disorders and the time has arrived to study it with energy and vitality', displaying, in turn, an essentialist, drive-led concept of sexuality, common to the times (1935: 3). One of Marañón's great interests was homosexuality, or, in his terms, *intersexualidad*. The endocrinologist lamented the state of Spanish society and culture and levels of awareness on sexuality in an observation he made in the prologue of the Spanish edition of Iwan Bloch's book on contemporary sexual life. Bloch had been travelling on a train and, noting the conversation and demeanour of a particular individual whom he thought interesting for his studies, asked if this person was a homosexual. The reply was affirmative, an impossible scenario in contemporary Spain (Marañón 1968, 1: 32).

Despite Marañón's leanings, which were progressive for the time, he viewed 'intersexuality' as a 'twisted branch in the progress of sexual life'. In order to remedy such a situation, it was necessary to 'strengthen differentiation between the sexes and to exalt manliness in men and femininity in women', an assertion that he wrote in the prologue to what he described as the first important literary contribution to the debate on 'sexual aberrations' (Marañón 1968, 1: 457–64).

In the wake of Marañón's and others' interventions, journals and other media began to emerge to meet the new needs of this sexual science. Two well-established medical reviews began to reflect these requirements: *El Siglo Médico* and *La Gaceta Médica*. These two reviews encapsulated the role of doctors and professionals in the promotion of the new sciences of sexology and social medicine, brought home their modernising role and established the basis for future events and developments. In *La Gaceta* Luis Huerta inaugurated a section on eugenics which gave a frequent account of new ideas on this subject. The fact that these issues began to appear in these two reviews is important for our account since they were the regular and official publications of the medical profession.

Other modern reviews were important in disseminating information on sexology such as the prominent *La Revista de Occidente*, established in 1923 by José Ortega y Gasset, a renowned intellectual and polemicist of the time. In this review there was a series of particularly influential contributions. George Simmel's ideas on masculinity and femininity were published here; the ideas of Enrique Casas on the ethno-anthropology of nuptial ceremonies, and polemics on machoism and Don Juan from Marañón, are some examples of the breadth of articles (Lázaro 1990).

An unprecedented event was the appearance in 1925 of the first weekly publication dedicated to the field: *Sexualidad*, edited by the psychiatrist Dr Antonio Navarro, who had written before on prostitution (1909). Nearly two hundred issues provide an unrivalled forum of debate on these matters. The slogan of the review was 'We ask you to be not chaste but cautious', words published in each issue and directed to the reader. The contents of this review were enormously varied but still await a detailed study.

The 1928 Eugenics Days as a prelude to the sex reform movement of the Second Republic

As noted above, the conflict between some sectors of Catholicism and more open attitudes towards sexuality and the attempt to open such questions up to a wider audience was clearly seen in the curtailment of the 1928 conference on eugenics. While eugenics, rightly so, has a poor press, it must not be assumed that all eugenics was essentially the same. In each country where eugenics had a following it was constructed in different ways, some forms were more authoritarian or genetics-based than others (Adams 1990). This relatively progressive event of 1928 brought together a number of scientists and professionals and even social Catholics of a reformist outlook. The conference, the first of its kind in Spain, caused a considerable furore which resulted in its outright condemnation by the Catholic newspaper *El Debate* and a resultant ban by royal decree which characterised the conference as 'a pornographic bonanza'. The intention behind the conference, however, had been to unite the various attempts, social and scientific, in order to address the question of sex reform and eugenics in the early twentieth century. The wave of opprobrium cast by the moribund *primorriverista* regime was a fierce one and prepared the way for stormy debates on sexuality, love, divorce and contraception in the following years (Alvarez Peláez 1988).

The consequences of the rise of this literature are ambiguous. Clearly the very fact that sex and sexuality were being discussed more openly was both a qualitative and a quantitative change in comparison with Catholic-driven statements on sexual morality. Sex became, as in many other European countries, an issue of great importance to wide sectors of Spanish society. Notwithstanding this, in part because sexology was becoming established in a repressive Catholic society, connections with dominant morality, rigid gender roles and a pathology of 'deviance' are evident. Some ideas were articulated to provide a revision of some of these constraints but others were utilised as a justification of the status quo, not this time a religious one but one ostensibly from the objective toolkit of science.

This process was evident in the first year of the Second Republic, when some moderate socialists proposed an amendment on 1 September 1931 to the women's suffrage bill, so that only men would be able to vote. It was in fact some of these socialists who most strongly opposed the right of women to vote, fearing that the electorate would swing rightwards. The following day, 'biological' arguments ensued. Dr Novoa Santos argued that women were not capable of displaying 'reflection and a critical spirit', that they allowed themselves to be carried away by emotion since 'hysteria' was intrinsic to women (Scanlon 1976: 275). This is an interesting example of how political expediency, 'left' politicians, a heavy dose of anti-feminism and deterministic 'science' could all quite comfortably sit together.

The Second Republic and the liberalisation of sexology

With the inauguration of the Second Republic in 1931, a climate of optimism was born within the more 'progressive' sectors of Spanish society. For many the Republic represented an opportunity to dissolve finally the tremendous inequalities in Spanish society and to curtail the power of the undemocratic forces of church, landed gentry and army. The Republic also represented the massive democratisation of knowledge; a good proportion of the deputies in the Parliament were educationalists, lawyers or scientists of one sort or another, a fact allowing for the categorisation of the new regime as 'the Republic of the intellectuals' besides being devoted to 'all the workers'. It was a period during which 'culture mattered' and the new regime attempted sweeping reforms in education and the bringing of 'culture' to remote villages. An example of this was the arrival of theatre and cinema in some villages for the first time (Graham and Labanyi 1995; Preston 1994).

The new Republican Constitution of 1931 guaranteed, at least on paper, equality for women before the law (article 25), equal rights to work (article 40) and the right for women over the age of twenty-three to vote (article 36), while article 43 declared that the distinction between legitimate and illegitimate children and the marital state of parents should disappear (Scanlon 1976: 263–4). In 1932 a reform of the Penal Code decriminalised homosexuality, except in the armed forces (García Valdés 1981). As a further measure, divorce was legalised in March 1932. The indignation provoked by this measure was tremendous, notably amongst conservative and Catholic sectors and this led in turn to a counter-attack by proponents of the measure. The socialist deputy Margarita Nelken, for example, reacted to Catholic opposition as follows: 'So, the Catholic religion does not allow divorce? Well, Catholics just don't get divorced, and that's that' (Scanlon 1976: 267). Three points regarding this legislation must be made here. First, merely because these advances were enshrined in law did not necessarily mean there was a change in attitudes in the population as a whole. Second, some of these measures, rather than overtly 'feminist', were in fact anti-clerical and seen as part of an overall process of modernisation. Third, their passing provoked either overt opposition or rancour that was left smouldering, to emerge in time as part of general opposition to the Republic.

Radical movements such as socialism and anarchism also endeavoured to contribute to this process with the overt organisation of unions, *Casas de Pueblo* (People's Houses) and rationalist schools which addressed questions of education and sexuality. Two contrasting but complementary aspects relating to sexuality were the establishment of a chapter of the World League for Sex Reform (WLSR) in Spain, and anarchist sex reform, both seen in their own way as part of the production of discourse on sexuality, even though they presented different solutions to the problems addressed.

The WLSR

The establishment of the Spanish chapter of the WLSR must be seen as an essentially middle-class, educated response to matters related to sexuality. In addition, the birth of the Liga Española para la Reforma Sexual sobre Bases Científicas should be understood within the context of the liberalisation process in Spanish society, the general opening up of ideas, and the 'management' of sexuality by doctors, experts and psychiatrists. This was evidently connected with wider European phenomena; the WLSR itself was established in 1928 in Copenhagen and congresses followed in 1929, 1930 and 1932. In the Spanish case the Liga published the first issue of its journal, *Sexus*, in late 1932. The committee of the Spanish Liga was composed mainly of doctors and jurists such as Luis Jiménez de Asúa, the scientist Gregorio Marañón, the jurist Mariano Ruiz Funes, the criminal law expert Quintiliano Saldaña and the sexologist César Juarros. The Liga produced a second and last *Sexus* in April 1933, and seems to have collapsed after the murder of its secretary, the sex reformer Hildegart Rodríguez. Before then the Liga did organise a conference from April to May 1933 which dealt with matters such as genetics, anthropology, ecology, prostitution, pre-natal and infant care, and politics and eugenics. The importance of the event is notable since, in contrast to the ill-fated 1928 attempt, this one was attended by the Minister for Public Education, Fernando de los Ríos, who inaugurated the conference, and the President of the Republic, Manuel Azaña, who gave the closing speech. Despite the short life of the Liga, its papers, and especially this conference, must be seen as part of an ongoing innovatory process and the 'scientisation' of ideas and discourses on sexuality (Cleminson 1995a). This development had already found fertile ground in a non-official movement: the powerful anarchist movement which had concentrated upon the sexual question for a number of decades.

The anarchists and sex reform in Spain

As has been documented elsewhere, the anarchist and anarcho-syndicalist movement of Spain was particularly well integrated into working-class experience, in the countryside and in the city. By means of a social and cultural dynamic tailored to the demands of workers and the limitations of the time, anarchist militants became effective proponents of a revolutionary change (Esenwein 1989; Heywood 1990). Anarchism attempted a cultural, political and sexual project which was intended to subvert dominant norms and provide solutions to the problems which cut deep into Spanish society (Ackelsberg 1991; Cleminson 1995b). Libertarians believed that one route towards revolution in the long term and improving working-class people's lives in the short term was through education, and great emphasis was laid on the publication of papers and journals. Anarchist journals would probably have been one of the first sources where workers could find out more about sexually transmitted diseases, contraception and questions of sexology. There were a number of explicit anarchist reviews in the 1920s and 1930s such as *Generación Consciente, Estudios* and *Iniciales* which devoted their pages primarily to matters of culture, sexuality and social struggle. The 'Questions and Answers' sections of some anarchist reviews such as *Estudios* attest to the diversity of issues to which anarchists attempted to provide solutions. A wide range of questions can be seen in such sections, including the alleged dangers of masturbation, the merits of vegetarianism, the characteristics of the future anarchist society and homosexuality.

Leftist movements in Spain, as in other European countries, had begun to tackle questions of sexual equality in the nineteenth century. The anarchist FTRE (Spanish Regional Federation of Workers) at its 1882 congress passed a motion allowing women to form unions within the union's structures (Kaplan 1977: 159). However, despite these efforts to integrate women into union structures and to alter the patriarchal attitudes of men in the movement, anarchist sexual politics often suffered from a huge contradiction between theory and practice. One measure towards resolving these problems was reflected in the creation of the anarchist women's organisation Mujeres Libres (Free Women), which claimed twenty thousand members in mid-1938 (Scanlon 1976: 305). The organisation attempted to alter male attitudes towards women, educate its members and generally empower them in the new libertarian society which the whole movement was attempting to construct (Ackelsberg 1991).

Membership of radical organisations did allow some women a more visible role. During the 1870s in the Andalusian town of Sanlúcar de Barrameda, anarchist women, in opposition to Catholic baptisms, undertook their own initiation ceremonies of young children. In such atheist ceremonies a boy was named 'Gateway to Human Progress' and a girl 'Anarchist Europe'. This phenomenon was seen on a wide scale, even though names were often somewhat simpler, such as 'Liberty' and 'Progress' (Kaplan 1977: 86).

In other places women were at the head of demonstrations and popular riots for food and lower rents. This was true of the Barcelona bread riots in the late 1910s. Women protesters against high prices and food shortages converged on the administration buildings and often refused to allow male protesters to join them. These demonstrations were part of an empowering strategy which was established by women themselves and, perhaps ambivalently, supported by some workers' organisations (Kaplan 1992).

Anarchist emphasis on what were understood to be the revolutionary aspects of sexuality was harnessed to emerging ideas on the importance of the sexual question. This is illustrated in the following declaration by the anarchist doctor Félix Martí Ibáñez (1937: 4–5) writing in *Ruta*, the paper of anarchist youth in April 1937: 'The Revolution, which represents the historic opportunity to provide a solution to the socio-economic problems of the youth, also provides the opportunity to resolve the daunting erotic question which has been present for so many years.' Clearly, the question of sexuality was not viewed as an isolated problem to be solved; it was seen as part of a wider problematic which encapsulated capitalism, relationships, education and culture.

What distinguished anarchist attempts at revolutionising sexuality from those of the Liga and 'official' sexology in Spain was precisely that anarchists endeavoured to politicise sexuality from an anti-capitalist, anti-statist position. The struggle for contraception or for meaningful relationships between people (despite their almost total denigration of homosexuality as an acceptable option) was linked to the overall transformation of society and its values. Anarchist sexologists and others active in the field believed that, through public access to education and knowledge on sexuality, ignorance would be defeated. This knowledge-bearing cultural project was rooted in a faith in science which verged on the 'scientism' seen in other radical movements of the time and, as such, was often uncritical of the value-laden aspect of science (Kaplan 1977; Mintz 1994; Cleminson 1995; Alvarez Peláez 1995).

Criticism can be levelled at this movement, which did not eliminate sexism from its ranks; men's egalitarianism often stopped at the front door. But it must be remembered that the anarchists, in the same way as the Liga and the academic disciplines of sexology, psychology and psychiatry, were operating in (and, in some cases, strengthened) highly gendered and repressive circumstances where military and governmental intervention was commonplace. Those anarchists and others who fought against dominant attitudes were open to sanction and public ridicule. For example, one anarchist male who had taught his wife to read and write, and who washed the clothes after his *compañera* came home from work tired out, was mocked as a *marica* (fairy) by older women in his village (Scanlon 1976: 287–8).

The Civil War and the destruction of 'progressive' sex reform

With the army revolt begun on 17 July 1936, Spain was plunged into Civil War and revolution. Amongst other aspects, the Civil War was a battle between tradition and modernity, a confrontation between the many different ideas on how society should be organised and how people should live their lives. The battle lines were refracted through politics, religion, class and sex. These conflicts are seen clearly in the words of Spanish bishops from 1 July 1937:

> The war is an armed plebiscite ... between a people divided: on the one side, the spiritual is revealed by the insurgents who rose to defend law and order, social peace, traditional civilisation, the fatherland and, very ostensibly in a large sector of the population, religion. On the other side there is materialism – call it marxist, communist or anarchist – which wants to replace the old civilisation of Spain by the new 'civilisation' of the Russian soviets.
>
> (in Fraser 1981: 413)

The opposition to sexual freedom, to the altering of rigidly cast gender roles, to any forms of sexual expression not condoned by the once again powerful Catholic church, were all characteristics of what many Spanish bishops had blessed as a *cruzada* against godless, lawless, immoral red Spain. What was at stake in terms of sexual morality had been shown by the founder of Spain's closest relative to a fascist party, the Falange. José Antonio Primo de Rivera declared before the Civil War with regard to the left:

> The character of the approaching movement is radically anti-Spanish. It is the enemy of the Fatherland. It despises honour, it encourages the collective prostitution of young working women in country sprees where all kinds of shamelessness are cultivated... It undermines the family, substituted in Russia by free love, by collective canteens, by facilities for divorce and abortion (have you not heard Spanish girls recently, shouting 'Children, yes, husbands, no!'?).
>
> (in Ellwood 1987: 8)

The attraction, for many, of fascism was its apparent ability to 'turn the clock back', to 'return' to a traditional Spain (Graham and Labanyi 1995: 105). After the collapse of opposition to Franco's troops, patriotism, the 'new Spain', motherhood and self-abnegation were all invoked:

> Women of Spain, in these grave moments for the country, your way of life cannot be that of frivolity, but austerity; your place is not in the theatres, the *paseos*, the cafés, but in the church and the hearth ... Your duty is not to procure for yourself an easy life, but to educate your children, sacrificing your pleasures and helping Spain.
>
> (in Esenwein and Shubert 1995: 182)

With the victory of these Nationalist forces in April 1939, the country's modernising process was arrested for decades and the Spanish people were immersed once more in the tradition of 'National Catholicism', this time enshrined in Franco's state (*Manual* 1941).

Notes

1   The works of Dominican Father Padre Ruiz Amado on the subject of the *noviazgo* were particularly successful. See, for example, *El secreto de la felicidad: Pláticas con las jóvenes de quince a veinte años*, Barcelona, Librería Religiosa, 1913. Also of interest are those works of the future Cardinal Gomá; see, for example, *El matrimonio*, 5th edition, Barcelona, Casulleras, 1931. After the Civil War this lineage was continued most significantly and prolifically by Padre Enciso, who published a large number of works with Athenas y Studium.

2   There are few references to Peratoner. One can be found in the *Diccionari biogràfic de Metges catalans*, Barcelona, Generalitat, 1984. More information can be seen in E. Amezúa (1991); Amezúa, 'Sexología, cuestiones de fondo y forma', *Revista de Sexología*, 49–50 (1992); and 'Los Hijos de Don Santiago: paseo por el casco antiguo de nuestra sexología', *Revista de Sexología*, 59–60 (1993).

Bibliography

Ackelsberg, M. A. (1991), *Free Women of Spain*, Bloomington and Indianapolis, Indiana University Press.

Adams, M. B. (1990), *The Wellborn Science*, New York and Oxford, Oxford University Press.

Alvarez Junco, J. A. (1995), 'Education and the Limits of Liberalism', in H. Graham and J. Labanyi (eds), *Spanish Cultural Studies: An Introduction*, Oxford, Oxford University Press.

Alvarez Peláez, R. (1985), 'Introducción al estudio de la eugenesia española (1900–1936)', *Quipu*, 2, 1, pp. 95–122.

— (1988) 'Origen y desarrollo de la eugenesia en España', in J. M. Sánchez Ron (ed.), *La ciencia y sociedad en España: de la Ilustración a la Guerra Civil*, Madrid, CSIC, pp. 179–204.

— (1990), 'La mujer española y el control de natalidad en los comienzos del siglo XX', *Asclepio*, 42, 2, pp. 175–200.

— (1995), 'Eugenesia y darwinismo social en el pensamiento anarquista', in B. Hofmann, P. Joan i Tous and M. Tietz (eds), *El anarquismo español y sus tradiciones culturales*, Frankfurt and Madrid, Vervuert/Iberoamericana, pp. 29–40.

Alvarez-Uría, F. (1983), *Miserables y locos: medicina mental y orden social en la España del siglo XIX*, Barcelona, Tusquets.

Alvarez-Uría, F. and J. Varela (1994), *Las redes de la psicología: análisis sociológico de los códigos médico-psicológicos*, 2nd enlarged edition, Madrid, Libertarias-Prodhufi.

Amezúa, E. (1991), 'Cien años de temática sexual en España: 1850–1950: Repertorio y análisis', *Revista de Sexología*, 48.

Aranguren, J. L. (1972), *Erotismo y liberación de la mujer*, Barcelona, Ariel.

Balcells, A. (1974), *Trabajo industrial y organización obrera en la Cataluña contemporánea (1900–1936)*, Barcelona, Laia.

Balfour, S. (1995), 'The Loss of Empire, Regenerationism, and the Forging of a Myth of National Identity', in H. Graham and J. Labanyi (eds), *Spanish Cultural Studies: An Introduction*, Oxford, Oxford University Press.

— (1997), *The End of the Spanish Empire, 1898–1923*, Oxford, Clarendon Press.

Barton, S. (1993), 'The Roots of the National Question in Spain', in M. Teich and R. Porter (eds), *The National Question in Europe in Historical Context*, Cambridge, Cambridge University Press, pp. 106–27.

Ben-Ami, S. (1978), *The Origins of the Second Republic in Spain*, Oxford, Oxford University Press.

Bloch, I. (1924), *La vida sexual contemporánea*, Madrid, Editora Internacional.

Brenan, G. (1943) *The Spanish Labyrinth*, Cambridge, Cambridge University Press, reprinted 1990.

Buxán, X. (1997), *Conciencia de un singular deseo*, Barcelona, Laertes.

Capmany, M. A. (1966), *La Dona a Catalunya*, Barcelona, Edicions 62.

— (1970), *El feminismo ibérico*, Barcelona, Tau.

Carr, R. (1983), *Spain, 1808–1975*, Oxford, Clarendon Press.

Cleminson, R. (1995a), *Anarquismo y homosexualidad: Antología de artículos de la Revista Blanca, Generación Consciente, Estudios e Iniciales (1924–1935)*, Madrid, Huerga y Fierro.

— (1995b), 'Werkstattnotizen zur WLSR in Spanien', *Mitteilungen der Magnus-Hirschfeld-Gesellschaft*, 20–1, pp. 45–9.

— (1995c), 'Beyond Tradition and "Modernity": The Cultural and Sexual Politics of Spanish Anarchism', in H. Graham and J. Labanyi (eds), *Spanish Cultural Studies: An Introduction*, Oxford, Oxford University Press, pp. 116–23.

Ellwood, S. (1987), *Spanish Fascism in the Franco Era*, London, Macmillan.

Esenwein, G. (1989), *Anarchist Ideology and the Working-Class Movement in Spain, 1868–1898*, Berkeley, Los Angeles and Oxford, University of California Press.

Esenwein, G. and A. Shubert (1995), *Spain at War: The Spanish Civil War in Context*, London and New York, Longman.

Forel, A. (1925), *El problema sexual*, Madrid, Editora Internacional.

Fortuny, C. (pseudonym of Alvaro Retana), (1929), *La ola verde*, Madrid, no publisher.

Foucault, M. (1973), *The Birth of the Clinic: An Archaeology of Medical Perception*, London, Tavistock.

Fraser, R. (1981), *Blood of Spain: The Experience of Civil War, 1936–1939*, Harmondsworth, Penguin.

García Lara, F. (1986), *El lugar de la novela erótica española*, Granada, Ediciones de la Diputación Provincial de Granada.

García Valdés, A. (1981), *Historia y presente de la homosexualidad*, Madrid, Akal.

González Calbet, M. T. (1988), 'El surgimiento del movimiento feminista, 1900–1930', in Pilar Folguera (ed.), *El Feminismo en España: dos siglos de historia*, Madrid, Editorial Pablo Iglesias, pp. 51–6.

Graham, H. and J. Labanyi (eds) (1995), *Spanish Cultural Studies: An Introduction*, Oxford, Oxford University Press.

Hall, L. A. (1991), *Hidden Anxieties: Male Sexuality, 1900–1950*, Cambridge, Polity Press.

Hernández-Catá, A. (1929), *El ángel de Sodoma*, Madrid, Mundo Latino.

Heywood, P. (1990), *Marxism and the Failure of Organised Socialism in Spain, 1879–1936*, Cambridge, Cambridge University Press.

Juarros, C. (1930), *La Sexualidad encadenada*, Madrid, Mundo Latino.

Kaplan, T. (1977), *Anarchists of Andalusia, 1868–1903*, Princeton, Princeton University Press.

— (1992), *Red City, Blue Period: Social Movements in Picasso's Barcelona*, Berkeley, Los Angeles and Oxford, University of California Press.

Kirkpatrick, S. (1990), *Las románticas: escritoras y subjetividad en España (1835–1850)*, Madrid, Cátedra.

Koch, M. (1891), *Higiene de las relaciones sexuales*, Madrid, Archivo.

Lannon, F. (1987), *Privilege, Persecution, and Prophecy. The Catholic Church in Spain 1875–1975*, Oxford, Clarendon Press.

Lázaro, O. (1990), 'La Revista (sexual) de Occidente', *Revista de Sexología*, 42, pp. 65–81.

Mainer, J. C. (1981), *La Edad de Plata (1902–1939): ensayo de interpretación de un proceso cultural*, Madrid, Cátedra.

Manual del Nacionalsindicalismo (Texto elaborado por el seminario central de Formación política y editado por la sección central de Rurales del Frente de Juventudes), Madrid, Del Frente de Juventudes.

Marañón, G. (1915), *La Doctrina de las Secreciones internas*, Madrid, Corona.

— (1924), prologue to Iwan Bloch, *La vida sexual contemporánea*, in his *Obras Completas*, 2nd edition, vol. I, Madrid, Espasa-Calpe, 1968.

— (1929), prologue to A. Hernández-Catá, *El ángel de Sodoma*, in his *Obras Completas*, 2nd edition, vol. I, pp. 457–64, Madrid, Mundo Latino, 1968.

— (1935), *Conferencia con motivo de los 25 años de Labor*, Madrid, Imprenta Hernando.

— (1968), *Obras Completas*, 2nd edition, Madrid, Espasa-Calpe.

Martí Ibáñez, F. (1937), 'El problema sexual y la juventud revolucionaria', *Ruta*, 27 April, pp. 4–5.

Martínez, J. (1990), 'Sexualidad y orden social: la visión médica en la España del primer tercio del siglo XIX', *Asclepio*, 42, 2, pp. 119–35.

Mintz, J. R. (1994), *The Anarchists of Casas Viejas*, Bloomington, Indiana University Press.

Mirabet i Mullol, A. (1985), *Homosexualidad hoy*, Barcelona, Herder.

Monlau, P. F. (1846), *Higiene privada*, Barcelona, Imprenta de D. Pablo Riera.

— (1850), *Madrid en la mano*, Madrid, Gaspar y Roig, Editores.

— (1853), *Higiene del Matrimonio o Libro de los casados, en el cual se dan las reglas e instrucciones necesarias para conservar la salud de los esposos, asegurar la paz conyugal y educar bien a la familia*, Madrid, Imprenta de M. Rivadeneyra.

Nash, M. (1991), 'Pronatalism and motherhood in Franco's Spain', in G. Bock and P. Thane (eds), *Maternity and Gender Policies: Women and the Rise of the European Welfare States 1880s–1950s*, London and New York, Routledge, pp. 160–77.

Navarro Fernández, A. (1909), *La Prostitución en la villa de Madrid*, Madrid, Ricardo Rojas.

Peratoner, A. (1874), *Los peligros del amor, de la lujuria, del libertinaje… seguido de un estudio del Dr Tardieu sobre la sodomía y la pederastia*, Barcelona, E. Miret.

— (1876), *Onanismo conyugal o fraudes en el cumplimiento de las funciones genitrices: ampliación de la obra del Dr L. F. E. Bergeret, inclusos varios extractos de distinguidos médicos*, Barcelona, E. Miret.

Pérez Sanz, P. and C. Bru Ripoll (1987), 'La sexología en la España de los años 30: Las jornadas eugenésicas de 1928 y 1933', *Revista de Sexología*, 30.

— (1989), 'La sexología en la España de los años 30. Tomo IV: Alvaro Retana El sumo pontífice de la variedades', *Revista de Sexología*, pp. 40–1.

Preston, P. (1994), *The Coming of the Spanish Civil War: Reform, Reaction and Revolution in the Second Republic*, London, Routledge.

Robinson, P. (1977), *The Modernisation of Sex*, New York, Harper & Row.

Rose, N. (1985), *The Psychological Complex*, London, Routledge & Kegan Paul.

Ruiz Amado, R. (1926), *Amor virginal*, Barcelona, Librería religiosa.

Sánchez Granjel, L. (1974), *El sexo como problema en la España contemporánea: pesquisa bibliográfica: cuadernos de la Historia de la Medicina*, 13, Salamanca, Universidad de Salamanca, pp. 111–31.

Scanlon, G. (1976), *La polémica feminista en la España contemporánea*, Madrid, Siglo xxi.

Simón Palmer, C. (1974–9), *La mujer en el siglo XIX: notas bibliográficas*, Madrid, Consejo Superior de Investigaciones Científicas, series Cuadernos Bibliográficos, 31 (1974), pp. 141–98; 32 (1975), pp. 109–50; 34 (1978), pp. 163–206; 37 (1979), pp. 181–211.

Smith, P. J. (1992), *Laws of Desire: Questions of Homosexuality in Spanish Writing and Film, 1960–1990*, Oxford, Clarendon Press.

— (1998), *The Theatre of García Lorca: Text, Performance, Psychoanalysis*, Cambridge, Cambridge University Press.

Suárez Casañ, V. (1903), *El embarazo*, Segunda Serie, vol. I, Barcelona, Maucci.

Trigo, F. (1908), *El amor en la vida y en los libros*, Madrid, Renacimiento.

Tuñón de Lara, M. (1970), *Medio siglo de cultura española (1885–1936)*, Madrid, Tecnos.

Vázquez García, F. and A. M. Mengíbar (1997), *Sexo y razón: una genealogía de la moral sexual en España (siglos XVI–XX)*, Madrid, Akal Universitaria.

Weeks, J. and J. Holland (eds) (1996), *Sexual Cultures: Communities, Values and Intimacy*, Basingstoke, Macmillan.

8

Sexuality and politics in Russia, 1700–2000

Igor S. Kon

It is not so much public opinion as public officials that need educating.

Oscar Wilde

After a long period of neglect and silence, the history of Russian sexuality and eroticism has become quite a fashionable topic in the 1990s, both in and outside Russia. We now have a few solid social history monographs (Levin 1989; Engelstein 1992; Pushkaryova 1997), general overviews of Russian sexual culture from pre-Revolutionary times until today (Kon 1995, 1997), monographs on Russian family history, gender socialisation, prostitution, abortion and birth control, homosexuality, psychosexual literary biographies, sociological surveys of current sexual attitudes and behaviours (Bocharova 1994; Bodrova 1996), a serial scientific publication of Russian underground erotic folklore and literature, and so on.

But is the 'Russian Eros' something solid, more or less stable and unchangeable across the centuries, or a vague and fluid cluster of values, attitudes, social representations and behaviours, which has had different meanings for different ages, generations, genders, social strata and subcultures? Was the Soviet sexual culture a continuation of traditional, 'genuine' Russian sexual values, or their negation? How do 'Russian' sex/gender stereotypes and sexual and romantic values relate to comparable 'western' phenomena? Have they always been in conflict with each other or are the differences relatively minor and explicable by the stages and tempo of socio-economic and cultural development?

IGOR S. KON

The unity of opposites

At practically every moment of its history Russian sexual culture was described both by foreigners and the natives in an extremely polarised manner, and these contrasting images are reproduced in contemporary scientific literature. The three main axes of this counterpoint are gender stratification, the bodily canon, and love and sexuality.

On the one hand medieval and early modern Russia was a patriarchal society, where women were brutally suppressed and oppressed in both social and domestic life; wife beating was considered an expression and proof of conjugal love even by the women themselves. The attitudes and practices of gender inequality, aggravated by centuries of serfdom, are abundantly reflected in Russian folklore and literature. On the other hand Russian social history, culture and folklore have always had a 'powerful woman syndrome'. In Russian fairy tales there are not only militant Amazons and faithful wives but an unusual, by western standards, image of a wise woman – Vasilissa Premudraya. Not a few women played important roles in political and public life. Foreign observers in the eighteenth and early nineteenth centuries were surprised by the relative freedom and social independence of Russian women. Since Hegel and German Romanticism, there has been a philosophical tradition which considers the 'Russian soul' or 'national character' to be feminine rather than masculine.

Equally contradictory is the Russian bodily canon and body politics, including soul/body opposition, social representation of the body, attitudes to nudity and the rules of decency. On one hand Russian character, lifestyle and mentality are often presented and represented as a realm of predominant spirituality (*dukhovnost*), in sharp contrast to western materialism, pragmatism and body-boundedness (*telesnost*). This ideology of disembodied spirituality, with the corresponding underestimation and denigration of the body and its physiological functions, is most clearly implemented in Russian Orthodox religious art (Flegon 1976). Western religious art from the late Middle Ages presents a view of the entire human body as living flesh, with only genitals covered. In Russian icons only the face is alive, while the body is fully covered or outlined in an emaciated, ascetic form. Russian Orthodox icon painting, made according to the Byzantine canon, is much stricter and more ascetic than western art. Secular nude painting appeared in Russia much later and under more stringent control than in the West. Whereas Italian painters were portraying the nude body in secular settings during the Renaissance, Russian artists gained that right only in the late eighteenth century. Even the extravagant Soviet prudery, with its bans and ideological campaigns against any kind of body display and nudity in art and everyday life, was historically rooted in this traditional religious mentality. On the other hand Russian everyday life and popular culture and language have always been anything but modest and sexually prudish. Foreign observers of the seventeenth to nineteenth centuries expressed surprise and shock at the Russian custom of nude mixed bathing in bath-houses and rivers, as well as at the richness and openness of Russian obscene language (*mat*), widespread in all social strata.

This exaggerated soul/body contrast is further projected into the incompatibility between romantic love and carnal lust (sexuality). On the one hand the normative image of love in classical Russian literature is extremely inhibited, chaste, spiritualised and opposed to sexual, carnal pleasure. Russian nineteenth-century literature created a wonderful language of romantic and sentimental love. Yet this literature also bore a strong imprint of what Freud believed to be a fundamental contradiction of male, especially adolescent male, sexuality: incompatibility between tender love and sensual attraction. Its moral emphasis was generally on self-control and restraint. Carnal passion, 'love for sex', had to be sacrificed either to the spiritual 'love for person' or to a serene marital 'love for wedlock'.

On the other hand Russian folklore, language and everyday culture have always been openly and crudely sexual. The so-called Russian erotic tales and proverbs describe naturalistically and in detail all kinds of sexual actions, they glorify the sexual exploits of polygamous heroes, such as the possession of a sleeping beauty, dishonouring (i.e. raping) a young woman in revenge for her refusal to marry the hero, and so on. The nature and even the existence of romantic love in Russia has been questioned from two absolutely different points of view. According to Nikolai Berdyaev (1989/1907: 17), 'there is something dark and tormented, obscure and often deformed in Russian love. We have not had genuine romanticism in love.' Yet the same fact (if it is a fact) is interpreted either as an effect of excessive idealism and romanticism, the affirmation of love at the expense of a more prosaic and realistic sensuality, or as the result of sexual permissiveness, serfdom, poor housing conditions, poverty and the peasants' traditional naturalistic outlook.

Historical trends

My point is that we must look not at whether the thesis or the antithesis of these oppositions is 'true' (both can be substantiated) but why their unity has been historically so stable.

According to the great Russian historian Vassily Klyuchevsky, the history of Russia is that of a country in the constant process of colonisation, extension of borders and conquest of new territories (Klyuchevsky 1987: 50). This extensivity of Russian history has had important consequences for the nature and development of Russian sexual culture.

The Christianising of Russia, stretching over several centuries and all the while involving new territories and peoples, was slow and in many ways inefficient and superficial. In popular belief, rites and customs, Christian norms not only co-existed with pagan norms but frequently incorporated them. Paganism influenced attitudes towards love and sexuality particularly strongly. Some pagan rites and customs, like *Skakaniya* or *Yarovukha*, survived in certain peasant communities until the end of the nineteenth century. The former took place on the eve of the wedding ceremony at the groom's house; the young guests would all stand in a circle, resting their arms on one another's shoulders and gallop, kicking their legs up high, the maidens lifting up their skirts, and all of them singing blatantly erotic songs, a group carouse which ended with them all sleeping side by side. *Yarovukha* (from Yarilo, the pagan god of fertility) was a gathering of young people at the bride's home for a party, after which they would remain and sleep side by side, with every liberty save the final intimacy being permitted. The sexual behaviour and mores of non-Russian ethnic groups were even more exotic from the Orthodox point of view. This mixed and heterogeneous pagan–Christian cultural heritage has been accentuated and made even more contradictory by huge territorial, regional and ethnic diversity. Russian provinces have always had very different sexual customs, attitudes and ideas about courtship, premarital pregnancy, and so on. It is impossible to generalise from one part of the country to another. Russian ethnography has always been regionally oriented.

Regional and ethnic diversity was intensified by the enormous cultural gap between educated and 'westernised' nobility and gentry, on one side, and the illiterate and enslaved peasantry, on the other. Social class and strata differences in Russia have been much more pronounced than in western Europe.

The extreme ethnic and cultural heterogeneity of the population made the position of the Russian Orthodox church difficult. Being incapable of exterminating and vanquishing the innumerable and immensely varied vestiges of paganism, the church had either to incorporate these or turn a blind eye to them. Russian Orthodoxy sometimes appears more 'realistic' and tolerant than Roman Catholicism, on, for example, such issues as the celibacy of the clergy, and it tried to balance these unwilling concessions against the spirituality and otherworldly asceticism of the church doctrine itself: thus creating a highly contradictory system of moral and aesthetic values.

The 'civilising process' of cultural modernisation and secularisation, including the emergence of new secular forms of social control over body and sexuality, domestication of body and language, and the introduction of new rules of propriety and 'good manners', was also somewhat different in Russia from that in early modern western Europe. In so far as it was related to and associated with the development of capitalism, urbanisation and the emergence of the middle classes, the 'civilising process' was belated in Russia, and was experienced and labelled as 'westernisation'.

Because of the peculiar strength of Russian absolutism, new forms of socialising and etiquette were often introduced from above, by the imperial court, and not as mere examples for more or less voluntary imitation but as arbitrary and compulsory prescriptions, under close administrative supervision, and with the utmost contempt and disregard for individual preferences and tastes. There is a sort of continuance between Peter the Great's masquerades and compulsory boyars' shavings and the Communist Party's crusades between the 1950s and the 1980s against long hair, beards, miniskirts, wide or narrow trousers, and so on. Ideologically these were quite opposite policies – in the first case it was a compulsory westernisation, and in the second anti-westernisation – but the administrative-compulsory methods and social-psychological consequences of these policies were similar.

Since it was introduced mainly by external and repressive, rather than internal and positive, means, and because of the general socio-economic and political weakness of the middle classes, the civilising process in Russia tended more to rigid conformity and uniformity than to pluralism, individualisation and diversity.

The differentiation of public and private life, with their correspondingly different means of social control, was underdeveloped in

Russia. For a considerable part of Russian history, civil society was either swallowed up in or completely controlled by the despotic state. No Russian man or woman of any estate could claim that their house was their fortress. There were no guarantees of the sanctity of private life. Social vulnerability to state interference was aggravated by housing conditions and strict control by the local peasant community, intolerant of any kind of nonconformity.

An important psychological correlate of imposed social control was a deep-rooted mass conviction that all aspects of personal life, and especially sexual life, could and should be strictly regulated and that everything was either right or wrong (as earlier it was either a sin or a virtue). Yet total control means equally total rejection. When individual judgement is underdeveloped, the people's only choice is between complete surrender to and complete rejection of the imposed norms: just as centuries ago, with the Christianising process, the Russian Empire was far too big and socially and culturally heterogeneous to be effectively controlled or 'civilised' by administrative means. Many 'pre-civilised' and even 'pre-Christian' lifestyles and attitudes to body and sexuality continued to exist under the surface and on the periphery of the official public life in both Czarist and Soviet Russia. As in a medieval society all forms of unorthodox sexuality were considered heretical, now they were looked upon not only as moral laxity, depravity and anomie (*vsedozvolennost*) but as political opposition. And since modernisation and civilising have been considered 'westernisation' in Russia, the opposition to their manifestations – whether gender equality, feminism or sexual tolerance – inevitably acquired a political and nationalistic flavour in the context of an old war between traditionalism/nationalism and modernism/westernisation.

Sexual culture and erotic art

In all Christian cultures basically different languages of love and sexuality have existed. At one pole there was the highly sublimated, spiritualised love lyric, emphasising noble and elevated feelings. At the opposite pole there was openly sensual and physiologically explicit popular carnival culture and aristocratic libertine art. To combine these contrasting images was extremely difficult. The missing link was a refined, sophisticated erotic art as a means of incorporating sexuality into 'high' culture.

But in Russia this was more difficult than in western Europe. The emotional vocabularies for the description and expression of sentimental and passionate love, as well as the corresponding literary genres, were created in eighteenth-century Russian literature, under the direct impact of French, English and German cultures. French libertines also had a strong influence in Russia. Young gentlemen of Pushkin's time enjoyed not only Denis Diderot's 'immodest treasures' but also Ivan Barkov's bawdy verses. But Barkov's obscene and sacrilegious poetry has nothing in common with elegant and playful western eroticism.

Obscene underground literature in Russia was firmly rooted in the popular culture, folklore and language, and it had important political functions (as a challenge to the authorities and to the established religious and social order) and psychological functions (relieving young men of their sexual tensions and at the same time teaching them 'how to do it'). But the existence of these two absolutely separate languages only enlarged the already existing psychological gap between love and sexuality.

Russian censorship, supported by the joint forces of the church and state bureaucracy, was strict and all-embracing. Erotica was considered not only corrupt but also alien, having nothing to do with the Russian national heritage. This idea was clearly expressed as early as the famous book by Prince M. M. Shcherbatov, *On the Corruption of Morals in Russia* (1786–9). Russian literary criticism was also extremely prudish. Not only frivolous French novels but even highly moralistic works by British sentimentalists were declared indecent. In the 1820s Romanticism came under virulent attack for its 'sensuousness'. And in 1865 the magazine *Sovremennaya letopis* discovered 'eroticism in its most cynical form' even in Russian writer Alexander Ostrovsky's plays.

None of this prudery was exclusively Russian. In France both *Madame Bovary* and *Les Fleurs du Mal* were in 1857 formally condemned by the court. And later Leo Tolstoy's American translator Isabel Hapgood refused to translate *The Kreutzer Sonata* because she found its language 'to be too excessive in its candour'. Erotica was attacked not only by the religious right and conservative middle class but also by the radical left. The so-called revolutionary democrats played an important part in forming nineteenth-century Russian literary and artistic culture. Aristocrats of Pushkin's time had received a good secular education from their childhood, and even while remaining deeply religious generally distanced themselves from official hypocrisy. This was much more difficult for the next generation of Russian intellectuals, who had been educated in religious seminaries and/or were themselves from ecclesiastical backgrounds. While breaking with some principles of their families, they were unable to overcome others.

Transplanted into an alien social milieu, many of them suffered acute shyness and tried to repress the desires of their flesh, the more so because not everything was 'orthodox' in their sexuality. The famous literary critics Belinsky, Chernyshevsky and Dobrolyubov suffered from unsatisfied sexual desires, masturbatory anxieties, feelings of sexual inferiority, unconscious homoeroticism, and so on. Similar experiences and feelings were typical for many young men of that period outside Russia. But unsuccessful inner battles, instead of helping ambitious Russian radicals to develop sexual tolerance, turned into a principled moralistic-aesthetic condemnation and renunciation of any sensuality as repulsive and unworthy. Unable either to restrain or accept his own sensuality, Belinsky was extremely disapproving of any of its manifestations, for example the poetry of Alexander Polezhayev. Reasoning from the standpoint of an imagined 'innocent young boy', who had to be protected from seduction in every way possible, the 'frenzied Vissarion' denounced Boccaccio in passing; he called a novel by Paul de Kock a 'squalid and ignoble work'.

These strong anti-sexual feelings and a general suspicious, circumspect attitude towards the body and sensuality, which were inherited by subsequent generations of Russian revolutionaries, Narodovoltsy and Bolsheviks, were not a simple manifestation of individual personal psychosexual problems and difficulties but a very clear-cut ideology. While the conservative right censured eroticism for undermining religious and family values, populists and social democrats could not fit it into their normative canon of giving up all energy to the liberation of the working classes. In comparison with this grand social design, everything else paled into insignificance. Even the subtle intimate lyrics of Afanasy Fet, Yakov Polonsky and Konstantin Sluchevsky seemed 'vulgar' to the radical critics of the latter part of the nineteenth century, who could see no difference at all between erotica and pornography. The sexual views of Russian feminists of the time were equally conservative: like many of their western European counterparts they saw male lust at the root of many social ills, and indeed constructed lust as specifically male.

In other words the inflexible rigour of the socio-political and moral attitudes and beliefs of the Russian democratic intelligentsia was becoming the militant foe of the quotidian, emotional and psycho-physiological realities out of which normal individual human life essentially took shape. Any artist or writer who attempted to deal with these realities came under withering attack simultaneously from both right and left, and this seriously hampered the emergence in Russia of any lofty, refined erotic art with corresponding language and vocabulary, without which sexuality and all talk of it inevitably appeared base and sullied.

The predominantly negative attitudes to sexuality, body and erotica began to change only in the last years of the nineteenth century and around the 1905 revolution, when 'the sexual question' (*polovoi vopros*) suddenly became one of the most urgent issues in philosophy, education, politics and the arts. The 'sexual question' of the period was fundamentally a gender issue concerning women's emancipation. Sexuality proper was discussed mainly in its most problematic and socially dangerous aspects – abortion, prostitution, venereal diseases and homosexuality. The sex education issue was practically reduced to the question of how to prevent adolescent masturbation, which was looked upon as extremely dangerous, although in western Europe views on the deleteriousness of 'self-abuse' were beginning to be moderated around this time, and the young were being reassured about the awful warnings carried over from previous generations.

The most important outcome was the emergence of a sophisticated erotic art. New Russian erotic art and philosophy used the same language and discussed the same problems as their western contemporaries. But the social possibilities were much more restricted. Early twentieth-century Russian philosophy of Eros was more metaphysical than phenomenological. Writers like Merezhkovsky, Gippius and Berdyaev tried to rehabilitate an abstract Eros, yet, as soon as the subject turned to real, everyday, bodily enjoyment, a barrier immediately rose. While this timidity certainly had its origins in the personalities of these authors, who were unable to accept some of their own sexual – especially homoerotic – feelings and inclinations, it was typical of the entire generation of thinkers.

Russian erotic art, poetry and literature were much more expressive and outspoken. But, like their European counterparts, they were openly decadent. Enchantment with unusual, strange, deviant, sombre, violent, 'perverted' forms of sexuality was liberating but at the same time repulsive and shocking. Decadent art openly declared itself to be immoral and amoral, and it was generally regarded as socially and educationally subversive. And it was not always easy to differentiate the arrogance of the experimental avant-garde art from the shamelessness of commercial erotica.

Russian society was not ready to differentiate between these variegated phenomena. In the minds of many prominent intellectuals they formed a single picture of a terrifying 'sexual Bacchanalia'. The logic of both left and right was practically one and the same: sexuality was a dangerous instrument of the class – or national – enemy, through which the enemy was undermining the spiritual and physical health of 'our side'. Conservative authors maintained that the current 'obsession with sex' was engendered by the revolutionary movement and godlessness. For the populist and social-democratic critics 'erotic individualism' and pornography were the products of dissolute bourgeois culture, the means through which the bourgeoisie was trying to infect the naturally spiritually healthy working classes. The social democrats claimed that 'sexomania' was part of the reaction to the defeat of the revolution of 1905, a consequence of intellectuals' disillusionment with public life and withdrawal into their own private lives. Both were right. The demands for 'sexual liberalisation' were an integral part of the social renovation programme which preceded the 1905 revolution. And the defeat of the revolution, while undermining people's interest in politics, encouraged them to seek compensation in their private lives, first and foremost in sexuality.

Soviet sexual experiment

Strict control over – indeed eventually the elimination of – sexuality was one of the main aspects of Soviet policies aimed at the formation of the 'New Soviet Man', but this was neither explicit nor deliberate. We may delineate three major stages:

First, 1917–30: disintegration of the traditional family structure; the social emancipation of women; the weakening of the institution of marriage and the sexual morality based on it; and normative uncertainty in regard to sexuality.

Second, 1930–56: the strengthening of marriage and the family by state administrative methods; establishment of totalitarian control over the individual; denial and repression of sexuality; and elimination of sexual culture.

Third, 1956–87: the replacement of totalitarianism by authoritarianism; gradual expansion of the sphere of individual freedom; transition from state administrative methods to moral administrative methods for protecting marriage and the family; and the shift from a policy of denying and repressing sexuality to one of medicalisation and pedagogisation.

Originally the Bolsheviks' sexual policy was not repressive. Soviet legislation and policy on issues of marriage and procreation in the 1920s were the most daring and progressive in the world. Women were accorded full equal rights with men in all social and private areas, including marriage and family relations. Medical services for mothers and children were expanded and improved and became entirely free. Yet the realities of life that confronted the Bolsheviks immediately after the 1917 Revolution presented more difficulties than they had anticipated. Many of the splendid advances towards equality were impossible to carry forward in the midst of economic ruin, poverty and lack of culture; these plans had to be put on the back burner for a time. And the costs associated with the subsequent breakdown in marriage and family patterns – unwanted pregnancies, fatherless children, prostitution, the spread of venereal disease – were great and provoked mounting concern. The Bolsheviks had to do what was necessary, rather than what was desirable, but these measures often had boomerang effects which only aggravated the original difficulties.

The liberation of women from the ecclesiastical bonds of marriage made them more vulnerable to sexual exploitation. The massive involvement of women in the labour force proved to be detrimental to family life and the education of children. The legalisation of induced abortion in 1920 produced a terrible decline in the birth rate. As attempts to improve social conditions proved to be a failure, the state had to turn to more and more restrictive social policies. The aim of changing social conditions, adapting them to the needs of individual human beings, which was the original essence of Marxist theory, was gradually reformulated into the task of adapting human behaviours, needs and even feelings to extant poor and inhuman social conditions. Social control took the place of individual freedom.

Ultimately the Bolsheviks had two alternative strategies in regard to sexuality: acceptance or suppression. The first, more liberal viewpoint was formulated by Alexandra Kollontai and was always marginal. The second, more rigid and dogmatic stance was taken by Aron Zalkind. Zalkind admitted the existence of a biological sexual drive in human beings and the harm of 'sexual self-corking'. At the same time, however, he proposed wholesale subordination of sexuality to the proletariat's class interests.

The means of legitimising this suppression and its phraseology were changeable. In the 1920s sexuality had to be suppressed in the name of the higher interests of the working class. In the 1930s self-discipline was advocated for the sake of Soviet state and Communist Party. In the 1950s state administrative control was gradually transformed into moral administrative regulations for the sake of the stability of marriage and the family. With all these ideological differences, the practical message regarding sexuality remained the same: Don't do it!

What were the real reasons for this sexophobia, unprecedented in the twentieth century and making sexuality literally unmentionable over one-sixth of the world's land surface?

First, as George Orwell put it so pithily, in order to ensure absolute control over the personality, a totalitarian regime endeavours to deindividualise it, to destroy its independence and emotional world. The link between sexophobia and deindividualisation was well recognised by such Russian Soviet writers as Mikhail Bulgakov, Yevgeny Zamyatin and Andrei Platonov. Sexophobia helped to confirm the fanatic cult of the state and the leader and also performed some 'applied' political functions – the authorities frequently used accusations of sexual perversion, decadence and the keeping or distributing of pornography for dealing with political opponents and dissidents.

Although sexophobia was the official state policy, it was also to a certain degree a 'people's policy'. As a result of industrialisation and collectivisation, as well as political repression, the social composition of the communist elite was rapidly changing in the early 1930s: yesterday's peasants were everywhere replacing intellectuals and members of the urban working class. This 'cultural revolution' was accompanied by a general upsurge in anti-intellectualism. For unsophisticated former peasants 'anti-sexual' arguments were far more convincing than they had been for the previous ruling elites. They could hardly renounce sex itself, nor had they any intention of doing so, but it was very easy for them to expunge it from the culture – and they did so with relish and sincerity.

Whereas the sexophobia of the 1920s had been reinforced by arguments about class interests and by mechanistic theories about the possibility and necessity of channelling individual 'sexual energy' into more exalted social goals, the authorities now propagated moral concern for shoring up marriage and the family. Promulgation of policies for strengthening marriage and family stability at any cost was invariably accompanied by attacks on 'anarchic' sexuality. People who, because of a lack of education and/or their own inhibitions, did not have the words to articulate and express intricate erotic experiences were now convinced that only perverts and decadents talked freely about sex. Sexual intolerance, behind which often lurked personal ignorance and anxieties, became an essential aspect of global social intolerance.

Stalinist sexophobia was an important element in the general cultural counter-revolution of the early 1930s aimed at liquidating social and cultural diversity and at establishing total control over the personality, its most important steps being the recriminalisation of homosexuality (1933), and bans on pornography (1935) and abortion (1936). But the liquidation of erotic culture and degradation of the elite to the level of the masses produced not so much a desexualisation of public and private life as its impoverishment, primitivisation and vulgarisation. Sexuality, driven underground and degraded to the level of a simple 'sex instinct', became more and more wild, and potentially aggressive. Forbidden erotica became a strong anti-Soviet and anti-communist symbol, pressing the people to make their choice – and their choices were often against the regime.

As for sexual culture proper, the net result of sexophobia was a practical liquidation of all sorts of erotic culture and the prohibition of sexual discourse, whether in the area of sex research, erotic art or medical information. Enforced silence strengthened traditional hypocrisy, which, in turn, was easily transformed into cynicism. Group sex came to flourish openly among every generation in the youth hostels and dormitories. All too common was what went on in the vacation homes and outdoor recreation centres: once out of sight of parents or spouses, young people (and the not-so-young) sometimes binged and caroused as if there was no tomorrow, fulfilling and overfulfilling the plan, making up for what was out of reach in everyday life.

The Second World War caused serious dislocation to marital and family relationships and sexual morality. It gave rise to innumerable temporary liaisons and children born out of wedlock. The penitentiary system had an ongoing negative effect on the family as well. Not only were millions of people torn apart from their families and deprived of normal sexual lives for years at a time, but they had to put up with the terrible cruelty – including sexual abuse – of the camps. This certainly affected their subsequent sexual lives. The lack of serious discussion about gender differences produced an extremely sexist everyday consciousness as well as a host of misunderstandings and mutual recriminations between men and women. The absence of sex education resulted not only in sexual ignorance but also in a growing generation gap. And, like the country's economic and social problems, resolution of these burning issues was postponed for many decades.

Gradual liberalisation and transformation of the Soviet regime after Stalin's death from totalitarian to authoritarian altered its sexual policy from one of brutal suppression to one of awkward taming. Until the 1960s sex was practically unmentionable; there was not a shred of public information available about it. Yet as soon as life became slightly freer, it became clear that both the value orientation and the sexual conduct of Soviet youth were moving in the same direction as those of their counterparts in the West: earlier sexual maturation and awakening of erotic feelings among adolescents; earlier onset of sexual life; growing social and moral acceptance of premarital sexuality and cohabitation; weakening of the 'double standard' of sexual conduct for men and women; enhanced significance of sexual satisfaction as a factor in making and sustaining a happy marriage; resexualisation of women; narrowing of the prohibited sphere within culture and an increase in public interest in the erotic; rising toleration in regard to the unusual, variant and deviant forms of sexuality, particularly homosexuality; and a growing gap between the generations in terms of sexual principles, values and behaviour.

These trends are common to the USSR and the West. But whereas in the West they have been openly discussed, and frequently over-exposed, over the course of several decades, thereby enabling the public consciousness to internalise and digest their potential consequences gradually (although conservative circles have been incapable of so doing), in the Soviet Union everything was swept under the carpet. While people's behaviour and values, particularly those of young people, have been changing, official society has pretended that nothing has been happening. Unmistakable symptoms of profound, long-term and irreversible transformations were treated as isolated incidents or extraordinary events engendered by the malicious influence of the 'decadent West', necessitating administrative discipline.

In the 1950s and 1960s some progressive Soviet education experts, doctors and psychologists began to talk of the need for some sort of sex education for adolescents. It must be said that these initial forays into the subject of sex education were by no means radical. 'Sex education' was conceptualised primarily as moral education; the idea of a special course in sexual enlightenment invoked dreadful panic amongst most progressive educators, who often declared it to be totally unnecessary. No one even dared contemplate the idea of acquainting adolescents with the fundamentals of contraception.

The reformist strategy in sexuality was just as much a failure as the Khrushchev and Kosygin reforms in economics. The Stalinist legacy was too sombre, and resistance to change too strong. Medicalisation of sexuality in the mid-1960s managed to take the first timid steps, culminating with the establishment of a medical sub-discipline named 'sexopathology', while pedagogisation (to use Foucault's term) remained generally at the level of appeals alone. The 'reformers' themselves had but a poor understanding of what they wanted. Sexuality remained an enemy for them, a dangerous wild beast that had to be bridled.

Disputes about whether the USSR needed sex education, and if so what exactly this should involve, lasted a good quarter of a century. Only in 1983 was a two-part course on preparation for marriage and family life formally introduced into Russian schools: 'Hygienic and Sexual Education' (twelve hours), taught to adolescents at the age of fifteen, within a course on human anatomy and physiology, and 'The Ethics and Psychology of Family Life', a thirty-four-hour course for those aged sixteen to seventeen. The course also included some elements of sex education. All the same, the programme remained largely on paper and in the late 1980s it was altogether eliminated from the schools.

Sexual revolution and counter-revolution (1987–97)

The breakdown of the Soviet regime has brought the Russian people their long-desired sexual liberation. But, as was also the case with the economy and politics, sexual freedom was immediately transformed into anomie and anarchy, and became a controversial symbol of social and personal liberation and the object of political speculation. Once again there are two poles: conservative traditionalists, nationalists and communists, with a common blending of sexophobia, homophobia, anti-semitism and anti-Americanism, on one side; and liberal 'westerners', on the other side.

The first and undeniable achievement of the current Russian sexual revolution is that sexuality has become visible. It is openly discussed and represented in mass media and advertising. A lot of erotic publications are available. Sexuality is recognised as an important element in culture and individual life. Questions about sexual attitudes and behaviours are included in national public opinion polls. People have become much more outspoken about sexual issues. Sexual tolerance is growing. After long debate, homosexuality was decriminalised in 1993. Despite high levels of homophobia, same-sex love is no longer a taboo topic, and the public tolerance, as reflected in the polls, is systematically growing, especially among younger, better-educated and urban people. Several voluntary associations for the promotion of sexual knowledge and safe-sex practices, including a Russian Planned Parenthood Association (RPPA) and a few local centres for sex education, have been formed (with western financial help).

At the same time sexual liberation means many difficult social problems. Contemporary Russian sexual culture is completely commercialised and Americanised, and this is highly frustrating for parents, teachers and intellectuals. As a consequence of the old Soviet reproduction policies, in 1989 Russia was a world champion for unwanted pregnancies and induced abortions. Thanks to the efforts of medical authorities and the RPPA, this statistic has somewhat improved in the last few years. According to official figures, in 1990 women aged fifteen to forty-nine reported having 114 abortions per thousand women, in 1992 98, in 1995 73 and in 1996 69 (Vishnevskii 1998). Nevertheless the abortion rate is still one of the highest in the world. And, because of the general sharp economic decline of the country, all other health indicators, including birth rate and infant and maternal mortality, are deteriorating. All sexually transmitted diseases have reached really dangerous proportions. 'The number of syphilitically infected people per thousand of population had risen from 1990 to 1996 forty-eight times and among children sixty-eight times' (Vishnevskii 1998). The country is on the verge of a real AIDS epidemic. Prostitution, and especially child prostitution, is growing, as well as sexual violence and rape.

The situation of adolescents is extremely difficult. According to recent surveys (Chervyakov and Kon 1993, 1995), the sexual behaviour and attitudes of urban adolescents are rapidly changing. In 1993 25 per cent of sixteen-year-old girls and 38 per cent of boys had had coital experience; in 1995 the respective figures had already risen to 33 per cent and 50 per cent. Among seventeen-year-olds the respective growth is from 46 per cent to 52 per cent (females) and from 49 per cent to 57 per cent (males). The absolute figures are comparable to the USA and western Europe but in Russia the change is going very fast; adolescent sexuality is strongly related to social class and is often violent and aggressive. Unprotected and uncontrollable early sexual activity has serious moral and epidemiological consequences. About 10 per cent of teenage girls experience sexual initiation under some degree of compulsion. No more than 5–7 per cent of rape is formally registered and even these cases are often ignored.

People of all ages complain about inadequate sexual knowledge. Intergenerational taboos on the exchange of sexual information within Russian families are very strong: parents are shy about discussing these matters with their children. According to a representative national survey, only 13 per cent of parents have ever talked with their children about sexual matters. In the Russian mass media there is a lot of soft porn and cheap erotica but no scientific educational programmes. In all national public opinion polls since 1989 the predominant majority of adults, 60–90 per cent, depending upon age and social background, strongly support the idea of systematic sex education in schools, with only 3–20 per cent against. Parents, teachers and students are equally positive about sex education but this is extremely difficult to organise.

The new sexual openness and the negative sides of the sexual revolution are used by the conservatives, fascists and communists as an ideological weapon against liberal reform.

The first massive attack against sexuality, in the form of an anti-pornography crusade, was initiated by the Communist Party in 1991. In whipping up a moral panic in the country, the Communist Party pursued very clear, though always unacknowledged, political goals. The anti-pornography campaign aimed at diverting popular attention from pressing political issues and blunting awareness of the government's economic failures. In defending morality and the family, the Party was deflecting blame from itself for the weakening and destruction of both morals and the family. Communist leaders

213

were trying to cement the developing alliance between the Party and conservative religious and national chauvinist organisations, including blatantly fascist groups. Anti-pornography slogans enabled the Party to direct popular fury and frenzy against the *glasnost* so hated by the Party apparatchiks, by branding the democratic mass media as a Jewish–Masonic conspiracy bent on corrupting the morals of young people, destroying traditional popular values, and so on. Under the pretext of concern for young people, the Party endeavoured to restore the control over them it had lost. Reactionary pundits invariably portrayed young people not as subjects of social activity but as the eternal objects of education, lost sheep vulnerable to any stupid influence (though never any sensible one), from which they had to be saved, by force if necessary, against their own will.

In spite of all efforts, this campaign failed, people did not swallow the bait, and the USSR Supreme Soviet's strong worded anti-pornography resolution remained on paper only. The leaders of the August 1991 coup also used anti-sexual phraseology.

In early 1997 a global attack on sexual culture, including the issues of women's reproductive rights, sexual/erotic culture and sex education, was renewed with fury by the communists, the extreme nationalists, the Russian Orthodox church and the members of 'Pro-life' and the Roman Catholic Goluba associations. The US anti-abortionists have no real support in Russia. In the national public opinion poll of 1994 women's right to abortion was recognised by 73 per cent of men and 88 per cent of women, with only 11 per cent and 8 per cent against. But there is considerable ideological and financial support from extreme-right US organisations and it was these who initiated this new campaign, the main arguments of which are that sex education, birth control, abortion, masturbation and homosexuality are exclusively western, non-Orthodox, anti-Russian subversive phenomena, deliberately aimed at degrading historical Russian culture and physically exterminating the nation by reducing its birth rate. All this is supported by wild imagination and lies.

The Russian Planned Parenthood Association is denounced by Christian fundamentalists as a 'satanic institution', propagating abortion and depopulation. The official slogan of the RPPA, 'The birth of healthy and wanted children, responsible parenthood', was represented in *Pravda*, the Communist Party periodical, and religious newspapers as meaning 'One child in a family'. The booklet *Your Friend Condom*, for young adults and teens, is described as if it were addressed to seven-year-olds. Influential Orthodox priests publicly proclaim that the International Planned Parenthood Federation is financed by the US and British governments and, at the same time, that it is formally banned by President Clinton.

Another target is school sex education. There is not and never has been any such thing in Russia. At the demand of the Russian Ministry of Education, the United Nations Population Fund (UNFPA) in collaboration with UNESCO gave a grant for three years' experimental work in sixteen selected schools, to develop workable curricula and textbooks 'for fourteen- to sixteen-year-olds, considering the importance of young people being able to make informed and responsible decisions before reaching the age of potentially starting sexual activities'. There was no cultural imperialism or any attempt to invent something uniform and compulsory for the whole country. In the introduction to the project it is emphasised that 'to ensure cultural acceptability, all curricula and text-books will be developed by Russian experts, making use of knowledge and experience from several countries, and with the input of technical assistance from foreign experts' (Kon 1997).

The project was initiated in October 1996. Its first step was sociological monitoring, trying to assess the sexual values and attitudes of children, parents and teachers of a few pilot schools, on a strictly voluntary basis. Similar controls were planned for the next stages of the experiment. Unfortunately, Ministry of Education officials, without consulting the experts, made a fatal mistake: they announced the inauguration of such delicate work without adequate political and psychological preparation. Even worse, the Ministry sent to thirty thousand schools a package of five 'alternative sex education programmes', negligently edited, never tested in the classroom and unrealistic (some of them required more than three hundred class hours). These programmes had nothing in common with the UNESCO project but are perceived as a part of it.

So before it was even born, the project came under heavy attack in the mass media as a 'western ideological subversion of Russian children'. In some small towns people were asked in the street: 'Do you want children to be taught in school how to make sex? If not, please sign the petition to ban this devilish project.' Priests and activists tell their audiences that all bad things in western life are rooted in sex education, that western governments are trying now to ban or eliminate it, and only a corrupt Russian government, at the instigation of the world 'sexological–industrial complex', is acting against the best interests of the country. This is supported with 'scientific' data: for example, that in England, at the instigation of irresponsible sexologists, boys begin masturbation at nine, and at eleven years they are already impotent.

Some prominent members of the Russian Academy of Education also attacked this 'western' spirit: 'We don't need the Netherlands' experience, we have our own traditional wisdom.' President of the Academy Dr Arthur Petrovsky strongly dissociated himself from this nationalist position as well as from suggestions to re-introduce moral censorship. But the general decision was that instead of special 'sex education' the country should improve adolescents' moral education 'with some elements of sex education' (this formula was used in 1962). At the insistence of some communist members of Parliament, the Attorney General's office has begun a criminal investigation into whether the questions about sexual anatomy in an anonymous questionnaire for pilot schools might be considered as 'depravity' and 'seduction'.

Freedom of artistic expression and the mass media are also under attack. The State Duma has approved the first reading of a law limiting the distribution and sale of products, services and performances of a sexual nature. Its intention is to control the spread of pornography and commercial erotica, especially among minors. But the most difficult issue of any such legislation is the differentiation between pornography and erotic art. In the draft law, prepared by professionals, this was taken into account. Yet later legislators deleted this limitation and instead of the 'unclear' concept of erotica introduced the notion 'products of a sexual nature', which is defined as 'products of mass media, any other printed and audiovisual products, including advertising, messages and materials, transmitted and received by computer networks, as well as different things and means, satisfying the needs, related to sexual drive, with the exception of medical drugs and products for medical purposes'. This definition is legally and scientifically meaningless. Everything can be used or interpreted in a sexual way. For the Greek youth who secretly copulated with the Aphrodite statue, the sculpture was definitely a 'sexual production', just as was Guido Reni's St Sebastian for Yukio Mishima. Does it mean that these objects of art and their reproduction should be distributed only in the 'special places' and children should be banned from the Hermitage museum? According to this draft law, Nabokov's *Lolita* should be banned from any public library. If this law is finally accepted, Russian art and culture will be once again at the mercy of corrupt state officials and their subservient and ignorant 'experts'.

What may be the possible outcome of these battles? In the short run almost anything can happen in Russia. But in the long run I am optimistic. The unique Soviet sexophobia was partly rooted in old Russian traditions but its main social strength was the under-development of private life and the fact that the USSR was a closed society. Both of these factors are now in decline.

Like some other aspects of Soviet/Russian life, sexophobia has been the offspring of the marginal, declassé lumpen-proletarians, ex-peasants who did not really belong to the town or the countryside. This segment of the population is gradually disappearing from the historical stage. By the year 2000 fewer than half of the forty-year-olds but over 60 per cent of the thirty-year-olds and 70 per cent of twenty-year-olds will have been born in the cities.

Current sexual attitudes and practices in Russia are highly diversified according to age, gender, education, cohort, and regional, ethnic and social background. In the near future this heterogeneity will probably increase and it may produce more cultural conflicts. Yet, in the long run, it is the younger, urban and better-educated people who will certainly have the upper hand in defining what is right and what is wrong. Any attempt by the state, church or local community to limit forcibly their sexual freedom is doomed to failure, and will be terribly detrimental to the authority of the institutions making the attempt.

Bibliography

Berdyaev, N. (1989/1907), 'Metafizika pola i lyubvi', *Eros i lichnost': filosofia pola i lyubvi*, Moscow, Prometei.

Bernshtam, T. A. (1988), *Molodyozh v obryadovoi zhizni russkoi obshchiny XIX–nachale XX v*, Leningrad, Nauka.

Berry, E. E. (ed.) (1995), *Postcommunism and the Body Politics*, New York, New York University Press.

Bocharova, O. A. (1994), 'Seksualnaya svoboda: Slova i dela', *Chelovek*, 5, pp. 98–107.

Bodrova, V. (1996), 'Russian Attitudes on Sex and Youth', *Choices*, 25, 1, pp. 10–11.

Chervyakov, V. and I. Kon (1998), 'Adolescent Sexuality in Russia', paper presented at the AIDS in Europe, Second European Conference, New Challenges for Social and Behavioural Sciences, Paris, 12–15 January 1998.

Costlow, J. T., S. Sandler and J. Vowels (eds) (1993), *Sexuality and the Body in Russian Culture*, Stanford, Stanford University Press.

Engel, B. A. (1994), *Between the Fields and the City: Women, Work, and Family in Russia, 1861–1914*, Cambridge, Cambridge University Press.

Engelstein, Laura (1992), *The Keys to Happiness: Sex and the Search for Modernity in Fin-de-siecle Russia*, Ithaca, Cornell University Press.

Flegon, A. (1976), *Eroticism in Russian Art*, London, Flegon Press.

Goldman, Wendy Z. (1993), *Women, the State and Revolution: Soviet Family Policy and Social Life, 1917–1936*, Cambridge, Cambridge University Press.

Golod, S. I. (1996), *XX vek i tendentsii seksuanykh otnoshenii v Rossii*, St Petersburg, Aleteya.

Heller, L. and P. Lang (eds) (1992), 'Amour et erotisme dans la littérature russe du XXe siècle', *Actes du Colloque de juin 1989 organisé par l'Université de Lauzanne, avec de concours de la Fondation du 450me anniversaire*, Geneva, Peter Lang.

Klyuchevsky, V. O. (1987), 'Kurs russkoi istorii' (1904), in *Sochinenia v 8 tomakh*, vol. 1, Moscow, Gospolitizdat.

Kon, I. S. (1995), *The Sexual Revolution in Russia: From the Age of the Czars to Today*, New York, Free Press.

— (1997), *Seksualnaya kultura v Rossii: klubnichka na beriozke*, Moscow, OGI Press.

Kon, I. S. and J. Riordan (eds) (1993), *Sex and Russian Society*, Bloomington, Indiana University Press.

Levin, E. (1989), *Sex and Society in the World of the Orthodox Slavs, 900–1700*, Ithaca, Cornell University Press.

Marsh, R. (ed.) (1986), *Women in Russia and Ukraine*, Cambridge, Cambridge University Press.

Pushkaryova, N. L. (1997), *Nevesta, zhena, liubovnitsa (chastnaya zhizn' zhensjchiny v doindustrialnoi Rossii X – nachala XIX vv*, Moscow, Ladomir.

Vishnevskii, A. G. (ed.) (1998), *Naselenie Rossii 1997: pyatyi ezhegodnyi demograficheskii doklad*, Moscow, Knishnyi dom Universitet.

Zakharov, S. I. and E. I. Ivanova (1996), 'Fertility Decline and Recent Changes in Russia: On the Threshold of the Second Demographic Transition', in J. DaVanzo with the assistance of G. Farnsworth (ed.), *Russia's Demographic Crisis*, Washington (DC), Rand.

Sexual science and sex reform

9

Medical science and the modernisation of sexuality

Harry Oosterhuis

In his influential *History of Sexuality* (1976) Michel Foucault argues that the modern idea of sexuality was historically constituted in the nineteenth century when medical science delimited perversion. Whereas earlier historians saw the 'medicalisation' of sexuality as a change only of attitudes and labels – for them, unchanging deviant sexual behaviours and feelings were no longer regarded as unnatural, sinful or criminal but simply became diseases, relabelled by physicians – Foucault and other social constructivist historians have challenged this interpretation. Not only are they critical of the view that the medical model was a scientific and humanitarian step forward but also they emphasise that nineteenth-century physicians, by describing and categorising non-procreative sexualities, were very influential in effecting a fundamental transformation of the social and psychological reality of sexual deviance from a form of immoral behaviour to a pathological way of being. Thus, by differentiating between the normal and the abnormal, the argument runs, physicians, as exponents of a 'biopower', were not only constructing the modern idea of sexuality but also controlling the pleasures of the body. Socially created out of disciplining powers and discourses of knowledge, sexuality was a nineteenth-century invention. Before medical theories emerged that lumped together behaviour, physical characteristics and the emotional make-up of individuals, there was no entity, according to Foucault, which could be delineated as sexuality.

I would be the last to reject this account totally, but my basic assumption is that the picture which has been drawn of the medicalisation of sexuality is rather one-sided. The disciplining effects of medical interference with sexuality have been overemphasised. Medical theories have played an important role in the making of sexual categories and identities. However, this does not necessarily mean that these were only scientific inventions, shaped systematically by the logic of medicine and imposed from above by the power of organised medical opinion. In order to explain how sexuality was shaped by nineteenth-century medical science, which is the subject of this chapter, the wider social context has to be taken into account. Arguing that new ways of understanding sexuality emerged not only from medical thinking in itself, I will focus on the connections between the contents of medical theories and their institutional and social settings. This chapter relies on my current research on the work of the German–Austrian psychiatrist Richard von Krafft-Ebing as well as on the work of other scholars.

Scientific interest in sexuality, originating in the Enlightenment, replaced the Christian view of sin and virtue with secular notions of nature. As a natural phenomenon, sexuality was open to two distinct moral meanings. On the one hand, leading Enlightenment thinkers like Rousseau believed that unspoiled nature offered a foundation for moral behaviour and harmonious relations between the individual and society. On the other hand, De Sade and others argued that natural drives were ethically neutral or even blindly amoral and thus could not provide a foundation on which to build society. Connected to these divergent interpretations of human nature, Enlightenment thinking on sexuality was ambivalent. To the extent that it contributed to procreation and was connected to harmonious heterosexual love, marriage, family and maternity, it was applauded, but, if sexuality was premature, illicit, excessive or motivated by sheer lust, it was considered socially subversive. As a basically irrational, unproductive and egoistic drive, sexuality undermined the optimistic idea of moral nature and posed a potential risk to social harmony. The preoccupation with the dangers of masturbation was typical of the Enlightenment approach to sexuality, relying on sanitary solutions and the beneficial effects of a healthy lifestyle, moderation and self-mastery. Not so much penal law but medicine, education and social hygiene were seen as the means to prevent deviance and shape a healthy sexuality capable of being integrated into society.

Next to the (economic) interest in the size and health of the population for which Malthus set the tone, the growing concern over public health issues in the nineteenth century, especially problems of sexually transmitted diseases, prostitution and public indecency, fostered medical interest in sexuality. After 1850 the scientific and social status of medicine was enhanced, especially in France and Germany where physicians were allied to the state. Physicians gradually replaced the clergy as authoritative personal consultants in the realm of sex. On the one hand, doctors could not escape from recognising that sexual passion was an essential part of human nature. Echoing the typical nineteenth-century model of the closed energy system, the (male) sexual drive was conceptualised as a powerful force that builds up from inside the body until it is released in orgasm. Many believed that, especially in males, unfulfilled drives would lead to (nervous) illness. On the other hand, giving oneself up to uncontrolled impulses was considered dangerous for the health of the individual as well as for that of society. The human sexual economy was believed to function according to a quantitative model of energy flow in which the 'spending' of semen meant a loss of energy in other areas of life and moderate expenditures were most consonant with health and fertility. Moderation and will-power were keynotes of the professional advice offered to the bourgeoisie.

It is questionable whether the medical profession as a whole did impose a sexual ideology on the lay public. Not only was there diversity of opinion in medical literature on sexuality, it is also necessary to differentiate between the bourgeoisie and the working class. Most medical practitioners were strictly dependent on the approval of their bourgeois clients. Sexual immorality was a special target for medico-moral campaigns aimed at surveillance and regulation of the working class and the urban poor. In the discourse of the public health movement of the mid nineteenth century, immorality, poverty and the spread of contagious diseases became condensed. Prostitution was a chronic concern. It was upheld by a double standard: bourgeois women were supposed to be protected, but promiscuity on the part of bourgeois men was tacitly condoned, with lower-class women providing a 'necessary outlet' for the male sexual drive. At the same time prostitution was seen as a problem because of the transmission of venereal diseases. In the course of the nineteenth century, police systems of registering prostitutes were implemented throughout Europe. The medical control of sexually transmitted diseases was tacked on to the existing police surveillance of the demi-monde of prostitution. At the same time the police increasingly took strong action against other forms of disorderly sexual conduct in the course of the nineteenth century. Same-sex practices of men – particularly in public places in cities as well as in such institutional settings as prisons, barracks, ships, schools and dormitories – were especially worrisome.

The extensive state-backed medical involvement in the regulation of female prostitution contradicted a crucial legal principle of both Enlightenment thought and nineteenth-century liberalism: non-interference by the state in citizens' private lives. Opposing the union of church and state, Enlightenment and liberal thinkers emphasised the distinction between sin, the province of the church, and crime, the concern of the state. However, the liberal separation of private and public spheres quickly ran up against its limits. Sexual conduct and its possible consequence, reproduction, came to be seen as critical social and political issues, since they involved the health and strength of nations. The compulsory medical examination of prostitutes and the medicalisation of deviant sexualities marked a transformation of private activity into behaviour that could be legitimately judged by standards of respectability and public health.

Whereas earlier medical interest had focused on masturbation, prostitution and venereal diseases, from the 1860s onwards prominent psychiatrists became concerned with deviant sexual behaviours that were usually considered immoral and that were often punishable. Although sodomy had been decriminalised in several European countries during and after the French Revolution (France, the Netherlands and Bavaria for example), new offences against morality such as public indecency were introduced, and also legal ages of consent for sexual contacts. Moreover, in the second half of the nineteenth century the criminalisation of homosexual behaviour was extended in Germany (in 1871) and in England (in 1885 and 1897). As a result of the growing persecution of immoral offences, physicians, as forensic experts in courts, were increasingly confronted with sexual deviance. Before the 1860s, medical interest in disorderly sexual conduct was intrinsically linked to forensic medicine, focusing on criminal acts like rape and sodomy. In general experts in forensic medicine confined themselves to physical diagnosis to furnish evidence of immoral offences. Thus the French professor of forensic medicine A. Tardieu claimed in 1857 that pederasts arrested by the Paris police possessed penises shaped like those of dogs, and their passive partners the soft and rounded contours of women. The forensic explanation of their behaviour was social rather than biological: the result of moral failure, unfavourable conditions of life, bad habits such as masturbation, and imitation. For the German psychiatrist H. Kaan, who published one of the first psychiatric classifications of sexual disorders (*Psychopathia Sexualis*, 1844), perversions were still ubiquitous bad habits, fostered by individual and social conditions; he did not yet consider the offender as a fundamentally different type of person.

In the first half of the nineteenth century it was not decided whether lewdness was a cause, a result or a form of insanity in itself. Various medical authorities assumed that, as with onanism, committing 'unnatural acts' could lead to physical weakness and insanity. However, around the middle of the century the connection between sexual behaviour and morbid deviation was reversed in some medical analyses. In their treatment of sodomy the French physician C. F. Michéa in 1849 and the German forensic medical authority J. L. Casper in 1852 shifted the focus from the physiological characteristics of the sodomitical act to the biological disposition of the offender. They were the first to assert that a preference for members of the same sex was often innate and involved femininity in men. Their approach set the tone for psychiatrists who began to connect sexual acts that were not aimed at procreation with diseases of the brain and the nervous system.

Psychiatric interest in the broader aspects of sexual deviance emerged from the forensic preoccupation with the psychological make-up of moral offenders. Whereas physicians had first believed that mental and nervous disorders were the *result* of 'unnatural' behaviours, psychiatrists supposed that they *caused* sexual deviance. More and more sexual disorders were viewed not just as forms of immoral behaviour but as symptoms of an underlying morbid condition, as a form of 'moral insanity' especially. Called upon to deliver expert testimony in court, the main thrust of psychiatrists was that the irresponsibility of moral offenders had to be considered in judging them. Certain categories of defendants should be sent to asylums and clinics rather than to prisons.

In the last decades of the nineteenth century several psychiatrists, especially in France and Germany, were classifying and explaining the wide range of deviant sexual behaviours they discovered. Basing their arguments on deterministic theories of hereditary degeneration and neurophysiological automatism, more and more psychiatrists subscribed to the new view that in many cases deviant sexual activities were not immoral choices but symptoms of innate characteristics. From around 1870 prominent German and French psychiatrists shifted the focus from a temporary deviation from the norm to a pathological state of being.

In 1869 the German psychiatrist C. F. O. von Westphal published the first psychiatric study of what he coined as contrary sexual feeling (*conträre Sexualempfindung*). R. von Krafft-Ebing's article published in a leading German psychiatric journal in 1877 can be considered as a direct precursor of numerous classifying works on sexual pathology. Whereas Krafft-Ebing in 1877 distinguished only four perversions – murders for lust, necrophilia, anthropophagy (cannibalism) and contrary sexual feeling – in the 1880s and 1890s he and his German and French colleagues created and underpinned new categories of perversion by collecting and publishing more and more case histories. After the terms 'uranism', 'contrary sexual feeling' (inversion) and 'homosexual' (and heterosexual) had been coined in the 1860s by, in succession, C. H. Ulrichs, Westphal and K. M. Benkert, exhibitionism was introduced in 1877 by C. Lasègue, the master-concept 'sexual perversion' in 1885 by V. Magnan, fetishism in 1887 by A. Binet, sadism and masochism in 1890 by Krafft-Ebing, and algolagnia in 1892 by A. von Schrenck-Notzing.

In the 1880s most leading French psychiatrists contributed to the development of sexual pathology, while after 1890 German and Austrian experts would set the tone; English, Italian and Russian contributions to this field, although substantial, were less numerous. Their and many other publications made a substantial contribution to the emergence of a medical discourse on sexuality so that at the end of the nineteenth century perversions could be recognised and discussed. Several taxonomies were developed, but the one that took shape in Krafft-Ebing's popular and much-quoted *Psychopathia Sexualis* eventually set the tone, not only in medical circles but also in commonsense thinking. The first edition (1886) of this highly eclectic encyclopaedia of sexual deviation was followed soon by several new and expanded editions and translations in several languages. With this book, containing extensive case studies and auto-biographies, Krafft-Ebing became famous as one of the founding fathers of scientific sexology. By naming and classifying virtually all non-procreative forms of sexuality, he was one of the first to synthesise psychiatric knowledge of sexual perversion. Although he also paid attention to several other derangements in sexual life, Krafft-Ebing distinguished four main perversions: sadism, masochism, fetishism and contrary sexual feeling. The last one was most prominent and it was explained as a biological and psychological mixture of manliness and femininity. Subsumed under this rubric of inverted gender were not only homosexuality but also various physiological and psychological fusions of manliness and femininity that in the twentieth century would gradually be reclassified as radically separate phenomena, such as hermaphroditism, androgyny, transvestitism and transsexuality.

Not only were psychiatrists concerned with labelling deviant behaviours and bracketing them as perversions, but they also tried to explain them as biological and psychological phenomena. The development of sexual pathology can be understood in the context of some major currents in late nineteenth-century psychiatry. Changing views of sexuality were congruent with trends in general theories of psychopathology: they embraced both the dominant somatic aetiological notions of late nineteenth-century psychiatry, the pathology of nervous tissue and degeneration theory, as well as the attempt to escape the limitations of the somatic model by elaborating a psychological understanding of mental disorders. In fact the modern meaning of sexuality came to the fore when the dominant physiological approach was superseded by a more psychological one. In the first half of the century the term referred mainly to the fact that an individual belonged to the male or female sex. Sex difference was explained from anatomical variation: the decisive benchmarks for evaluation of sex identity were the genitals, secondary sexual characteristics and functional potency with a normally constituted member of the opposite sex. There was an evolution over the nineteenth century from medical explanations stressing anatomical features to those placing more weight on the sexual instinct and psychology. Only gradually was the term 'sexuality' used to indicate *desire* for the opposite sex (or the same sex), an attraction that was based on a physical and psychological polarisation and matching of male and female elements.

In explaining perversions several psychiatrists tried to integrate them with current biomedical thinking. Late nineteenth-century psychiatry was characterised by a growing and pervasive emphasis on heredity as a key factor in the aetiology of mental illness. Although many psychiatrists continued to believe that perversion was sometimes acquired through bad environmental agents, seduction and corrupt habit-formation like masturbation, they increasingly stressed that sexual disorders, like many mental diseases in general, were inborn. Following the dominant somatic approach in psychiatry that situated mental disorders in the nervous system and particularly in the cerebral organs, many psychiatrists supposed that not only physical but also intellectual and moral traits were hereditary. In addition to the pathology of nervous tissue, Darwinism and the theory of hereditary degeneracy played an important part in psychiatric explanations of mental illness in general and sexual disorders in particular. It was argued that while reproductive heterosexuality was the result of evolutionary progress, sexual deviance showed that natural processes could also move backwards in a sort of process of devolution; nature was capable of producing monsters, or, as the British psychiatrist H. Maudsley and Krafft-Ebing put it more mildly, 'step-children of nature'.

Krafft-Ebing and his French colleagues were deeply influenced by B. A. Morel, who had devised a theory of degeneration to explain several pathological phenomena by the influence of environment as well as inheritance. According to Morel, acquired disorders could be inherited from 'tainted' relatives and, once mental illness had a hold, it followed its inevitable course in the 'neuropathic family': it was handed on to the descendants and deteriorated over the generations until the line died out. The analysis of degeneration was embedded in a critique of the increasingly frantic conditions of modern civilisation, stressing the vast range of novel stimuli which produced nervous exhaustion, fatigue and mental disturbances. Degeneration was associated with lack of inhibitory control of the 'higher' faculties over the more primitive levels of the central nervous system: modern people were less and less governed by moral law and had become more and more slaves of their physical desires.

The concept of hereditary degeneration became a central organising concept of late nineteenth-century psychiatry, especially in France, not because it offered a more precise understanding or better treatment of mental disease but because of the possibility of gaining scientific legitimacy. Although the belief that insanity was an organic disease was hardly confirmed by contemporary anatomical and physiological evidence, degeneracy theory was attractive for psychiatrists because it offered a naturalist model of mental pathology that seemed to make sense of their clinical data in scientific terms. The theory also facilitated psychiatry's annexation of sexual deviance because it enabled psychiatrists to extend the boundaries of mental pathology by including among their patients a substantial number of people who behaved erratically yet were rarely believed to be completely mad. Strengthening the association between mental disorders and social evils, degeneration theory not only gratified specific professional needs for late nineteenth-century psychiatry but also served a larger and more covert political role. Indicating that within humankind lay the seeds of inevitable decay, it became a dominant cultural idea that articulated anxieties in society at large, and it marked a crisis of the social optimism that had characterised liberalism. The concern with biological decline and depopulation became something of an obsession affecting many nations by the late nineteenth century, especially France but also Britain, Germany and Italy. Hereditary degeneracy summed up for late nineteenth-century Europeans the terrible human costs of modernisation and it expressed deep fears of the disorder of 'mass society' and of the 'dangerous' classes in big cities. The Enlightenment and liberal concept of human nature that stressed the fundamental commonalities shared by all was superseded by increasing emphasis on inborn differences and 'natural' hierarchy. Degeneration theory, like Social Darwinism, rationalised social inequalities as facts of nature.

Whereas the first historians of sexology, often psychiatrists themselves, emphasised that superstitious beliefs and cruel practices had been replaced by sound medical science and humanitarian treatments, more recent historical work has associated medical theories of sexuality with social, political and moral control. Not only has psychiatric interference with sexual deviance often been characterised as the climax of the medicalisation of sexuality, it has also been considered as a typical expression of conservative bourgeois morality and Victorian hypocrisy by several historians. True, as the eager reception of degeneration theory by psychiatrists illustrates, there are elements that would substantiate such a judgement. They often relied uncritically on conventional standards of sexual conduct in their diagnosis of perversion, thereby confusing mental disorder with mere nonconformity. Uncontrollable sensuality was pictured as a severe threat to civilisation; in the medical view the history of mankind was a constant struggle between animal lust and morality. Psychiatrists indeed surrounded sexuality with an aura of pathology, and they echoed, for example, nineteenth-century stereotypical thinking on masturbation, masculinity and femininity.

However, psychiatric theories were far from static and coherent and they cannot be regarded only as a disqualification of sexual aberration. Different national sexological traditions are relevant here. In France the concern about effeminacy and the depressed fertility rate determined psychiatry's interference with sexuality in the defence of the heterosexual family ethic and the proper roles of men and women. In Germany, Austria and Britain the development of sexology in the last decade of the nineteenth century was also connected closely with efforts to abolish laws outlawing homosexual behaviour – Krafft-Ebing, Hirschfeld and Havelock Ellis are cases in point. Ironically, this difference in national sexological traditions – the German, Austrian and British ones more innovative than the French – can be explained by the fact that disorderly sexual conduct, such as homosexuality, was not punishable in France, while German, Austrian and British law codes laid down penalties for 'unnatural vice'. In France fears of depopulation, national decline and male impotence influenced the rather conservative orientation of medical research into sexuality.

In the 1890s, when Austria (Vienna) and Germany (Berlin) replaced France as the centre of medical research into sexuality, the emerging new science of sexology – the term *Sexualwissenschaft* was introduced in 1906 by Bloch – underwent some important theoretical innovations. First, there was a change in emphasis from a somatic to a psychological interpretative framework. Second, there was a shift away from a classification of disease categories within clear boundaries to a tentative understanding of 'normal' sexuality in the context of perversions as extremes on a graded scale of health and illness, normal and abnormal, and masculine and feminine. Third, the significant step from a predominantly forensic focus and a physiological explanation to the considerable broader goal of addressing general psychological issues of human sexuality meant that sexuality was more and more disconnected from reproduction. Fourth, some sexologists began to consider the impact of cultural differences in explaining various forms of sexual behaviour.

A striking case in point was Krafft-Ebing's sexual pathology. Influenced by degenerationist thinking, his biological approach to sexuality has often been contrasted with Freud's psychological one. However, around 1890, when he introduced fetishism, sadism and masochism in his *Psychopathia Sexualis*, the focus shifted from a physiological to a more psychological understanding. Bodily characteristics and actual behaviour were less decisive in the diagnosis of perversion than individual character, personal history and inner feelings: psychological motives, emotional life, dreams, imagination and fantasies. At the same time an associationist explanation of perversion was proposed by psychiatrists such as Binet and Schrenck-Notzing. They asserted that the major forms of sexual pathology were psychologically acquired by exposure to certain accidental events. Although the underlying causes of perversion remained degeneration and heredity, Krafft-Ebing, Binet, Schrenck-Notzing, and others shifted the medical discussion away from explaining sexuality as a series of interrelated physiological events to a more psychological understanding. In this new psychiatric style of reasoning, perversions were disorders of an instinct that could not be located in the body. Already – before Freud – the idea gained ground that sexual disorders could result from unconscious psychological causes which originated in childhood.

There was another way in which the psychiatric approach to sexuality foreshadowed Freud's. Whereas the differentiation of healthy and pathological sexuality – reproduction being the touchstone – was the basic assumption in his work, in Krafft-Ebing's discussion of the main perversions for example, at the same time the barriers between the normal and abnormal were subverted. Sadism, masochism and fetishism were not only disease categories but also terms which described extremes on a graded scale of health and illness, and explained aspects of 'normal' sexuality. In his view sadism and masochism were inherent in normal male and female sexuality, the former being of an active and aggressive, and the latter a passive, submissive nature. Also the distinction between fetishism and 'normal' sexuality was only gradual, quantitative rather than qualitative. Fetishism was part and parcel of normal sexuality, Krafft-Ebing explained, because the individual character of sexual attraction and, connected to that, monogamous love were grounded in a distinct preference for particular physical and mental characteristics of one's partner. This was in line with Binet's assertion that all love was to some extent fetishistic, thus indicating that it was a general tendency at the heart of sexual attraction.

In addition the barriers between masculinity and femininity became diffused in medical theory. The extensive discussion of several forms of physical and mental inversion – often connected to homosexuality – highlighted the idiosyncratic and chance character of sex differentiation and signalled that exclusive masculinity and femininity might be mere abstractions. Whereas earlier Krafft-Ebing and many of his colleagues had tended to identify inversion with degeneration, in the mid-1890s the concept of sexual intermediacy was grounded in contemporary embryological research and in evolutionary theories. The first stressed that the early state of the human embryo was characterised by sexual neutrality and the second suggested that primitive forms of life lacked sexual differentiation. Echoing E. Haeckel's law of recapitulation, humanity appeared to be of a bisexual origin from a phylogenetic as well as an ontogenetic perspective.

Although Darwinism had often been used to prove that heterosexuality was a natural norm for higher forms of life and that perversions like homosexuality were necessarily degenerate, evolution theory could also be invoked to undermine the conventional sex differentiation. Darwin viewed masculinity and femininity not as static properties but as malleable functions that depended on the contribution any given trait made to the survival and reproductive success of the organism. Hirschfeld, the leader of the first homosexual rights movement in Germany and the founder of the first sexological journals, was profoundly indebted to Darwinian notions of evolution. Differentiating between successively anomalies in the sex glands, the genitals, secondary sexual and psychological characteristics and sexual orientation, he argued that there was a seamless continuum of human sexual types ranging between fully male and fully female: hermaphroditism, androgyny, transvestitism and homosexuality (the concept of transsexuality would be coined in the 1940s). Also from a more psychological perspective, the absolute distinction between masculinity and femininity as well as between homo- and heterosexuality was undermined. According to the German psychologist M. Dessoir, sexuality during puberty was still undifferentiated and indefinite. He concluded that not only homosexuality but also heterosexuality was acquired in culture.

It should be clear that, as far as the scientific discussion about sexuality is concerned, Freud was not a radical pioneer but built on psychiatric theories of sexuality that had been formulated in the 1880s and 1890s. Psychiatric theories opened up a new continent of knowledge, not only by treating sexual abnormality as disease instead of sin and crime, but even more because they made it clear that the nature of sexuality was significant for the whole existence of the individual and society, and therefore deserved serious study. Krafft-Ebing pointed to the danger of the sexual instinct threatening civilisation, but at the same time he drew attention to its constructive role in culture and society. For him love, as a social bond, was inherently sexual, and he tended to value the longing for physical and psychological union with a partner as a purpose in itself. As far as the relational aspect of sexuality was concerned, Krafft-Ebing, at the end of his life, was inclined to the opinion that homosexuality was the equivalent of heterosexuality and therefore not an illness.

The exclusive naturalness of the reproductive instinct became problematical, and more and more primacy was assigned to the satisfaction of desire. The German sexologist A. Moll broke new paths by positing two major instincts as basic for what he called the 'libido sexualis': discharge (*Detumescenztrieb*) and attraction (*Contrectationstrieb*). The first referred to the sexual act proper, the second to social needs. In his *Untersuchungen über die Libido sexualis* (1897) Moll explicitly detached the sexual impulse from propagation and compared normal and abnormal sexual forms side by side. Reproductive heterosexuality lost its naturalness and became increasingly understood as the result of a developmental synthesis of component impulses. Accepting sexuality, not just procreation, as a vital physical force, sexologists like Moll, M. Marcuse and H. Ellis began to discuss whether sexual abstinence was harmful and to recognise the relative normalcy of infantile sexual manifestations. Theories of sexuality began to centre on desire instead of reproduction. Sexology's tendency to make sexual variance imaginable enlarged the sphere allotted to idiosyncratic desires and from this it was only a small step to Freud's lusting 'libido' and 'pleasure principle', according to which sexual desire's only built-in aim is its own satisfaction. The modern concept of sexuality that was constituted around the turn of the twentieth century was not only a reaction against Victorian prohibitions but also an epistemological transformation: an individualisation and psychologisation of sexuality. The emergence of sexual identity and desire, irrespective of its reproductive potential, is central to the modern sexual ethos.

Several historians of sexuality have more or less damned late nineteenth-century contributions to sexual pathology as medical imperialism. Although Foucault stressed that sexuality was shaped rather than repressed by the scientific will to know, the purport of his argument, and even more that of some of his followers, is that 'perverts' were trapped in a medical discourse through which not only power relations and social control of deviant sexualities but also sexual subjects themselves are constituted. The radical implication of Foucault's reasoning is that before, say, 1870 there did not exist 'perverts' like homosexuals, fetishists and masochists, nor their counterparts, 'normal' heterosexuals. Perhaps this contention can be defended, but the problem is that the conclusion has too readily been drawn that new categories and identities were merely constructed by a monolithic medical discourse. The exclusive focus on medical theories entails that the voices of the individuals, from which doctors drew their observations and demonstrated their theories, remain silent. However, sexology was unlikely to have gained momentum without the particular impetus created by the intimate confessions of 'perverts' themselves. In the development of sexual pathology (auto)-biographical accounts played a central role; for a large part doctors were influenced by the people concerned as they furnished them with life stories and sexual experiences. The works of Krafft-Ebing and Havelock Ellis, for example, were illustrated with hundreds of case histories and autobiographical accounts.

The subjects of Krafft-Ebing's case studies were drawn from different social groups. Whereas hospitalised patients and suspected moral offenders on whom he wrote forensic reports had no other choice than to conform to standard medical procedures, and have their stories recorded by Krafft-Ebing and his assistants, many of his aristocratic and bourgeois patients, who generally had contacted him of their own accord, were given ample opportunity to speak for themselves. These individuals – most of them economically independent, and, for the most part, living in large cities and outside of the traditional family – had contacted Krafft-Ebing as private patients, or corresponded with him because they had recognised themselves in published case histories. Some of them sent in an autobiography in order to have it published in a new edition of *Psychopathia Sexualis.* Whereas most cases in his early work were on the whole rather short and factual, later publications contained more extensive ones. By publishing autobiographies and quoting the patients, many case studies especially focused on the patients' subjective experience.

Homosexual men especially, but also fetishists and masochists, were usually eager to reveal their lives to Krafft-Ebing. Whereas he had probably expected them to be nervous 'degenerates', many indicated plausibly that they enjoyed perfect health and that they were physically indistinguishable from their fellow men. Written by educated and often cosmopolitan men, some of the autobiographies were full of learned and literary references, speculations about the causes of their odd feelings and detailed self-analysis. They linked perverse desire to the experience of the self and they were clearly seeking a confirmation of their sexual urges. Also they vividly demonstrated a considerable degree of subjective suffering, not so much because of their sexual orientation as such but because of the social condemnation, the legal situation, the need to disguise their real nature, and the fear of blackmail and of losing their social status. Several men stressed that their sexual behaviour could not be immoral or pathological, because they experienced their desire as 'natural'. By publishing such arguments and remarking that they strikingly illustrated the feelings and suffering of 'perverts', Krafft-Ebing must have made a powerful statement for those concerned. In new editions of *Psychopathia Sexualis* he included more and more extensive autobiographies, the writers of which made clear that they did not seek a cure since it was not their disposition that made them unhappy but the social condemnation.

Homosexuals especially did not play by definition a passive role *vis-à-vis* the psychiatrist. The revision of medical views on homosexuality at the end of the nineteenth century did not only involve medical theorising. Next to physicians the impetus for scientific investigations into contrary sexual feeling had come from self-proclaimed homosexuals themselves, especially the German lawyer Ulrichs, who introduced the concept of uranism in 1864. Krafft-Ebing's views were influenced not only by Ulrichs but also by like-minded patients and informants. After having published several autobiographies which showed the harmful effects of penalisation, he began to favour judicial reform. When, at the end of the nineteenth century, homosexuals began to organise protest movements, they referred to Krafft-Ebing as a scientific authority who was on their side; and he indeed supported the homosexual rights movement which was founded in Berlin by Hirschfeld in 1897.

One can find different, even contradictory sets of values in Krafft-Ebing's *Psychopathia Sexualis*, and it was open to divergent meanings. Quite evidently contemporary readers interpreted the book in various ways. Although intended for physicians and lawyers, it served not only as a guide for professionals but also as a mouthpiece and panel for the individuals concerned. By publishing letters and autobiographies and by quoting statements of his patients verbatim, Krafft-Ebing enabled voices to be heard that were usually silenced. The active role of several subjects of his case studies in the genesis of his sexual pathology suggests that medical sexology not only facilitated medical treatment and other forms of restraint but also created the possibility for the individuals concerned to speak out and to be recognised. For them the book could give the initial impetus to self-awareness and self-expression. To a large extent individuals who recognised themselves in Krafft-Ebing's cases could give their own meaning to their sexual feelings and experiences. Some of the autobiographers took the opportunity to express their criticism of current social norms and even those of the medical profession.

'Perverts' began to speak for themselves, and they were looking for models with which to identify. Despite the medical bias, many case histories in *Psychopathia Sexualis* served as go-betweens, linking individual introspection – the (often painful) recognition that one is a deviant kind of person – and social identification – the often comforting sense of belonging to a community of the like-minded. Because Krafft-Ebing distinguished himself as an expert who had made a stand against traditional moral-religious and legal denunciations of sexual deviance, individuals approached him to find understanding, acceptance and support. For many of Krafft-Ebing's clients his work was an eye-opener; they made references to its salutary effects and a few even stated that it had saved them from despair. In fact they did not need medical treatment, because pouring out one's heart was something of a cure in itself. The writing of their life history, giving coherence and intelligibility to their torn self, might result in a 'catharsis' of comprehension.

Krafft-Ebing and many of his upper-class clients shared the same cultural background and the same bourgeois values. In a way they co-operated: 'perverts' who wanted to make their voice heard in public depended on sympathetic physicians like him because medical science was the only respectable forum available, and in his turn Krafft-Ebing had to rely on their confessions to validate empirically his sexual pathology. Generally, psychiatric accounts and case histories as published by him were not simply a means of coping with or controlling deviant sexualities but also offered a space in which sexual desire in the form of autobiographical narrative could be articulated. In the long run the greater ability to be recognised and discussed facilitated medical treatment and other forms of restraint, as well as self-awareness. The way several of his patients and informants read his work illustrates that the sexual domain became a contested field and that it was but one step from the admission of the individual's right to sexual fulfilment.

New ways of understanding sexuality emerged not only from medical thinking in itself: changes in the context of psychiatry, both the immediate professional, institutional settings and the wider social environment, should be taken into account. The development of sexology within psychiatry was closely connected to the professional endeavour of broadening and diversifying psychiatry's territory outside the mental asylum by changing the institutional settings in which psychiatrists worked. Psychiatry's interference with sexual deviance grew out of its fundamental weakness rather than its strength. Psychiatrists were far from being the powerful agents of social control suggested by many historians of sexuality and of psychiatry. During the first half of the century psychiatrists had won dominion over the most serious and dangerous forms of mental dysfunction, but in general their authority was confined to the walls of the lunatic asylum, housing the chronically insane of the pauper classes. Moreover, even in the second half of the century, psychiatrists had difficulties in convincing other scientists and the public that as physicians they had an exclusive and scientific insight into the nature of insanity. The lack of anatomical and physiological evidence of the somatic basis of mental illness and the therapeutic futility of the asylum underlined the vulnerability of psychiatry. When psychiatrists began to theorise on sexuality around 1870, their professional status was rather fragile. So, I would suggest, rather than explaining how psychiatrists used their power to control and discipline sexual deviants, the question should be why they interfered with sexuality as a way to promote their specialism and to extend their professional domain.

In the last decades of the nineteenth century leading psychiatrists shifted their activities away from the mental asylum, in which care and management of ever-expanding numbers of chronic and poor patients had taken the place of expectations of cure, to the university clinic and private practice. The psychological approach provided psychiatry with both a new clientèle and a vastly enhanced social authority. Psychological thinking enabled psychiatrists to appropriate middle-class patients who were just slightly mentally deranged, who showed relatively mild disturbances and who did not need to be hospitalised in asylums. By meeting the needs of bourgeois clients, psychiatrists created the possibility to build up a private practice, and this entailed a shift in the social background of their clientèle. Psychiatrists indeed played a key role in the construction of the modern concept of sexuality, but the emerging medical theories became established as facts about sexuality only because they were linked to relevant social groups from the beginning.

Case histories and autobiographies of Krafft-Ebing's patients and their social and cultural settings make clear that medical knowledge of sexuality could be successful only because it was embedded in society. The construction of modern sexual identities was realised in a process of social interaction between individuals, who contemplated themselves, and physicians, who shaped perversion as a psychiatric field. Self-conscious sexual identities clearly evolved among well-educated, urban and often cosmopolitan bourgeois and aristocratic circles. It was in the context of rapidly expanding urban life and emerging consumer culture that the individual's particular and unique desires became significant. Psychiatric theories reached a public that was already provided with a great number of literary and other medical works on the subject of sexuality. Sexual themes were emerging as topics for novels and the stage. There was a market for a psychologically orientated psychiatry that responded to the need for self-knowledge.

Psychiatric discourse reflected as well as shaped sexual experiences. It indicated and provoked a growing preoccupation not only with sexuality but also with the searching scrutiny of the inner life. In late nineteenth-century bourgeois society sexuality was privileged as the quintessence of privacy and the individual self. The rise of sexual pathology in psychiatry only magnified the effects of this need for self-comprehension. This does not necessarily mean that individual meanings of the sexual self should be considered as reflections of an internal, psychological essence. Neither psychiatric case histories nor autobiographies are unmediated sources for the voices of 'perverts'. Sexual identities crystallised as patterned narratives, and as such their content and form were of a social rather than of a psychological origin. Sexual identity appeared as a script, on which individuals modelled their life history. Psychiatry offered a fitting framework to look at and make sense of one's self, and in this way it was crucial to the new sexual self-consciousness and the public conception of sexuality. In the absence of traditional social routines or moral certainties, self-contemplation was a cause for anxiety and uneasiness; yet, as many of Krafft-Ebing's case histories illustrate, it also created some space for individuality and self-expression.

'Perverts' appealed to ideals of authenticity and sincerity to bestow moral value on their sexual identity. In nineteenth-century bourgeois society individual authenticity had become a pre-eminent value and a framework for introspection, self-contemplation and self-expression. The constitution of desire as the clue to the inner self can be explained only as a consequence of the reconstitution of the function of sexuality in modern society. Whereas in traditional society sexuality, as a function of social behaviour, had no distinct existence, the differentiation of public and private entailed the ever greater dissociation of sexuality from its embeddedness in fixed, putatively 'natural' patterns of behaviour. The rise of the ideal of romantic love – 'true' love became the reigning standard to justify sexuality – entailed that sexuality was gradually differentiated from a transcendental moral order and from its traditional instrumental integration with reproduction, kinship and social and economic necessities. Personal sentiment and attraction gradually replaced the calculus of familial advantage in choosing a partner, and sexuality became located in the separate sphere of intimacy, dating, courtship and romantic love. This, in its turn, created the possibility for medical science to define it as a distinct impulse and to discover its internal physical and psychological laws. Whereas in premodern society sexuality was dominated by a reproductive imperative – the crucial differentiation was between reproductive sex within marriage and acts that interfered with procreation within marriage (adultery, sodomy, bestiality and masturbation) – and it was more or less embedded in social patterns of behaviour, the emergence of 'perversions' reveals that in modern experience the sexual domain began to generate its own meanings. Sexuality became associated with profound and complex human emotions and anxieties.

Physicians may have purposefully heightened the problem of sexuality as a matter of health and disease in order to enhance their professional status, but this does not mean that the modernisation of sexuality can be reduced to medicalisation. Medical labelling and the

disciplining effects of scientific interference have been overemphasised as the major determinants in the process creating sexual
identities. A critical attitude towards the concept of sexuality as a
stable, 'natural' psycho-biological unity – in culture a diversity of
inferences can indeed be made *vis-à-vis* 'nature' – should not lead to
losing sight of sexuality as part of social reality. The argument that
sexual identities are culturally shaped rather than rooted in biological or psychological essence does not mean that they are not more
or less stable *social* realities. The process of medicalisation has to be
seen in the context of broad changes in the social structures of sexuality.
Medical explanations of sexuality took shape at the same time as the
experience of sexuality in society was transformed and it became a
subject for introspection and obsessive self-scrutiny in the bourgeois
milieu.

Bibliography

Birken, L. (1988), *Consuming Desire: Sexual Science and the Emergence of a Culture
of Abundance, 1871–1914*, Ithaca and London, Cornell University Press.
Bullough, V. L. (1994), *Science in the Bedroom: A History of Sex Research*, New
York, Basic Books.
Davidson, A. I. (1987), 'Sex and the Emergence of Sexuality', *Critical Inquiry*, 14,
pp. 16–48.
— (1990), 'Closing Up the Corpses: Diseases of Sexuality and the Emergence of
the Psychiatric Style of Reasoning', in G. Boolos (ed.), *Meaning and Method:
Essays in Honor of Hilary Putnam*, Cambridge, Cambridge University Press.
Dowbiggin, I. (1991), *Inheriting Madness: Professionalization and Psychiatric
Knowledge in Nineteenth Century France*, Berkeley, University of California
Press.
Ellenberger, H. F. (1970), *The Discovery of the Unconscious: The History and Evolution
of Dynamic Psychiatry*, New York, Basic Books/Harper Torchbooks.
Foucault, M. (1976), *Histoire de la sexualité, vol. I. La Volonté de savoir*, Paris,
Gallimard. English translation (1980), *The History of Sexuality, Vol. 1: An
Introduction*. New York, Vintage.
Gallagher, C. and T. Laqueur (eds) (1987), *The Making of the Modern Body:
Sexuality and Society in the Nineteenth Century*, Berkeley, University of
California Press.
Greenberg, D. F. (1988), *The Construction of Homosexuality*, Chicago and London,
University of Chicago Press.
Hekma, G. (1985), 'Geschiedenis der seksuologie, sociologie van seksualiteit',
Sociologische Gids, 5–6, pp. 352–70.
— (1987), *Homoseksualiteit, een medische reputatie: de uitdoktering van de homo-
seksueel in negentiende-eeuws Nederland*, Amsterdam, SUA.
— (1989), 'The Beginnings of the End of Sodomy and the Making of the

Homosexual', in K. Gerard and G. Hekma (eds), *The Pursuit of Sodomy: Male Homosexuality in Renaissance and Enlightenment Europe*, New York and London, Harrington Park Press.

Katz, J. N. (1995), *The Invention of Heterosexuality*, New York, Dutton.

Lanteri-Laura, G. (1979), *La Lecture des perversions: histoire de leur appropriation médicale*, Paris, Masson.

Luhmann, N. (1982), *Liebe als Passion: zur Codierung von Intimität*, Frankfurt am Main, Suhrkamp Verlag.

Mort, F. (1987), *Dangerous Sexualities: Medico-moral Politics in England since 1830*, London and New York, Routledge & Kegan Paul.

Müller, K. (1991), *Aber in meinem Herzen sprach eine Stimme so laut: Homosexuelle Autobiographien und medizinische Pathographien im neunzehnten Jahrhundert*, Berlin, Rosa Winkel.

Nye, R. A. (1984), *Crime, Madness, and Politics in Modern France: The Medical Concept of National Decline*, Princeton, Princeton University Press.

— (1989), 'Sex Difference and Male Homosexuality in French Medical Discourse, 1830–1930', *Bulletin of the History of Medicine*, 63, pp. 32–51.

— (1991), 'The History of Sexuality in Context: National Sexological Traditions', *Science in Context*, 4, pp. 387–406.

— (1993), 'The Medical Origins of Sexual Fetishism', in E. Apter and W. Pietz (eds), *Fetishism as Cultural Discourse*, Ithaca and London, Cornell University Press.

Pick, D. (1989), *Faces of Degeneration: A European Disorder 1848–1918*, Cambridge, Cambridge University Press.

Porter, R. and L. A. Hall (1995), *The Facts of Life. The Creation of Sexual Knowledge in Britain, 1650–1950*, New Haven and London, Yale University Press.

Porter, R. and M. Teich (eds) (1994), *Sexual Knowledge, Sexual Science: The History of Attitudes to Sexuality*, Cambridge, Cambridge University Press.

Sulloway, F. J. (1979), *Freud: Biologist of the Mind: Beyond the Psychoanalytic Legend*, New York, Basic Books.

Wawerzonnek, M. (1984), *Implizite Sexualpädagogik in der Sexualwissenschaft 1886 bis 1933*, Cologne, Pahl-Rugenstein Verlag.

Weeks, J. (1981), *Sex, Politics and Society: The Regulation of Sexuality since 1800*, London and New York, Longman.

— (1985), *Sexuality and Its Discontents: Meaning, Myths and Modern Sexualities*, London, Routledge & Kegan Paul.

Wettley, A. (1959), *Von der 'Psychopathia Sexualis' zur Sexualwissenschaft*, Stuttgart, Ferdinand Enke Verlag.

10

The World League for Sexual Reform: some possible approaches

Ralf Dose

Translated by Pamela Selwyn

An organisational overview

The World League for Sexual Reform (WLSR) was the final organisation founded by Magnus Hirschfeld, following the Scientific Humanitarian Committee (Wissenschaftlich-humanitäres Komitee) in 1897 and the Institute for Sexual Science (Institut für Sexualwissenschaft) in 1919. It officially came into being on 3 July 1928 at the congress in Copenhagen; the groundwork for its establishment had already been laid in 1926/7, so that the invitation to the Copenhagen congress could already be sent out on the League's letterhead. Membership cards were also issued before the official foundation.

The League existed until 1935 and later counted the First International Conference for Sexual Reform on the Basis of Sexual Science (held from 15–20 September 1921 in Berlin) as its first congress, so that the four conferences that followed were considered the second to fifth meetings. These took place in Copenhagen, 1–5 July 1928, London, 8–14 September 1929, Vienna, 16–23 September 1930 and Brno, 20–6 September 1932. An invitation was issued for a conference in Moscow to be held in May 1931, for which the date was later changed to June 1932, but it, like the meetings planned for Paris (September 1933) and the USA, was not to take place.

There were a number of publications under the aegis of the League. There were proceedings of the congresses of 1921 (Weil 1922) (while not a publication of the League, this volume belongs thematically in this context), 1928 (Riese and Leunbach 1929), 1929 (Haire 1930) and 1930 (Steiner 1931). The conference volume for which subscriptions were solicited in the 1932 programme was apparently never published; all that exist are journal articles about the congress (e.g. Weisskopf 1933; Scize 1933a, 1933b; Emde Boas 1932, 1933; Rosenthal 1932). The League made two attempts at establishing an international journal entitled *Sexus*, but neither attempt got beyond the first edition. The editorial board for the 1931 issue of *Sexus* was based in Vienna (Chiavacci 1931). In early 1933 another attempt was made at the Institute for Sexual Science in Berlin, using the publishers Wilhelm Kauffmann (Institut für Sexualwissenschaft 1933). There were also publications on the national level. In the Netherlands the WLSR had a publications series (*Sexueele Hervorming*). *Sexus*, published in Spain (Huerta and Hildegart 1932–3) and *Le Problème Sexuel*, published in France (Albrecht 1933–5) were journals put out by the League's national sections and associated with them.

By the end the League claimed 190,000 members worldwide (Emde Boas 1932), including 182 individual members (in 1930); the rest belonged to member organisations. The German National League for Birth Control and Sexual Hygiene (Deutscher Reichsverband für Geburtenregelung und Sexualhygiene) brought in twenty thousand members. Other corporate members were the Scientific Humanitarian Committee, the British Society for the Study of Sex Psychology and the League for the Protection of Motherhood and Sex Reform (Bund für Mutterschutz und Sexualreform). Further member organisations can only be guessed at, since no membership lists have survived. Of the individual members in 1929/30 some sixty, one-third, belonged to the British section alone. There were approximately 190 British members in 1932/3; in 1935 there were still at least 142 members in Britain, 68 of them active participants (figures extrapolated from the correspondence of the League's British section preserved in the papers of Dora Russell).

A brief review of the literature

There is surprisingly little scholarly work on the WLSR, apart from the following studies. An (unpublished) Dutch *skripsie* by Leontine Bijleveld (1984) is devoted to the four constant themes of WLSR congresses: women, abortion, contraception and homosexuality. There is an essay by the Danish sexologist Preben Hertoft (1988 and 1990) on the demise of the WLSR, with the thesis that the main purpose in founding the WLSR had been mutual reinforcement for sex reformers, who tended to be marginalised in their home countries. A short essay by Annegret Klevenow (1986) on the eugenic positions represented within the WLSR is, unfortunately, remarkably vague in both documentation and argument. Richard Cleminson (1993 and 1994/5) has endeavoured to describe the influence of Wilhelm Reich and of the anarchists on the short-lived Spanish section under Carmen Rodriguez, who used the name Srta Hildegart (see also Pérez Sanz and Bru Ripoll 1987, and Cleminson and Amezúa, Chapter 7 of this volume). Llorca Díaz (1995) has recently published an account in Spanish of the WLSR which arose in close collaboration with the Centre for Research on the History of Sexology (Forschungsstelle zur Geschichte der Sexualwissenschaft) of the Magnus Hirschfeld Society (Magnus-Hirschfeld-Gesellschaft). Dose's article in *Mitteilungen der Magnus-Hirschfeld-Gesellschaft* (Dose 1993) provides a similar overview of the organisation and objectives of the WLSR. Finally, in a study of Soviet sexology after the Revolution, Susan Gross Solomon (forthcoming) has also dealt with its relationship to the WLSR.

Most of these works are based on printed sources, particularly the proceedings of the four WLSR congresses, and in the case of the Spanish section on an analysis of its journal. Hertoft also includes the well-known debate between Haire and Leunbach in Reich's journal (Haire 1935; Haire and Leunbach 1935; Leunbach 1935) and the – also published – correspondence between Reich and A. S. Neill (Placzek 1989). Until recently apparently nobody felt moved to search out and analyse unpublished sources. While looking at this late date for the central files kept by Wilhelm Kauffmann at Hirschfeld's Berlin Institute, which were confiscated by the Nazis, would not be a promising line of action, there may well be existing papers worthy of attention relating to people close to the national sections or to the congress organisers. A basic group of documents relating to the League's British section survives in Amsterdam among the papers of Dora Russell, who together with Norman Haire organised the 1929 WLSR congress in London and later the British section, and from leads thus provided connections could easily be made to other archival sources. In regard to the Spanish section there is extensive correspondence between Srta Hildegart and Havelock Ellis in the British Library. But what of the French section around Berty Albrecht? What of the Dutch section? And above all: what happened to the work done before and after the congresses at Vienna and Brno? Nobody has bothered to look, or even to collect, let alone evaluate, the contemporary response in the press.

Naturally the many works on the sex reform movement of the 1920s and early 1930s make almost 'ritual' references to the WLSR: supposedly the congresses brought together everybody who was anybody in the areas of sexology and sex reform. Atina Grossmann (1995) recently mentioned Hirschfeld's Institute, which also housed the WLSR offices, as the 'headquarters of sex reform'. But apparently all those who have dealt with the League simply note its disappearance, accept the contemporary explanations for its demise and consider the case closed, whereas closer examination might be worthwhile. On the one hand, there were national sections in a number of European countries which had their own activities. These deserve closer attention and evaluation in the context of their respective 'competitors' in the fields of sex reform and sexology.

On the other hand, although there is no reason to question the usual explanation that the WLSR broke up over political differences after Hirschfeld's death, so far a critical evaluation of the WLSR's true achievements beyond conference tourism is lacking. Historians also need to look beyond 1935 and in addition need to acknowledge that, parallel to the WLSR congresses, there were two other groups of congresses and scholarly organisations which must be examined together with the WLSR in order to gain a better understanding of what led to the WLSR's failure – if indeed it was one. These were Margaret Sanger's congresses on issues of world population and birth control and the two sexological congresses held by Albert Moll's International Sexological Society (Internationale Gesellschaft für Sexualforschung, INGESE). Only a comparison of the three lines of development will allow the drawing of conclusions about the significance and function of the WLSR – and about its failure.

There are several reasons for the neglect of the WLSR by scholars. The first is probably Wilhelm Reich's (and J. H. Leunbach's) verdict, rediscovered along with the WLSR in the late 1960s, that bourgeois sex reform was doomed to failure and that the liberation of sexuality from outdated constraints would be possible only under socialism. To be sure, this argument was already showing cracks by 1936, at the latest, but it remained influential none the less.

A second reason doubtless lies in the complex nature of the WLSR's objectives: it offered something for and by everyone. There was no successor organisation or movement that wanted to or could take up the WLSR tradition. For the homosexual movement after

1969, Hirschfeld's politics of integration was no longer of interest, and in the WLSR congress proceedings homosexuals are mentioned only in passing. The same applies, however, to issues of birth control, which the WLSR dealt with far more extensively: after all, the International Planned Parenthood Federation (IPPF) made a conscious decision not to place itself in the tradition of the (German and foreign) 'layperson's' organisations close to the workers' movement but instead to ally itself with middle-class medical doctors. There was also another, 'more successful' line or tradition that led in the same direction: Margaret Sanger's congresses.

Finally, for the new women's movement the male-dominated League was much too stuffy and patriarchal; and indeed, despite the declaration under Point 2 of its platform calling for political, social and sexual equality for men and women, the WLSR was scarcely on the front line of the struggle for gender equality.

A complete overview of the WLSR cannot be offered. Instead, after a brief overview of its objectives, it will be examined from three different perspectives: as Hirschfeld's strategic attempt to form coalitions; a comparison of its success with that of other organisations; and as one stage in the process of handing down impulses for sex reform.

The WLSR's objectives

The League sought to unite a number of very differently structured sex reform discourses, as the 'planks', as Norman Haire referred to them, in its programme reveal. The integration of all these 'planks' was unsuccessful; they continued to exist side by side. And just as no melding of the various sex-reform discourses within the League occurred, there was also no central guiding force. At the Copenhagen congress the League elected Magnus Hirschfeld (1868–1935), Havelock Ellis (1859–1939) and August Forel (1848–1931) to its executive board. Ellis and Forel, who never participated actively in the League's work, were named honorary presidents in 1930. J. H. Leunbach and Norman Haire took their seats on the executive board. A working committee was also chosen, composed at first of Hertha and Walter Riese of Frankfurt am Main, Paul and Maria Krische of Berlin and J. H. Leunbach of Copenhagen (until he became a member of the executive board in 1930). They were joined in 1930 by Grigorij Batkis of Moscow, Josef Friedjung of Vienna and Pierre

Vachet of Paris, and in 1932 by Benno Premsela of Amsterdam. The League did have executive organs: the executive board, the working committee and the international committee. The last, however, does not seem to have had any activities of its own and appears to have been merely a name on a letterhead (the names are listed in the congress proceedings and also in the appendix to Bijleveld 1984). The working committee must have met a few times to prepare for the London and Vienna congresses but scarcely performed any authentic leadership function. The programme for each congress was developed at the conference site. Even resolutions of the WLSR's business meetings do not appear to have been very binding: in Vienna, for example, a programme was resolved for the planned congress in 1931 in Moscow, but the congress held instead in 1932 in Brno took up almost none of the recommendations.

The WLSR programme initially contained the following ten demands, in Haire's English translation:

1. Marriage reform. Wedlock must be raised to the position of a living comradeship between two people. This necessitates a reform in the marriage contract, conjugal rights and divorce.
2. The position of women as members of society. Women have not by any means everywhere as yet won the equal rights that are their due in political, economic, social and sexual spheres.
3. Birth control, i.e. a greater sense of responsibility in the begetting of children. We believe in making harmless contraceptives known, and combating on the other hand both abortion and the penalising of abortion.
4. Eugenics in the sense of Nietzsche's words: 'You shall not merely continue the race, but move it upward!'
5. A fair judgement of those who are unsuited to marriage, above all the intermediate sexual types.
6. Tolerance of free sexual relations, especially protection of the unmarried mother and the child born out of wedlock.
7. The prevention of prostitution and venereal disease.
8. The conception of aberrations of sexual desire not as criminal, sinful or vicious but as a more or less pathological phenomenon.
9. The setting up of a code of sexual law, which does not interfere with the mutual sexual will of grown-up persons.
10. The question of sexual education and enlightenment.

These demands were clearly not the product of lengthy international discussion, but rather were drafted by the founder Magnus Hirschfeld. Norman Haire had originally intended such a discussion to take place at the London congress, and planned to reformulate the ten demands before that congress in order to make them more palatable to the English public. In a letter of late 1928 to Dora Russell he wrote: 'Draft the planks of the League's platform in a new shape, less likely to offend the English public. I already have some ideas for this. When we have got this done, we can send it to Berlin for their opinion, and it would come up for consideration and voting at the business meeting which must be held one evening during the Congress.' But the minutes of this business meeting do not say anything about a discussion of the ten demands.

Between the version included with the congress announcement, i.e. Hirschfeld's formulations, and the version voted on in Copenhagen, changes were made to the text. In the final approved version the disappearance of 'tolerance of free sexual relations' (Point 6 in the *Werbebrief* or membership appeal) was particularly striking. It seems highly likely that Norman Haire intervened, as such a demand would have made him appear completely frivolous in England. 'Free love' did not reappear until the 1932 suggestions of the Vienna economist Rudolf Goldscheid, couched in terms of the 'right of man and woman to satisfy their sexual drives, also outside of marriage'.

Express reference to abortion was also lost (just as, however, other explanatory additions were also removed). However, resolutions on the subject of abortion legislation were formulated both in Copenhagen and in London. The German and English versions of the demand regarding birth control differed in another significant point. The English version emphasised self-determination over conception or non-conception: '3. Control of conception [in Vienna: birth control], *so that procreation may be undertaken only deliberately*, and with a due sense of responsibility' (emphasis added). The German version, in contrast, mentioned only '3. Birth control in the sense of responsible procreation'. This divergence rested on a programmatic difference which can be better understood by looking at the resolutions on the subject of birth control. The Copenhagen resolution on birth control not only regarded it 'as a means to limit offspring according to the economic, physical and mental resources of the parents and their children' but 'as a means to make unsuitable married couples refrain voluntarily from procreation', clearly pointing to the eugenic dimension of birth control. Such a position could not be asserted in London, despite the participation in the congress of Marie Stopes as well as the Malthusian League and the Eugenics Society, and the 1929 resolution simply 'declares that no child should be born of unwilling parents', and with that aim in view advocated free access to the necessary knowledge. Obviously British birth controllers involved in the WLSR and the organisation of its congress were much less interested in eugenic justifications of birth control than were their German counterparts.

The differences between the two resolutions were never addressed. It could be argued that one was as non-committal as the other, or that anyone could work with the text that s/he preferred while still referring to the WLSR resolutions. Comparing resolutions passed at different times and by different national sections, it is striking that wording adopted by the French and Spanish sections was not a translation of the WLSR platform but developed independently. Both sections were founded comparatively late and were scarcely under the influence of Hirschfeld.

Perspectives on the League's work

Coalition strategy

Magnus Hirschfeld – who undoubtedly instigated the foundation of the League – was one of the outstanding figures in sexology and the homosexual movement before 1933. For him homosexuals would attain emancipation via two paths: with the help of science and through the integration of the homosexual movement into other sex reform movements. He pursued this objective even before the First World War through his collaboration with Helene Stöcker's Bund für Mutterschutz, and after 1919 several steps, each building on the other, led to the founding of the WLSR. The first stage of these attempts at integration was the founding in 1920 of the so-called Action Committee (Aktionskomitee) as an attempt to bring together the various existing German homosexual organisations in order to fight for the abolition of article 175 of the German Penal Code. Second was the formation in 1925 of the Cartel for the Reform of the Sexual Penal Code (Kartell zur Reform des Sexualstrafrechts) – a coalition, much respected in legal circles, of organisations calling for changes in German sex crimes legislation and, more generally, in all legal regulations of sexual life. The Cartel's participation in this campaign rested on the recognition that isolated opposition to the anti-homosexual article 175 was doomed to remain ineffective. The impetus for the search for coalition partners was the publication of the official draft of a new German Penal Code in 1925.

At the beginning of 1927 the Cartel presented a counter-draft, which contained, for the first time, the entire spectrum of proposed reforms – as far as they were relevant to criminal law – which were also formulated within the League. It would be no exaggeration to call the Cartel a sort of national predecessor to the League, a successful trial run of the combination of demands of the most diverse origins. It seemed logical to attempt this beyond the merely national level. On the one hand, propaganda about the developments in marriage and sex crimes legislation in the Soviet Union was already common property among the German left and elsewhere. On the other, in many countries of western Europe efforts were also under way to establish birth control as a right (and/or as a eugenic duty).

Finally, in a third step, this integration of the homosexual movement was internationalised – at a time when it was becoming clear that the Cartel's efforts in Germany would remain unsuccessful. For homosexuals, however, this meant integration at the price of watering down or neglecting their own demands, rather than a normalisation of their relations with other reform movements. For its part the League participated in the (failed) efforts in the early 1930s in Berlin aimed at unifying the 'layperson's' organisations dedicated to birth control. Whether, and to what extent, the demands of the homosexual movement found their way into the publications of the German 'layperson's' organisations for birth control remains to be investigated. But it is clear from the congress reports after 1928 that on an international level the demands of homosexuals were more and more marginalised.

Competing international conferences

It is questionable whether the League's congresses (i.e. the international level of its work) should be viewed only in comparison to and in continuity with each other. In the 1920s and 1930s there were three parallel organisational structures on an international level devoted to questions of sexology and sex reform. The circles of participants overlapped, although the central figures in each kept their distance from each other (e.g. Margaret Sanger and Hirschfeld) or were openly hostile (e.g. Albert Moll and Hirschfeld). Each of the three structures had its own, quite telling fate.

The congresses of INGESE, held in 1926 in Berlin under the chairmanship of Albert Moll and in 1930 in London under the chairmanship of Francis A. E. Crew, claimed to be 'purely scientific' and to stay away from all reform projects. In the five volumes of proceedings from the 1926 congress, however, it soon becomes apparent that this standard was not met, with certain speakers becoming heatedly political and moralistic. Nevertheless, some scientifically significant papers were given, for example Aschheim and Zondek on hormonal sterilisation (in Marcuse 1927–8, vol. 1). Also striking, however, is what neither contemporaries nor later writers seem to have noticed: Albert Moll's well-grounded and clear-sighted critique of eugenics (in Marcuse 1927–8, vol. 4). Questions of sex reform were notably absent from the two volumes from the 1930 INGESE congress in London, full of biological essays in which the study of sexuality returned to its animal origins (Greenwood 1931). This type of congress had no apparent continuity beyond 1930. It stands for the disintegration of a still barely existent sexology into component disciplines: (social) gynaecology, hormone research, genetics and psychoanalysis.

In contrast to the INGESE congresses, attended by individual scientists, the League brought together not only researchers but also delegates of organisations known from the medical perspective as 'layperson's organisations'. (A presumptuous term, for who is a 'layperson' in regard to his or her sexuality? But it demonstrates the physicians' claim to expertise and the right to make definitions.) To the extent that these 'layperson's' organisations dealt with questions of birth control and contraception (and depending on national context) they were often close to the workers' parties. Within the League science was the underpinning of the desired reforms. Thus the papers and addresses given at these four (or five) congresses focused less on presenting research results than on extensive justifications for reform projects or reports on practical experiences. As regards the further development of *sexology*, the WLSR could justifiably be claimed as insignificant: the continuities of *sex reform* are discussed below.

There were also overlaps between the participants in the WLSR congresses and those of the third group, Margaret Sanger's World Population or Birth Control Congresses (Sanger 1927; Sanger and

Stone 1931). These overlaps were most apparent at the 1930 congress in Geneva whence the participating physicians went on to the WLSR congress in Vienna. In contrast to the spectrum of topics treated at WLSR congresses, Margaret Sanger chose a single organising theme, and was primarily concerned with taking stock of the current state of the art and organising funding for research. In the long term this proved the most successful strategy, ultimately leading to the founding in the early 1950s of the IPPF. As Atina Grossmann (1995) has shown in the German case, this process occurred in conjunction with the exclusion of lay persons (and organisations) and the surrender of control over the reproductive function (and even perhaps of sexuality) to the experts.

Continuities

There is a third thematic aspect: that of continuities beyond 1933 and 1945 (with the break in 1933 being a specifically German one), manifested in two very different examples.

Continuity seems to have been clearest in Britain. After the disbanding of the British section of the WLSR its members continued to meet within three organisations: the Sex Education Society (1936–9, with an attempted revival after Haire's return from Australia after the Second World War), the Federation of Progressive Societies and Individuals (FPSI), later called the Progressive League, and the British Sexology Society, founded in 1914 as the British Society for the Study of Sex Psychology. Nearly all of the participants in and supporters of the 1929 WLSR congress could also be found in one or another of these organisations. The Sex Education Society's programme was very close to Hirschfeld's programme for the League. The FPSI had a Sex Reform Group, of which Stella Browne was for some time co-chair, as well as a general commitment to sex reform aims. Even the Society for Sex Education and Guidance, established after the Second World War, though unconnected with the Haire group, began with almost exactly the same programme, and among the names of the officers and supporters were many familiar names from the rank and file of the WLSR.

Some of the people who fought for the liberalisation of the laws on homosexuality in Britain in the 1950s also emerged from these organisations. Although individuals who had something to do with the League in 1929 were not among the drafters of the Wolfenden and Griffin Reports during the 1950s, the relevant names crop up somewhat later. On 12 May 1960, after two years of rather quiet work, the Homosexual Law Reform Society made its first public appearance. Jeffrey Weeks has described the speakers at this event as 'what was to become a familiar mix of liberals and clergymen – Mrs Anne Allen, a magistrate and popular Sunday "problem" journalist, the Bishop of Exeter, Kingsley Martin, editor of the *New Statesman*, Dr L. Neustatter, a psychiatrist' (Weeks 1983: 170). Mrs Allen and Dr Neustatter had figured in the membership lists of the League, the *New Statesman* was the organ of the left-liberal British intelligentsia and its editor Kingsley Martin was an old chum of Bertrand and Dora Russell from Cambridge University days – many League supporters were recruited from this group – and a member of the Progressive League. While we should not attribute to the League an influence that it does not deserve, there is much evidence that its British branch was rooted in an intellectual milieu which was still relevant enough in 1960 to serve as an advertisement for the cause.

There was also a path leading back to Germany, although its origins were no longer known and also not recognisable: the books of Eustace Chesser and Norman Haire's 1934 *Encyclopaedia of Sexual Knowledge*. Chesser was already a leading member of the Sex Education Society in the 1930s. His books were published in large German-language editions from 1948 on in Switzerland and from 1950 on in the Federal Republic as well; his best-known work was the 1940 *Love without Fear*, much read in Germany into the 1960s under the title *Liebe ohne Furcht*, which went into at least twenty-six editions. In his book *Odd Man Out* (1959, published in German in 1961 as *Menschen auf Abwegen*) Chesser argued just as Hirschfeld had that homosexuality should not be criminalised since homosexuals cannot be depraved, unable as they are to change themselves: 'The adult who becomes conscious of his situation is not responsible for it' (translated from p. 13 of the German edition). Chesser was concerned, too, to promote an appropriate understanding of this behaviour among the public, which could be achieved only by a better knowledge of the conditions under which it arose. The scientific foundations, however, were different: Chesser described sexual development in psychoanalytic terms.

For Chesser the goal was to change the law and society's attitudes as well as family life so that homosexuals did not arise in the first place – little remained of the intentions expressed by the

League and to some extent by the Sex Education Society. Though it may seem surprising that this book was ever considered progressive, it nevertheless represented the breaking of a taboo – not only in Britain.

The second example is even more frightening. The *Encyclopaedia of Sexual Knowledge*, published for the first time under Norman Haire's name in 1934, sold over five hundred thousand copies in several new and updated editions until the late 1950s. On closer examination, it appears that Haire edited it and added a few articles of his own (on Sterilisation, Abortion and Contraception), but that it was largely written by others. As editor, though, Haire always commented upon the positions of authors he disagreed with in footnotes – and he frequently disagreed. A German translation was published in 1961 by Pfister Verlag, and a paperback edition in 1965 by List, just in time for the incipient sex wave. A book club, the Deutsche Bücherbund, put out its own edition (undated) and an expanded edition appeared in 1969. It was clearly quite a successful book.

The German edition of 1961–5 includes long passages from the English version of 1934 (the English edition from the late 1950s on which the translation is supposedly based may differ substantially from this earlier edition: the translators claim to have adapted the text to German conditions), but an examination here of a few chapters whose original author was definitely Norman Haire makes clear the difference between his attitudes and what was being sold under his name in West Germany in the 1960s.

As regards contraception: information about and free access to contraceptive devices were central demands of the sex reform movement in the 1920s. Though in his 1934 introduction Norman Haire emphasised that a woman reached her full potential only through motherhood, and a man only through assuming responsibility for a family, he went on to give a thorough and precise account of the arguments, both medical and social, in favour of contraception. He demanded that physicians should be acquainted with contraceptive methods and also expressly mentioned the existing advice centres spread across Britain. The German edition of 1961, in contrast, began with a long excursus on the positions of the Catholic and Protestant churches, raised pro-natalist population policy arguments and only then remarked, rather generally, that there might be medical reasons for recommending contraception. The only social reason mentioned as acceptable was that giving birth too frequently could endanger the mother's health and thus her capacity to raise her children properly. Unmarried couples, for example, who wanted to have sex but not children, were not mentioned; in 1935 Norman Haire had quite definitely taken this eventuality into account. Nor was there a word about advice centres – not surprising since scarcely any existed in the Federal Republic of Germany in 1961.

Haire offered very detailed and practical instructions for the use of various means of contraception, and addressed objections to specific methods. The 1961 German edition was significantly less precise, but paid close attention to Knaus/Ogino and the temperature method – only, however, to say that they are very uncertain – instead of stressing the more effective methods which were available even at that time. To do so would have gone against the intentions of the translators, though, who expressly emphasised: 'we are of the opinion that it is inappropriate to recommend birth control to young, healthy, childless married women because woman is most fertile when young' (p. 337).

In the 1934 edition Haire described everything that was being attempted concerning abortion, provided an overview of the legal situation and argued for a change in the penal code. He was not for abortion, but considered the operation itself safe when carried out under medically proper conditions.

The German version recommended that religious women should first consult their clergymen before suffering later pangs of conscience. The editors countered the arguments of those who believe that the decision should be placed in women's hands with arguments from population policy (which played no part in Haire's work). In contrast to Haire, who mentioned a number of abortifacients and methods by name, the German translators did not wish to lead 'rash' women 'into temptation' and offered no graphic descriptions. The statement that medically correct abortions were relatively safe in comparison to back-street abortions was also absent, as well as the appeal for the removal of abortion from the penal code.

On homosexuality, the English edition of 1934 offered various explanatory models, presented various treatments as unsuccessful and ended by citing Havelock Ellis, who denied homosexuals any hope of satisfying sexual relations. The assertion at the end of the chapter on perversions (intended to apply to all perversions) that neither prisons nor mental institutions were the proper means of treatment remained very general; in individual cases, it suggested, castration might be appropriate. All of this contrasted starkly with the positions developed in Germany and with the intentions pursued by Hirschfeld in the WLSR. In order to understand this chapter the almost complete impossibility, well into the 1950s, of discussing homosexuality publicly in England must be taken into account.

The German edition of 1961 first described Kinsey's findings on the incidence of homosexuality, and then offered extensive psycho-analytic case histories on the development of so-called 'full homo-sexuality', which was purportedly rooted in family constellations before puberty and was incurable. This was contrasted with bisexual behaviour, which arose after puberty as a result of homosexual experiences. There was no weighing of possible therapies and, strikingly, no critique of the penal code, although in England at the time there was intense discussion of the Wolfenden Report, the text of which was also circulating in German translation.

In short, what came to West Germany in the 1950s and early 1960s under the name of authors close to the League was no longer recognisable as the result of a sex reform movement. There was no longer any vision of social politics, political demands had disap-peared, and all that remained of the WLSR line were individual advice manuals which supported the family policy of the Adenauer regime.

Conclusion

Only a few aspects of the WLSR's work have been touched on here. The state of research is completely unsatisfactory. The question of the significance of the WLSR in its own time as well as of its influence in later years remains open. More needs to be learnt about actual connections with national reform movements and about how individual demands were rooted in national discourses, but an analysis of the interrelationships with other international organisations working at the same time is also necessary. A continuity or resumption of reform projects or discourses beyond 1935 or 1945 appears to have been possible and observable mainly in those countries not subject to direct fascist control (Britain, Sweden), but perhaps this thesis should be tested using the Dutch and Danish cases.

Bibliography

Albrecht, B. (ed.) (1933–5), *Le Problème sexuel: Revue trimestrielle. Morale – Eugénique – Hygiène – Legislation*, Paris, no. 1, November 1933 – no. 6, June 1935.

Bijleveld, L. (1984), *Seksuele hervorming in het interbellum: Het internationale kader de Wereldliga voor Seksuele Hervorming 1928–1935. Vrouwen – Abortus – Voorbehoedmiddelen – Homoseksualiteit*, Utrecht, Rijksuniversiteit, Vakgroep Geschiedenis.

Chesser, E. (1951), *Glück und Gefahr der Liebe: die Formen sexuellen Verhaltens*, trans. Conrad Couronne, Stuttgart, Hans E. Günther.

— (1961), *Mensch auf Abwegen: die Homosexualität des Mannes und der Frau*, trans. Ilse Custer, Stuttgart, Hans E. Günther.

Chiavacci, L. (ed.) (1931), *Sexus: Internationale Monatsschrift für Sexualwissenschaft und Sexualreform – Organ der Weltliga für Sexualreform*, general ed. Magnus Hirschfeld, Vienna and Leipzig, Verlag für Sexualwissenschaft, Schneider & Co., no. 1.

Cleminson, R. (1993), 'Einheit von Anarchismus und Marxismus? Wilhelm Reich und der Anarchismus in Spanien', *Mitteilungen der Magnus-Hirschfeld-Gesellschaft*, 19, pp. 73–84.

— (1994/5), 'Werkstattnotizen zur WLSR in Spanien', *Mitteilungen der Magnus-Hirschfeld-Gesellschaft*, no. 20/1, pp. 45–9.

Dose, R. (1993), 'Thesen zur Weltliga für Sexualreform – Notizen aus der Werkstatt', *Mitteilungen der Magnus-Hirschfeld-Gesellschaft*, 19, pp. 23–39.

Emde Boas, C. van (1932), 'Het Vijfde Internationale Congres der Wereldliga voor Sexueele Hervorming', *Verstandig Ouderschap*, 17, 11, pp. 2–3.

— (1933), 'Het 5de Wereldcongres der Wereldliga voor Sexueele Hervorming', *Nederlandische Tijdschrift voor Geneeskunde*, 77, pp. 414–17.

Greenwood, A. W. (ed.) (1931), *Proceedings of the Second International Congress for Sex Research, London 1930*, London and Edinburgh, Oliver & Boyd.

Grossmann, A. (1995), *Reforming Sex: The German Movement for Birth Control and Abortion Reform, 1920–1950*, New York and Oxford, Oxford University Press.

Haire, N. (ed.) (1930), *Sexual Reform Congress, London 8–14. IX. 1929, World League for Sexual Reform, Proceedings of the Third Congress*, London, Kegan Paul, Trench, Trubner & Co.

— (ed.) (1934), *Encyclopaedia of Sexual Knowledge*, by A. Costler, A. Willy and others, London, Francis Aldor.

— (1935), 'Ein Brief von Norman Haire', *Zeitschrift für politische Psychologie und Sexualökonomie*, 2, 2, pp. 81–90.

— (n.d.), *Geschlecht und Liebe heute*, Stuttgart and Hamburg, Deutscher Bücherbund.

Haire, N. and J. H. Leunbach (1935), 'Mitteilung an alle Mitglieder und Sektionen der Weltliga für Sexualreform', *Zeitschrift für politische Psychologie und Sexualökonomie* 2, 2, p. 98.

Hall, Lesley A. (1995), '"Disinterested Enthusiasm for Sexual Misconduct": The British Society for the Study of Sex Psychology, 1913–1947', *Journal of Contemporary History* 30, 4, pp. 665–86.

Hertoft, P. (1988), 'Norman Haire, Jonathan Høegh von Leunbach und das Ende der Weltliga für Sexualreform', *Zeitschrift für Sexualforschung*, 1, pp. 242–62.

— (1990), 'Hvem var Norman Haire? – en kontroversiel reformist', *Nordisk Sexologi*, 8, pp. 77–93.

Huerta, D. L. and Srta Hildegart (Carmen Rodriguez) (eds) (1932–3), *Sexus: Organo de la Liga Española para la Reforma Sexual sobre bases científicas*. The following issues definitely appeared: tomo 1, año1, núm. 1 (Oct.–Nov. 1932) and tomo 1, año 2, núm. 2 (Apr.–May 1933).

Institut für Sexualwissenschaft, Berlin (ed.) (1933), *Sexus: Internationale Vierteljahresschrift für die gesamte Sexualwissenschaft und Sexualreform*, Berlin, Wilhelm Kauffmann Verlag, no. 1.

Kartell für Reform des Sexualstrafrechts (ed.) (1927), *Sittlichkeit und Strafrecht: Gegen-Entwurf zu den Strafbestimmungen des Amtlichen Entwurfs eines Allgemeinen Deutschen Strafgesetzbuchs über geschlechtliche und mit dem Geschlechtsleben im Zusammenhang stehende Handlungen (Abschnitte 17, 18, 21, 22, 23) nebst Begründung*, Berlin, Verlag der Neuen Gesellschaft.

Klevenow, A. (1986), 'Geburtenregelung und "Menschenökonomie": die Kongresse für Sexualreform 1921–1930', in H. Kaupen-Haas (ed.), *Der Griff nach der Bevölkerung: Aktualität und Kontinuität nazistischer Bevölkerungspolitik*, Nördlingen, Greno.

Leunbach, J. H. (1935), 'Antwort an Norman Haire', *Zeitschrift für politische Psychologie und Sexualökonomie*, 2, 2, pp. 91–7.

Llorca Díaz, A. (1995), 'La Liga Mundial para la Reforma Sexual sobre Bases Científicas (1928–1935)', *Revista de Sexología*, 69.

Marcuse, M. (ed.) (1927–8), *Verhandlungen des 1. Internationalen Kongresses für Sexualforschung: Berlin, vom 10.–16. Oktober 1926, veranstaltet v. d. Int. Gesellschaft für Sexualforschung*, 5 vols., Berlin and Cologne, A. Marcus & E. Weber's Verlag.

Pérez Sanz, P. and C. Bru Ripoll (1987), 'La sexología en España de los años 30. Vol. II, Hildegart o la historia de Aurora Rodriguez Carballeira, su madre', *Revista de Sexologia*, 32.

Placzek, B. R. (ed.) (1989), *Zeugnisse einer Freundschaft: der Briefwechsel zwischen Wilhelm Reich und A. S. Neill 1936–1957*, Frankfurt am Main, Fischer Taschenbuchverlag.

Riese, H. and J. H. Leunbach (eds) (1929), *Sexual Reform Congress, Copenhagen 1–5. VII. 1928, W.L.S.R. World League for Sexual Reform, Proceedings of the Second Congress*, Copenhagen, Levin & Munksgaard, and Leipzig, Georg Thieme.

Rosenthal, M. (1932), 'Warum Sexualreform? Bericht über den fünften Internationalen Kongress der Welt-Liga für Sexualreform 1932', *Die neue Generation*, 28, pp. 175–9.

Russell, D. (1989), *The Tamarisk Tree*, London, Virago.

Sanger, M. (ed.) (1927), *Proceedings of the World Population Conference, held at Salle Centrale, Geneva, August 29th to September 3rd, 1927*, London, Edward Arnold.

Sanger, M. and H. Stone (eds) (1931), *The Practice of Contraception: An International Symposium and Survey, from the Proceedings of the Seventh International Birth Control Conference, Zurich, Switzerland, September 1930*, Baltimore, Williams & Wilkins.

Scize, P. (1933a), 'Le Congrès de la Ligue Mondiale pour la Réforme Sexuelle de Brno', *Sexus* [Berlin], 1, pp. 38–47.

— (1933b), 'Visión panorámica del Congreso de Brno', *Sexus* [Madrid], 1, 2, pp. 92–4.

Solomon, S. G. (forthcoming), 'Soviet Sexology after the Revolution: Balancing International Concerns and the Domestic Agenda'.

Steiner, H. (ed.) (1931), *Sexualnot und Sexualreform: Verhandlungen der Weltliga für Sexualreform, IV. Kongress, abgehalten zu Wien vom 16. bis 23. September 1930,* Vienna, Elbemühl.

Weeks, Jeffrey (1983), *Coming Out: Homosexual Politics in Britain, from the Nineteenth Century to the Present,* London, Melbourne and New York, Quartet Books.

Weil, A. (ed. on behalf of the Institute for Sexual Science) (1922), *Sexualreform und Sexualwissenschaft: Vorträge gehalten auf der I. Internationalen Tagung für Sexualreform auf sexualwissenschaftlicher Grundlage in Berlin,* Stuttgart, Püttmann.

Weisskopf, J. (1933), 'Der Brünner Sexualkongress', *Sexus* [Berlin], 1, pp. 26–33.

Wereldbond voor Sexueele Hervorming (WLSR) (ed.), *Sexueele Hervorming: een reeks geschriften van de Afdeeling Nederland van den Wereldbond voor Sexueele Hervorming (W.L.S.R.),* Amsterdam, Kosmos. Up to 1934 the following thirteen titles were issued:

Polak, Leo, *Sexueele ethiek.*

Mennicke, C., *Gelijkgerechtigdheit van man en vrouw op sexueel gebied.*

Wibaut-Berdenis van Berlekom, M., *Gelijkgerechtigdheit van man en vrouw op economisch gebied.*

Goudsmit, G. B., *Gelijkgerechtigdheit van man en vrouw op juridisch gebied.*

Cannegieter, H. G., *Het sexueele problem in de opvoeding.*

Premsela, B., *Geboorteregeling.*

Valkhoff, J., *Het vraagstuk van de Abortus Provocatus.*

Polak-Rosenberg, C. L., *De ongehuwde moeder en haar kind.*

Vorrink, Koos, *Coëducatie.*

Valkhoff, J., *Uitbreiding van echtscheidingsgronden.*

Hoop, J. H. v d., *Homosexualiteit.*

Stokvis, Benno J., *Homosexualiteit en strafrecht.*

Frets, G. P., *Huwelijk en eugeniek (rasverbetering).*

Index